On the Other Hand . . .

Also by Herbert Stein

PRESIDENTIAL ECONOMICS: THE MAKING OF ECONOMIC POLICY FROM ROOSEVELT TO CLINTON, Third revised edition (AEI 1994)

AN ILLUSTRATED GUIDE TO THE AMERICAN ECONOMY: A HUNDRED KEY ISSUES (with Murray Foss, AEI 1992)

THE FISCAL REVOLUTION IN AMERICA, Revised edition (AEI 1990)

GOVERNING THE $5 TRILLION ECONOMY (1989)

On the Other Hand . . .

Essays on Economics, Economists, and Politics

Herbert Stein

The AEI Press

Publisher for the American Enterprise Institute
WASHINGTON, D.C.

1995

Library of Congress Cataloging-in-Publication Data

Stein, Herbert, 1916–
    On the other hand—essays on economics, economists, and
politics / Herbert Stein.
        p. cm.
    Includes bibliographical references.
    ISBN 0-8447-3876-X : $25.95.—ISBN 0-8447-3877-8 (pbk.) : $16.95
    1. United States—Economic policy. I. American Enterprise
Institute for Public Policy Research. II. Title.
HC103.S758 1995
338.973—dc20   94-24823
                                                    CIP

The AEI Press
Publisher for the American Enterprise Institute
1150 17th Street, N.W., Washington, D.C. 20036

Distributed in Europe, the Middle East, Africa, and selected territories outside the
United States by Eurospan. For more information, contact Eurospan, 3 Henrietta
Street, London WC2E 8LU, England.

Printed in the United States of America

To Mildred

Contents

1

Introduction

The title of this book is inspired by President Truman's remark that he wished he had a one-armed economist, who would not say, "On the one hand . . . and on the other hand. . . ." But the president was wrong. He needed an economist who would say on the other hand, and sometimes on a third or fourth hand. On few economic policy issues in the United States is all the plausible evidence on one side. Presidents, pundits, and even economists frequently need to be reminded of that.

Much of my writing in the past five years has been saying on the other hand: "On the other hand, taxation is not a sin. . . . On the other hand, a budget deficit is not a disaster. . . . On the other hand, Japan's economic success is not a loss for us." And so on.

In an introduction to a collection of his essays, George Will, whom I admire, said that such collections were "necessarily episodic, but there are certain continuities, and mine are conservative convictions." I could say something like that. My essays are necessarily episodic, but there is a certain continuity, which is the absence of conservative convictions and also of liberal ones. I do not vote the straight ticket, either conservative or liberal.

In my fifty-six years in Washington, I have seen eleven presidents in action. The period was almost equally divided between Democratic and Republican administrations. Liberals, conservatives, and neo-cons, Keynesians, monetarists, and supply-siders have come and gone; I have not seen that any of them had a monopoly on wisdom or on folly. An old saying goes that whoever is not a Socialist when young has no heart and whoever is still a Socialist when old has no head. I say that whoever is not a liberal when young has no heart, whoever is not a conservative when middle-aged has no head, and whoever is still either a liberal or a conservative at age seventy-eight has no sense of humor. Obviously, orthodox certainty on matters about which there can be so little certitude must eventually be seen as only amusing.

I did not arrive at this agnostic condition only when I reached an advanced age. In one degree or another, I have been there for a long time, and I relate how I got there in the first essay in this collection. A subsequent article gives an account of the development of the American economy since 1929 from this standpoint—as a triumph neither of a consistent conservatism nor of a consistent liberalism but of a continuous process of adaptation to changing circumstances.

In disavowing liberal or conservative convictions, I do not mean to suggest that I have no convictions. But my convictions do not all fit comfortably within either the liberal or the conservative box, and I am hesitant about the derivation of policy decisions in particular cases from general ideologies or attitudes. The principle that seems to me to require the least qualification is that the government should not intervene in the heart of the market—in the determination of relative prices and the allocation of labor and capital among various industries. But beyond that, the policy issues are more difficult and require more case-by-case discrimination. I believe that the government has major responsibilities for maintaining conditions in which high employment can be achieved and the general level of prices will be stable, in which the poor and disadvantaged are assisted, and in which competition is preserved. But how far these objectives should be pursued, by what means, and with what expectations for success are issues that should be considered open-mindedly and with full awareness of the limitations of our knowledge. We will not find the answers in the back of the textbook. Some of the policy questions now facing the country are discussed, I hope in this open-minded way, in parts of this book.

I have also tried to describe without partisanship or ideological bias some aspects of my experience as an economist in Washington, including service as an adviser to the president. The essays that deal with the state and history of economics as I understand them may partly explain my own attitudes.

Newspapers and television now bathe Americans in a flood of "information" about economics and about economic policy. It is my hope that the essays in this book will help the reader to appreciate the significance and, what is often more to the point, the insignificance of this information. I also hope that despite the cliché about "the dismal science" readers may find some enjoyment in these reflections on economics.

Many of the essays included here were written at the American Enterprise Institute for Public Policy Research. I want to thank AEI for giving me complete freedom and a comfortable environment in which to work.

PART ONE
General Perspective

2

My Life as a Dee-cline

That every boy and every gal
That's born into the world alive
Is either a little Liberal,
Or else a little Conservative!
　　　　　—Gilbert and Sullivan

Gilbert and Sullivan were wrong about me. For a large part of my life, when I lived in Maryland, I was a Dee-Cline. In Maryland one could register as Democrat, Republican, or Dee-Cline. If you were a Dee-Cline you could not vote in the primaries. I was a Dee-Cline until 1964, when I registered as a Democrat in order to vote against George Wallace in the presidential primary. I am now a registered Republican but not a very hard-rock one.

I am uncomfortable with ideologies and ideologues, with people who know the answer to everything, with political parties and teams. I have been on a team from time to time, and have enjoyed it for a while, but there was always some reservation, as if that wasn't my true life and I was half an observer of what the other half of me was doing. I dislike serving on committees that are going to draft statements, because I know there is going to be something I cannot go along with. People ask me to sign petitions with which I am basically sympathetic, but there is always a sentence I cannot sign.

Surely the reasons for this attitude are largely matters of private personality in which there is no reason for others to be interested. But the reasons are partly more objective and may throw some light on the state of policy discussion today. This may explain the consistency of inconsistency and the rationality of the commitment to being uncommitted.

Politics and Public Policy

I don't remember having ideas about politics or public policy until I was in college. That may seem rather late, but I went to college at an early age. Anyway, I was in college from 1931 to 1935—that is, in the depths of the depression—and my family lived in Schenectady, New York, which was terribly hard hit during the depression. My father was unemployed for much of this time. I found only one day's work for myself during all of my vacations from college.

The state of the economy made a strong and lasting impression on me. It made me think that the economy left by itself might not work very well. It also made me think that there were a lot of poor people out there who were miserable through no fault of their own. These were the casual observations of a naive mind. A sophisticated economist and econometrician might be able to disprove them. But those ideas stuck with me.

These ideas contributed to my decision to major in economics. I thought that economics was the path to reform, and I was a reformer, what would now be called a liberal. I was ignorant of the different degrees of leftishness that existed. Some time, probably in my junior year, our college had a visit from John Strachey, a fashionable British Communist. I wrote a sarcastic article about him in the college literary magazine, because I thought that he did not know any economics, which was true, and I thought that I did, which was untrue. But we also had a visit from a vice president of the Chase Bank, and I enjoyed the thought that I had heckled him with difficult questions. So I was already neither here nor there.

Economic Agnosticism

After college I went for graduate study in economics to the University of Chicago, and that was another great influence in the direction of agnosticism or ambivalence, which may be a surprise to people who think of Chicago as a center of dogmatism. I did not choose Chicago because I thought it had any brand of economics different from what I would have found at any other first-rate university, but mainly because it was recommended to me by a professor to whom I was close.

I went to Chicago thinking I wanted to concentrate on labor economics, which seemed closest to the problems of the unemployed and the poor. I soon gave up that idea, however. I discovered that labor economics as it was then taught was impossibly dull, having mainly to do with the struggles of the cordwainers' union in the nineteenth century. My dissatisfaction was intensified by the fact that the courses in labor economics were taught at eight o'clock in the morning and that Colonel McCormick had arranged for Chicago to stay on daylight-saving time through the winter. So it was very cold walking along the Midway to an eight a.m. class in January. More important, I discovered the marvels of "the market" and of general equilibrium. I learned about the economy as a balanced aquarium in which everything was permanent and for the best.

This discovery created a conflict for me. There was a conflict between the idea that "the market" was the best of possible systems and my observation that something was in fact quite wrong. This conflict was resolved for me by a remarkable economist, Henry Simons. The essence of his philosophy was summed up in the title of a pamphlet he had written in 1934, "A Positive Program for Laissez-Faire." The "laissez-faire" part of the title indicated a rejection of the notions of a planned economy that were then very common in the country, especially in some Washington circles. The "positive" part of the program indicated his rejection of the notion that nothing needed to be done other than to get the government out of the way. Government had a positive responsibility to create the conditions in which the benefits of the market would be realized, but this was a strictly limited responsibility. Government was not to intervene in the "heart of the market," which was the price system.

A Laissez-Faire System

Government had three important functions in a laissez-faire system:

- Since the market by itself would not ensure aggregate equilibrium—would not prevent inflation or unemployment—government had a responsibility to use its fiscal and monetary policies to maintain the macroeconomic conditions in which the market could work well.

- Since the market would not necessarily exist by itself, at least in the form in which it would yield its maximum benefits, the government had a responsibility to maintain the necessary character of the market, especially competition and the availability of information.

• Since the market by itself would not yield a desirable distribution of income, the government had a responsibility to affect the distribution of income in the desired direction, while interfering as little as possible with the workings of the market that generated income efficiently. Simons said that he found extremes in the distribution of income, as of power, "unlovely." The use of that particular word removed the subject of income inequality from arguments about efficiency and justice, and simply asserted the right of the society to have and implement a preference about the distribution of income. The use of the word *extremes* showed how far he was from the radical equalizers of his time. And expressing the same distaste for extreme inequality in the distribution of power was his warning against pushing too far any of the responsibilities he assigned to government.

Thus, Simons distinguished himself from both the conservatives and the liberals of his time. On the one hand, the conservative reaction was later epitomized in William Buckley's book *God and Man at Yale,* in which Buckley cites the use of Simons's work in economics courses as evidence of the radical influences at work in New Haven. On the other hand, liberals clearly regarded Simons as a conservative, one of the founders or forerunners of the Chicago school that was a synonym for conservatism in economics.

Influences on Economic Thought

Simons's attitude has remained a major influence on me in the fifty years since I left Chicago. Others who encountered Simons in the 1930s and were similarly influenced then have since changed their ideas significantly. Mainly, they have become much less tolerant than he was of government intervention in the economy. Perhaps that is because I have spent the past fifty years in Washington, which they have not. Whether that means that I have been corrupted or that they have been insulated is not for me to say.

Simons was the colleague and protégé of another Chicago economist, Frank Knight. Simons spelled out some policy implications of Knight's economics and philosophy. Although I studied under

Knight I did not at the time get much out of him. Only later did I realize how much support I would find in his writing. He was a master at the rigorous and comprehensive elaboration of the conditions implicit in the economists' model of a competitive market economy. At the same time, he recognized the large gap between those conditions and the real world. Knight regarded economics as a description of how things *would* be if these conditions were fulfilled, and of how the real world *is* insofar as those conditions are fulfilled, which might not be very far. Also, he recognized, or claimed, that even if the real world did fulfill those conditions, the resulting state of the economy would not necessarily be the best conceivable or the best achievable. Thus, he left a lot of room for the *possibility* of appropriate government interventions in particular cases for particular reasons, while retaining a great deal of skepticism about government management as a general method of economic organization. Knight was an argument against dogmatism, whether "conservative" or "liberal."

It was while I was a student at Chicago that Keynes's *General Theory* was published, quickly dividing the world of economics between Keynesians and non-Keynesians. Here again the Chicagoans took a middle-of-the-road, "none of the above" point of view. They accepted much of what Keynes had to say about the short-run behavior of the economy and about short-run antidepression policy, only complaining that it was not new and they had always known it. But they denied that he had any general theory, and they particularly rejected the prescriptions for permanent reordering of the economy that some of his more devout followers drew from the book. So they were neither Keynesians nor non-Keynesians, and were excluded and rejected by both. This position I also absorbed and carried with me through much of my later life.

New Deal Economics

Armed with these ideas, I went to Washington in 1938. There I encountered some real conservatives and liberals and became even more aware than I had been that I did not belong in either camp. I worked at the Federal Deposit Insurance Corporation for an economist named Homer Jones, who was an alumnus of the Brookings Institution. Brookings was then the Alamo of pre–New Deal conservatism. Perhaps it is more accurate to say that some of the Brookings people, like Harold Moulton, who had been open-minded researchers before the New Deal, became sullen defenders of the past record as soon as FDR came into office. Anyway, observing their complete negativism, I felt no kinship with them.

My exposure to the Keynesians and the liberals was more intense and painful. A militant and extreme Keynesianism was coming into Washington in 1938 at about the time I came to town. This was stagnationist, holding that private investment would be permanently below the saving that would be generated at full employment and that government had to fill the gap permanently. It was redistributionist, holding that low-income people saved a smaller share of their income than upper-level income people, and that a transfer of income from rich to poor was a good way to overcome the secular excess of saving. It had also absorbed a desire for a variety of government investment programs and other government interventions, even though that was not readily deducible from Keynes's theory.

These ideas were embodied in a little book, *An Economic Program for Economic Democracy,* by seven Harvard and Tufts economists, that received much attention in 1938. The ideas attracted a lot of publicity from testimony by Alvin Hansen and others before the Temporary National Economic Committee in 1939. And they were the unifying doctrine of a group of politically active economists in the Department of Commerce, the Budget Bureau, the Federal Reserve, and the Treasury. They were an ideological and social "set," and I did not belong to it, ideologically or socially.

My difference from all those people became most acute in 1940 and 1941 when I became involved in questions of defense economics. I joined a team of economists in the Price Stabilization Division of the National Defense Advisory Commission. We regarded as our objective the avoidance of inflation during the defense buildup, without resort to price controls. Toward the end of 1940, the head of the division, Leon Henderson, took on another team of economists, who were equally devoted to the idea that price controls were essential. A struggle went on between these two teams during much of 1941. Finally the price-controllers won. This left me with the feeling not only that I was not a member of the Keynesian liberal team but also that they were my enemies.

Wartime Economics

The war had another important effect on my thinking insofar as it is measured on the liberal-conservative scale. It made me a consistent supporter of defense expenditures and especially resistant to the idea that defense spending in the United States had to be severely limited by ideas of what we could afford. In 1940 and 1941, there was a debate in Washington about the scale of our defense buildup. Many believed that it had to be kept small because of the budgetary and economic costs. I was firmly of the opinion that there was no cost to building up the defenses rapidly that could be nearly as great as the cost of failing to do so. After Pearl Harbor, it became clear that we had been nowhere near economic limits to our defense program and that we would have been much better off if we had rearmed more rapidly.

I think that I have not neglected the logical point that defense, like other good things, has its costs and that at some point the costs are not worth bearing. But I have been terribly impressed by the costs of being unprepared militarily, and terribly unimpressed by the magnitude of the costs when the defense program is of the size that has been under consideration ever since World War II. This attitude toward defense put me at odds with the "liberal" community after Vietnam. But in a peculiar way it also put me at odds with much of the "conservative" community. It made me unable to accept the view that government spending per se is bad and that limits should be placed on total government spending. It created for me the possibility that if total spending is limited by some general ceiling, defense spending might be cut too much, and the adverse consequences of that would exceed whatever gains there might be from the limitation of total spending. Also, if I accept the proposition that defense spending may be too low, I am unable to accept the proposition that there is some flaw in the political process that universally makes government spending too high. And if I accept that exception for defense spending I am bound to ask whether other kinds of expenditures may fall into the exceptional category also, and be too low.

This attitude makes it impossible for me to go along with conventional conservative strictures about government spending. But that in turn makes it impossible for me to go along with conventional strictures about taxation. One of the arguments in favor of low taxation most commonly used by conservatives is that if taxes are higher "they" (Congress, or politicians generally) will spend more. But if you think some of the additional spending will be for purposes for which spending would otherwise have been too low, you cannot be sure that increasing taxes causes a net loss.

Committee for Economic Development

But I am getting ahead of my story. At the end of the war, I went to work for the Committee for Economic Development, and there I felt that I was a number of a team, at least for about ten years. But it was the kind of team that especially appealed to me because it was itself outside the main ideological and political groupings of the time. CED was an organization of businessmen, but they were unorthodox businessmen, rebelling against the business establishment of the time, as represented by the National Association of Manufacturers and the U.S. Chamber of Commerce. CED had a strong University of Chicago orientation, and the idea behind it originally came from discussions at Chicago. The first chairman and guiding spirit, Paul Hoffman, was a trustee of the university. One of the leading members, Beardsley Ruml, had been dean of the social sciences at Chicago, and the first director of research, T. O. Yntema, was a professor at Chicago. (The next two research directors, Howard Myers and I, were also products of the University of Chicago.) My mentor, Henry Simons, wrote a report on taxation for the CED.

Paul Hoffman described the position of the CED as "neither left nor right, but responsible," and that became the watchword of the organization. Basically, its policy position was what I have described as the position of Henry Simons. It asserted an active role for government in maintaining high employment and economic stability by the use of its fiscal and monetary policies. Its fiscal policy was, as I later called it, "domesticated Keynesianism," relying on Keynesian analysis but rejecting as unworkable the fine-tuning prescriptions of Keynes's more devout followers. But on "micro" matters, CED was strongly free-market, opposing price controls (which was an issue at the end of the war) and opposing protectionism (which would be a continuing issue).

This Keynesianism, even though tempered, and this free-trade attitude irritated the conventional business leadership. At the same time, CED was not embraced by the orthodox Keynesians and liberals. The standard attitude of mainstream economists of the time was that CED was pretty good for a group of businessmen, and certainly better than other businessmen, but not really liberated from old taboos and interests.

The CED position of being outside both the business mainstream and the economists' mainstream, and of having consciously chosen to be outside, was very congenial to me. The situation did not last, however. CED was to be a victim of its own success. The committee had been formed originally by a group of maverick businessmen who were not the heads of the largest corporations. But as the CED received increasing amounts of attention and seemed to have influence on public and official thinking, it attracted more and more leaders of the big corporations. Consequently, the committee became more and more conventional. This did not mean the members became more "free-market." On the contrary, on some matters they became less so. In a statement on inflation in 1958, for example, they insisted, despite my arguments, on making an appeal for voluntary restraint on wage and price increases that I regarded as a dangerous opening toward price and wage controls. During work on a statement about labor relations, it became clear that many members were not concerned about the power of unions as long as all the firms in an industry dealt with the same union and had the same contract. An attempt to write a policy statement about antitrust policy turned out to produce a sermon on the social responsibility of business. I felt that the ideology of the CED was becoming the fashionable liberalism of, for example, the editorial page of the *New York Times*.

So, after about 1957 I became more and more disaffected with CED. At the same time, I found no other attachment. I was still identified with an organization of businessmen that everyone considered "conservative."

The Homeless Economist

My homelessness was evidenced by two incidents in 1964. During the Johnson-Goldwater campaign, the word *conservative* had the same implications of danger to the nation that the word *liberal* was to have in the Bush-Dukakis campaign, and with about as little reason. I tried to clarify the situation with an article in the *Washington*

Post entitled "Varieties of Conservatism: Wall Steet, Main Street and the University of Chicago." This was not only an effort at exposition. It also distanced me from the Wall Street variety, which fairly described the CED, and the Main Street variety, which fairly described the Republicans in Congress. I thought I was identifying myself with the Chicago variety. But I soon learned from a good friend at the university that I was not orthodox in that sect either. I continued to believe, following Simons, that vigorous enforcement of the antitrust laws was essential, whereas the Chicagoans of 1964 had rejected that idea. Indeed, it was to become clearer in later years that whereas I still clung to, or was stuck with, Simons's idea of the "positive program for laissez-faire," the new Chicagoans were elevating the laissez-faire aspect of that prescription and downplaying the positive program part.

But I did not fit in with the other team either. In 1964 the CED decided to give me a sabbatical for the year 1965–1966, after twenty years of service. I would have the year off with full pay and could go anywhere. Having a hankering to live in Paris, I asked the Council of Economic Advisers to name me as the U.S. representative on an international committee of economists who would advise on a study of fiscal policy to be done by the Organization for Economic Cooperation and Development. I thought that I had demonstrated enough expertise and objectivity on that subject to be eligible for the appointment, and I did not have to be paid. My request was denied, however. I was later told by an "insider" that I would have been appointed if I had been a "card-carrying Democrat." I do not regret missing Paris, because I did some of the best work of my career spending my sabbatical at the Center for Advanced Study in the Behavioral Sciences, but the incident illustrated what it meant to belong or not belong to a team.

In 1967, after twenty-two years, I left the CED and moved to Brookings, which was then in a liberal phase. I chose Brookings not because of any ideological affinity—rather the contrary—but because at Brookings I could do my own thing rather than writing statements to be signed by people with whom I was not much in sympathy. But I soon found that doing my own thing, at least in that stage of my life, was unsatisfactory, not ideologically but existentially. I felt that I was missing out on the most exciting part of life in Washington, and possibly in the United States, which is the life of politics, because of my reluctance to commit myself.

Sometime in 1968 I read part of a novel (I never finished it) by Sartre about the Spanish Civil War, in which there is a conversation between a French Communist and a friend. The Communist is urging his friend to join the party, but the friend says he is not committed. The Communist then replies: "Join and you will be committed."

In this mood I decided to join. I offered my services in the campaign for the Republican presidential nomination, characteristically, to Nelson Rockefeller, the least Republican of the Republicans. In the upshot, I chaired a task force on the budget for the Nixon campaign and then joined the Nixon administration as a member of the Council of Economic Advisers.

The Republican Mainstream

Although I had joined, I was not fully committed. I had just completed a history of the making of fiscal policy in the previous forty years and told myself that I was only entering the government as an observer, to be a "fly on the wall" to see how things looked from the inside. My initial intention was to take only one year's leave from Brookings, but its president, Kermit Gordon, who had been a member of the CEA in the Kennedy administration, told me that I would not get the hang of things in less than one year. And although I did stay for five and a half years, I was never "fully" committed. There was always part of me in observer status, expecting that the clock would strike twelve and return my car and driver to a pumpkin and mouse. Or, as I told George Shultz after one meeting in the White House, "I have the feeling that we are a troop of boy scouts invited into City Hall for a day to act as if we are the City Council."

But still, I was more committed, and felt more a part of a team, in the Nixon administration than I have before or since. That was basically because a number of people who could not have been more different from me—starting with Richard Nixon himself—treated me as part of the team. And yet it is consistent with my attitude as I have described it that the team I joined was rather unusual. It did not have a rigid doctrine. Mr. Nixon, as I and others have said, was "a conservative man with liberal ideas." He was, after all, the proponent of revenue sharing, the Family Assistance Plan, and the Environmental Protection Agency. He supported the idea that the budget should be balanced at high employment, and took pleasure in thinking that made him a "Keynesian." He floated the dollar, removed production controls from agriculture, and initiated a round of international tariff reduction. His great sin, in the field of economics, was the imposition of price and wage controls, but he at least recognized that it was a sin. Everything could be discussed with him: there were no forbidden subjects, as increasing taxes was to be in the Reagan administration.

When I left the government, at the end of August 1974, I was comfortable in feeling that I was part of the Republican mainstream, and that the Republican mainstream was broad enough so that being part of it imposed no serious limits to my independence of thought. By 1978, however, I found that mainstream to be too narrow. In the early days of the Carter administration, I had been asked to serve as chairman of an advisory committee on economic policy to the Republican National Committee. I declined because I did not want the responsibility it involved, but I did accept membership. I soon found myself at odds with that team. The other members of the advisory committee, and the RNC as a whole, were infatuated with the idea that reducing taxes would raise revenues and that the politically attractive promise of cutting taxes could thus be made consistent with the traditional Republican devotion to balancing the budget. I argued against this in the advisory committee and at a hearing that the RNC held, but to no avail, obviously. It was not so much that I was opposed to cutting taxes, although I was already worried about the effect of a tax cut on the defense program. Mainly I was offended by the use of the shoddy "Laffer curve" argument.

In 1980, I favored the selection of George Bush as the Republican presidential candidate, and was especially pleased that he recognized the deception in "voodoo economics." After Ronald Reagan became the candidate, I worked with an independent committee that raised $3 million on his behalf, which relieved me of any direct contact with his rhetoric. I wrote an article in the *Wall Street Journal* explaining that I was for Reagan despite his ideas about the tax cut, because I thought he would be stronger for defense and against inflation than Carter. This was a precisely limited endorsement.

After the election, the administration created a committee called the President's Economic Policy Advisory Board (PEPAB), consisting of former Republican economic officials, almost all of whom had worked on the campaign. I was not initially invited to join, but I told my friend, George Shultz, who was to be the chairman, that I would like to participate, and he included me. So at the infrequent meetings that PEPAB held before it disappeared at the end of 1986, I grumbled and dissented, mainly about the tax policy but also more generally about the absence of any logical foundation for the administration's whole budget policy.

But my dissatisfaction with what had become conventional conservative Republicanism did not make me any happier with the opposition. It was too protectionist, too dovish, too inflationist, too redistributionist, and too tempted by grandiose ideas of economic planning for me. I sometimes felt that there were people commonly identified as "liberals" who were as unhappy with their team as I was with mine. I think of an article by Charles Schultze effectively debunking the idea of "industrial policy." But we were not about to form a new team called "None of the Above."

Dissent from Convention

I have concentrated here on economic issues. I am aware that now the difference between liberals and conservatives is at least as much about social or moral issues as about economics. On these other matters, I have less experience than on economics, but I feel about them the same ambivalence, the same inability to swallow whole the doctrine of any party or sect. These areas are filled with hard questions to which the answers are painfully uncertain. Abortion is a good example. There are heart-rending conflicts of rights and interests, and I find it impossible to say that one never or always dominates the other. So the answer probably depends on times and circumstances, which will be hard to define with confidence but will be better than "always" or "never." Capital punishment is a similar case. My "instincts" are against capital punishment—it is so irreversible. But I cannot say that Israel was wrong to make an exception and execute Eichmann. And if Eichmann, who else? Do we then logically go to chopping off the hands of purse-snatchers? Decisions have to be made, and people will disagree about what the decisions should be, but no one will have a strong claim to moral or intellectual superiority.

As time has passed, I have come to recognize that my dissent from the conventional parties, ideologies, and schools is less a matter of policy than of talk. I have become less confident that I know what good policy is. Also, I have come to think that differences of policy within the range of options usually under consideration in the United

States are not terribly important. Defense policy is an exception to that, but I do not pretend to know what defense policy should be. I only know that what is commonly said about the economics of the matter is nonsense.

But it is the talk, and not only from the Right but also from the Left, and not only from the politicians but also from the "intellectuals," that is most distressing. People routinely say with apparent certainty serious things that are if not patently false at least highly uncertain. And there is no debate, no confrontation of facts or analysis. The things people say are not meant to be measured on the scale of truth. They are only the signs by which one indicates which team one belongs to, like the "identification-friend-or-foe" signals that warplanes emit. Perhaps this low quality of the discussion does not hurt, but it is surely "unlovely," in Henry Simons's favorite word of disapproval. *(April 1989)*

3

The Future of the Adaptive Society

In 1989, I wrote an essay giving a synthetic history of the
economic policy of the previous sixty years. The beginning of
this period saw capitalism entering upon its greatest agony, the
Great Depression, from which it recovered in great strength. The
end of the period saw the collapse of communism.

Continuous Adaptation

The history of the sixty years could have been written as the story
of the triumph of capitalism over communism, and in a crude sense
that was the story. But the point, as I saw it, was that the capitalism
that had triumphed was not the capitalism of Herbert Hoover—or of
any of the presidents who had followed him. It was the triumph of a
society that, while retaining certain fundamental features, had
adapted almost continuously, in one direction or another, to emerg-
ing problems, perceptions, and theories. So I called my essay "The
Triumph of the Adaptive Society," chapter 4 in this volume.

In this addendum to my earlier essay, I offer comments on the
situation as it appears five years later. At the end of my 1989 essay,
I wrote:

> The main lesson of the past is not to be proud. Previous
> beliefs that we have found the final answer to economic
> problems have been disappointed. There are people who

think that the answer has been found in the varieties of capitalism that exist today and most particularly in Reaganism-Thatcherism. The disillusionment this time may be less painful than in the earlier cases. But we will discover—I believe we have already discovered—problems for which this formula is inadequate. We will have to adapt, and will. We will do better if we are not too inflated with the idea that we already live in the Golden Age.

Five years later, it is clear to almost everyone that we do not live in the Golden Age. Moreover, it is clear that we are not and have not been on the path to a Golden Age. In a peculiar way, Leninism and Reaganism are parallel in this respect. Lenin "pointed the way" to a Golden Age that would exist in the future and that his program would achieve. Of course, most of us always knew and now almost everyone knows that there is no Golden Age in his direction. Reagan pointed the way to a Golden Age that had existed in the past—before Kennedy and before Roosevelt, before Martin Luther King and Rachel Carson and Gloria Steinem. But there had been no Golden Age, and there was no going back. I don't want to push this comparison very far. Lenin's path to his Golden Age was immeasurably brutal. Reagan's was only mildly negligent.

No Going Back

By 1989, when the magical Reagan was replaced by the prosaic Bush, reality began to set in. It became obvious that we were not going back. Government expenditures were rising. Taxes were as high as ever. Government regulations were increasing. The Reagan Revolution was over and had left some trace but not much. Devout Reaganites were disappointed, and some were infuriated. They believed that Bush had betrayed the revolution. But these trends were already evident in the latter days of Reagan. It was not that Bush had betrayed the revolution but that reality—economic and political—had left the revolution behind.

The Reagan charm was a local anesthetic that kept the country pain free, while the essential operation of ending the cold war by a combination of strength and negotiation took place. But when the operation was over and the anesthetic wore off, many problems became apparent.

At this point, I should explain what I mean by saying that

problems became apparent. A problem becomes apparent when there is a serious disparity between the conditions that are believed to exist and the conditions that are desired and expected. The expectation also implies some notion of the means by which the desired conditions could be achieved. And to say that the disparity is serious implies something about the priority given to some conditions over others.

So when I say that some problems became apparent, I do not necessarily mean that the conditions complained of actually existed or that the expectations were reasonable, or that the implied policies were likely to be effective or that the goals sought were the most important. My own ideas on any of these points are not relevant to my immediate question, which is the nature of the adaptation the society is now trying to make, although I shall return later to some thoughts about the probable success of that adaptation.

Concerns of Americans

With this disclaimer, I can sketch the long list of problems with which many Americans have been concerned since I wrote my 1989 essay:

• Total output and average per capita incomes have been growing significantly more slowly than in the years 1948–1973.

• The incomes of some part of the population have been growing much less than the average, or even declining. Just which part of the population this is and why are open questions.

• There is worry that this generation of Americans, or the next, cannot expect to live as well as their parents, and so they will not live "the American Dream."

• The proportion of the population in poverty has not fallen in about twenty years. The proportion among blacks and children has remained especially high.

• In parts of many cities, not only poverty but also crime, persistent unemployment, illiteracy, illegitimacy, drug and alcohol abuse, and other pathologies are common.

• Relations among the races seem to be deteriorating.

• The quality of American primary and secondary education is disappointing and may have been deteriorating.

• The U.S. lead over other countries in economic performance has been diminishing, and in some respects we have fallen behind.

- The United States has a large, persistent federal budget deficit.
- The United States has a large, persistent trade deficit with the rest of the world, especially with Japan.
- Many Americans are without health insurance, and many who have insurance are unhappy about the cost and the paperwork involved.
- The U.S. economy fell into a recession in 1990 from which it recovered unusually slowly. Viewing the history of the past twenty years from a position in this recession contributed to the view that economic performance in the two decades as a whole had been unsatisfactory.

These conditions—real or alleged—came into the national consciousness through media that reported and interpreted them, since most people could not observe most of these conditions directly. Also, of course, some politicians found it in their interest to exploit the possibilities for dissatisfaction with the Reagan-Bush administration by emphasizing these conditions.

Intellectual Entrepreneurship and Boredom

Moreover, two processes that I had noted in the essay on the period 1929–1989 were at work. One was intellectual entrepreneurship—the process by which intellectuals construct out of fragmentary evidence of what is going on theories and interpretations that at the minimum sell books and may also bring them into positions of influence with political powers. Thus, we had theories of economic decline, associated with the name of Lester Thurow, and of basic structural change, associated with the name of Robert Reich.

The other factor at work was boredom. The public mood seems to alternate between seeking relief from political activism and intrusiveness, on the one hand, and boredom with government inertia on the other. The charm of Ronald Reagan held off public boredom with do-nothing government for a while, but the personality of George Bush only accentuated the restlessness with a government that seemed unknowing and unresponsive.

The election of Bill Clinton was a reaction to these conditions—to what people believed were America's problems, partly as they had been made to seem by intellectual entrepreneurs, and to boredom with inactive government. In the two years since Clinton's election, it has become clear that we are in a phase of more active government, which indeed began with Bush but in a more apologetic way. But, also clearly, the new activism will not try to deal with all the complaints about the national condition that were loudly voiced during the 1992 campaign. The administration's proposals to deal with the nation's problems will not be radical or revolutionary, and the opposition will aim only to moderate somewhat the move toward a larger role for government, not to stop or reverse it.

Activism Constrained

At present, the move toward greater activism seems to be constrained by budget considerations—essentially by the reluctance to raise taxes and by the need to show at least a decline in the budget deficit. But some increase in taxes, relative to GDP, is apparent. There will also be some increase in expenditures for social programs made possible by the reduction in defense spending. As a contribution to dealing with the lagging incomes of low-income workers, the Earned Income Tax Credit program is being increased. New measures of government intervention are taking place outside the budget. Thus, environmental and safety regulations are increasing. The government intends to promote the development of selected industries and products by small injections of federal funds. There is a search for ways to reform, and improve, the welfare system without spending much more money, and that may involve more government control of the way welfare recipients behave.

The largest increase in the government's role in the economy under consideration in 1994 relates to the health care industry. How that will come out is still uncertain. Some of the proposals on the table involve curtailment of the freedoms of some patients and of some health care providers, while increasing the options open to some others. But already in 1994 a tendency to withdraw from the more compulsive aspects of proposals for health care reform is visible.

Taken all together, what is now in sight is not a descent along the "road to serfdom." Except possibly in the case of health care, where the issue is still in doubt, no serious infringement of freedom is involved. Americans will have large and rising incomes to dispose of as they will, and freedom to move, to change jobs, and to engage in other activity without serious hindrance. Taxation, government spending, and government regulation will be lower here than almost anywhere else in the world.

Of course, if the image of alternating phases of active and passive governments is realistic, we must recognize that in 1994 we are still in the early days of an activist phase. Possibilities of government control greater than now in sight remain, especially since some of the steps being considered are unlikely to achieve the desired goals. But the probability also remains of another turn at some point toward a government that would not reverse what is now happening but that will slow down further interventions. *(May 1994)*

4

The Triumph of the Adaptive Society

O ctober 1989 marked the sixtieth anniversary of the onset of capitalism's greatest crisis. It has also been about this long since some seemingly intelligent and objective observers thought that communism, as then being put into practice in the Soviet Union, was the great hope of the world. Now we are celebrating the success of capitalism and the failure of communism. This celebration is well deserved. While I do not want to be misunderstood as not joining in the celebration, I want to bring a note of realism to the party.

Capitalism Transformed

Capitalism survived its crisis and went on to great successes. But the capitalism that survived and succeeded was not the capitalism of 1929. The capitalism that will succeed in the next sixty years may not be the capitalism of the late twentieth century. Capitalism succeeded in large part because it adapted. Capitalism is not a blank slate upon which anything can be written; it has a central core that must be preserved if it is to remain capitalism. But the large penumbra around that core can change without ending capitalism, and it has to change from time to time if capitalism is to survive.

The central core of capitalism, without which a society would not be capitalist, is freedom. But absolute freedom is impossible, and no one has satisfactorily defined the amount and kind of freedom that is essential to qualify as capitalism. Undoubtedly, the adaptations of American capitalism in the past sixty years have rearranged freedoms, redistributed them among individuals, and changed their character. People are no longer free, for example, to spend as large a part of their incomes as they formerly were. If some of the leading figures of 1929 were to be confronted with the picture of the American society as it is now, they would say that this society is neither free nor capitalist. But very few Americans living today would doubt that we qualify as both free and capitalist, nor would there be much doubt that countries as diverse as, say, Sweden and Singapore qualify.

Our adaptations have not all been in the same direction. There has been an increase in the size and functions of government. But all change has not been in that direction. There have been withdrawals of some powers and functions, and we have adapted to or around others.

Some adaptations have been led by public policy, some by private behavior. The genius of the system is that both policy and behavior have been free to adapt to changing circumstances and needs and to each other. The freedom of the private sector to adapt to conditions created by public policy has disciplined public policy. When public policy creates inefficiencies, the private sector has a strong incentive and much opportunity to overcome the effects of the policy. The private sector, for example, adapted to government regulation of the interest paid on bank deposits by developing money-market mutual funds with many of the features of bank deposits but without the regulation on the interest they paid. In 1962, Milton Friedman complained of the limitation of freedom implicit in the federal government's monopoly of the post office business. The private economy adapted by express mail service and by facsimile transmission. But in this essay I shall concentrate on the adaptations of public policy because they have been most critical to the survival of the system.

One might say that capitalism succeeds simply because capitalism is a very productive system, per se. But that capitalism was productive, in the sense that we now measure by gross national product, was never in doubt, and questions about the survival or success of capitalism were not usually questions about its productiveness. Analysis and experience show that capitalism in some forms and manifestations leaves large gaps between expectations and performance, despite its productiveness. Capitalism might have survived even if these gaps had not been closed, but it surely could not have been the success we now consider it to be. Adaptation of public policy has been essential to closing those gaps.

Capitalism 1929–1939

I shall review the adaptations of the past sixty years and then discuss the adaptations that may lie ahead. I especially want to address the changes that occurred from 1929 to 1939, because that history is too much forgotten or misunderstood and because it carries the most dramatic lessons of the need for open-mindedness and whatever intelligence we can muster.

Confidence in the System. Three aspects of the situation as it was in the late 1920s and early 1930s are important to recall and difficult to appreciate or even believe today:

- the confidence in the economic system as it existed at the time of the crash and the persistence of that confidence even for a year or two after the crash
- the severity of the depression
- the disappearance of confidence in the economic system as the depression deepened, the lack of consensus on alternatives or correctives, and the willingness to accept almost any proposed remedy

That the American people should have had great confidence in their economic system in the 1920s was perfectly natural. Not only were they, except possibly the farmers, more prosperous than they had ever been, but they were for the first time obviously more prosperous than any one else in the world.

The system in which they had confidence was not the free-market system of atomistic competition, of the Invisible Hand. It was the business system, which is a different thing. In this system, the benefits flowed from the character and wisdom of identifiable businessmen. They were the heroes whose pictures I used to see in the *Saturday Evening Post* and *Colliers*. They were not driven by the market: they were to tame and rationalize the market. It was the responsibility of government to help them do that. One of Herbert Hoover's main interests as secretary of commerce was helping trade associations organize to avoid destructive competition and overproduction, in part by providing more statistics. These business-men were to be protected from foreign competition by high tariffs. And high tax rates that might discourage these geese from laying their golden eggs had to be avoided.

Of course, some economists knew that the system had a tendency to fluctuate. They also had ideas about how these fluctua-tions could be moderated, including the idea of contracyclical public works spending. While Herbert Hoover was aware of work going on in this field and had encouraged it, the danger did not hang over him or the country. Aside from the "adjustment" after World War I, it had been a long time since our last "panic," and we now had the Federal Reserve System to prevent that kind of thing.

As usual, a few intellectuals complained about the state of American society. But in the 1920s, unlike earlier periods, their complaints were not much about the economy. In a way, they complained because the economy was too successful: we were too materialistic, and our heroes were vulgar money seekers. A few thought that the Soviet Union was giving the world a model of an economic system that was superior to capitalism and would replace it. Lincoln Steffens had seen the future, in Moscow, and found that "it works." But this view was more common in Europe than here. Bertrand Russell was probably the leading example. In a book published in 1920, he said: "The fundamental ideas of Communism are by no means impracticable, and would, if realized, add immeasur-ably to the well-being of mankind."[1] (Incidentally, he republished the book in 1949 without any revision on this point.)

General confidence in the economic system persisted for some time after the stock market crash, certainly well into 1930. A little book, *Oh, Yeah,* published in the early 1930s, contains a collection of statements by leading figures of the time about the imminence of the recovery.[2] Even today, almost sixty years later the book is a frightening reminder of the degree of confidence placed in the utterances of people in authority. It ought to be required reading for all public figures, or at least for their press secretaries. These reassurances came mainly from government officials, starting with

---

1. Bertrand Russell, *The Practice and Theory of Bolshevism* (London: Univer-sity Books, 1920), p. 90.
2. Edward Angly, *Oh, Yeah* (New York: Viking Press), p. 1031.

the president, and business tycoons, who were motivated in part by the hope that their statements would help moderate the economic decline and possibly divert attention from their own failures. But they also seemed to have some belief in what they were saying, and it was not only such people who felt so confident.

That confidence should have persisted for many months, perhaps more than a year, after the stock market crash is not entirely surprising. Most of the statistics by which we now measure economic performance did not exist then, and people were less bathed in economic news, except for the stock market averages, than they are now. The best general measure of the economic performance then available, the index of industrial production, declined between 1929 and 1930 by less than between 1920 and 1921. There was no official or generally accepted measure of unemployment, and the rate of unemployment was a subject of dispute throughout the 1930s. But by the estimates we now have, the unemployment rate in 1930, although it had jumped from 1929, was still less than it had been in 1921. Thus, no one would tell that we were going through something different and immensely more serious than we had experienced before. But by 1931, everyone knew.

The Depression. I have to devote a little time to describing the depression, although I have no new information to present about it. We are running out of the generation of people with personal memories of the depression. Economists now use data sets that begin with 1946 at the earliest. It is important to keep retelling this story to remind successive generations that the history of capitalism is not one of progress from 1776 interrupted only by minor fluctuations around the trend that can be ironed out retrospectively by statistical techniques or made to disappear by sophisticated analysis. The depression was a real crisis of capitalism, especially of American capitalism, in the course of which capitalism changed substantially. Whether capitalism could have survived in any form without those changes is uncertain, but certainly it could not have survived in the form of 1929.

By estimates that we have now, but did not have at the time, the real gross national product declined 30 percent from 1929 to 1933. The largest previous decline since the Civil War had been 8 percent from 1918 to 1921, which was attributed to the adjustment after World War I. In what had once been thought of as the great depression of 1893, the real GNP fell by 3 percent. Real GNP began to rise after 1933, but it did not regain the 1929 level until 1939. For the whole decade from 1930 through 1939, average real GNP was 13 percent below the 1929 level.

The decline in per capita consumption, which roughly measures how people were living, was not so large as the decline in GNP; it declined by 22 percent from 1929 to 1933. Much of the decline of output was absorbed by the decline of investment.

But these aggregate statistics, shocking as they are, do not tell the real story. One could say that the collapse to 1933 only brought real per capita consumption back to the level of 1921 and real GNP back to the level of 1918, neither of which in the span of history looks so terrible. The real problem was the tragic distribution of the pain: the unemployment rate rose to 25 percent in 1933, according to estimates we have now but did not have then, and was still 17 percent in 1939. Real farm income fell by almost 50 percent.

Even these figures are only suggestive, because we do not know how these losses were distributed. We do not know how many people experienced unemployment, or for how long, and how many farmers lost everything while others at least survived reasonably. We do know that there were people who did fairly well—like tenured professors, whose real incomes rose as the cost of living declined. For other people who were continuously employed and confident of staying that way, the situation was not too bad. Real hourly compensation of manufacturing production workers rose during the depression.

Aside from not knowing the more or less objective facts, we do not know the psychological condition of the people at the time in any comprehensive way. Popular representations of the period are not helpful. We have on the one hand the happy movies of the period— screwball comedies and Broadway musicals. We know that they were not realistic pictures of the decade, but their popularity may reflect the readiness of a large part of the public to be mollified by superficial escapism.

On the other hand, many of the so-called realistic portrayals, of which the best known are the photographs of migrant workers, destitute farmers, and breadlines, were taken by photographers working for the Resettlement Administration. The mission of this government agency was to bring back pictures that would justify an appropriation request. We know now, from research done subsequently, that some of the most affecting pictures were the result of the artistry of the photographer imposed on a more banal actuality. In addition, some of the photographers were disappointed with the difficulty of finding subjects appropriate to their purpose, because many whose objective situation seemed most depressing were surprisingly optimistic.

But if it is impossible to be precise and comprehensive in describing how miserable conditions were during the depression, there is no doubt that they were miserable to a degree not experienced before or since in the American economy. Large numbers of people were destitute, living on handouts. Many lived in severely straitened circumstances, working intermittently, or supported by relatives. Even many who were working fairly steadily lived in great anxiety over falling into the unemployed class. And some people did not suffer at all, even thrived on the situation.

These conditions were made even more intolerable than they would otherwise have been by the general realization that much of the suffering was totally unnecessary. That is, it was not the result of any inadequacy in the number and skill of the labor force or in the quantity of capital or in the state of technology. It was no good saying that we were as well off, on the average, as we had been only ten years earlier. We were, even on the average, much worse off than we could be. And the cause of the most resentment was the uneven distribution of the pain of the depression. We had poverty in the midst of plenty in two senses—poverty in the midst of potential plenty for the society as a whole and poverty in the midst of actual plenty for some members of the society.

The strong feeling of the unfairness of the situation was important for the subsequent adaptations, many of which were largely motivated by that. Before the depression, the inequality in the distribution of income in the existing system could be justified by the argument that inequality was associated with such rapid general progress that even the poor were becoming rich. In 1932, that was no longer a credible story.

The depth of the crisis is represented for me by the fact that William Green, the notoriously mild-mannered president of the notoriously conservative American Federation of Labor, told a congressional committee in 1931 that if something was not done promptly there would be violence. In fact, it is surprising how little violence there was. The most forceful demonstration of protest during the whole period was the bonus march in 1932, when 20,000 veterans of World War I came to Washington to present their demands to the government. And what did they demand? They did not demand a change in the capitalist system: they demanded that the bonus for their war service, which had been promised them for 1945, should be paid then, in 1932. And when Congress rejected their demand, all but a handful of them went home peacefully. The lack of violence did not, however, indicate satisfaction or confidence in the economic system. Rather, it indicated confidence in the political system as an instrument for meeting the society's needs, as was evident after the 1932 election.

The state of the American political and economic system was analyzed by a not unsympathetic German economist, Moritz J. Bonn, in *The Crisis of American Capitalism,* published in 1932:

> And quite spontaneously the question arises in thousands of hearts and brains: Is the capitalist system any longer justified if, in the richest country in the world, it is incapable of shaping an order which will guarantee to a comparatively sparse population, admittedly industrious and capable, a subsistence consonant with the human needs developed by modern techniques, without millions being from time to time reduced to beggary and to dependence on soup kitchens and casual wards. . . . The real significance of the American crisis consists in the fact that today it is not merely the present economic leadership or economic policy that is being questioned, but the capitalist system itself.[3]

Bonn said that the condition of American capitalism was made especially critical because, unlike earlier periods, although "an existing socialist system may be execrable or even disastrous[,] it cannot, however, be dismissed as 'impossible' " (p. 202).

While Bonn's analysis is representative of much thinking at that time, it contains a fundamental error, which still pervades much of today's thinking and talking. That is, he thought a unique thing called "capitalism" or "American capitalism" was in crisis and had to be compared with a distinctly different unique thing called "socialism." That view is parallel to the current one that a unique thing called "capitalism" has succeeded where another unique thing called "so-

---

3. M. J. Bonn, *The Crisis of Capitalism in America* (New York: John Day Co., 1932), pp. 188–89, 190, 202.

cialism" has failed. The fact is, the crisis of the 1930s was the crisis of 1929-style American capitalism, which died forever and was succeeded not by socialism but by American capitalism of a different style.

The New Deal. The American people, insofar as one can judge from the discussion of the time, from their voting in elections, and from what the government did and the public applauded, were not interested in either capitalism or socialism. Although they wanted something done, they were not concerned about either retaining or rejecting capitalism or about embracing or repelling socialism. Possible actions were not measured on that ideological scale.

There were a few Communists in the country, who got a good deal of attention, because they included some people with access to the media. There were a few non-Communist sympathizers. But communism held little attraction for Americans. It was associated with godlessness, bomb-throwing, free love, and, sufficiently disquieting for many American workers, trying to enlist Negro activism. The fact that the Soviet Union had a five-year plan and reportedly had no unemployment contributed to interest in the idea of national planning. One did not have to be a Communist to be a planner. Some of our leading businessmen were urging national planning. In the 1932 election, the Communist party got two-tenths of 1 percent of the vote, and some of that was from people who just wanted to register their disgust at the whole political-economic situation but neither wanted nor expected a Communist regime in America.

The Socialist party did better in the election of 1932, with 2 percent of the vote. Its candidate was, after all, a white Protestant clergyman, which seemed safe enough. But America did not need the Socialist party to get the kind of change the Socialists offered. The country could get almost all the Socialist program through one of the major parties, and within about ten years it did.

Americans voted in 1932 for a change, without ideological limits or directions, and they got it. They got in Franklin Roosevelt the perfect instrument for such a change—a president who was not inhibited, as Hoover had been, by prior ideas about economics or by prior ideas about the limits of government intervention in the economy.

One of my economics professors was asked sometime in the 1930s to give a lecture on the economics of the New Deal. He began his lecture by saying that there was no economics in the New Deal; there was no consistent theory or ideology in it. Its basic rationale was to take the most direct approach to any apparent problem.

If people were running on the banks, we would close the banks. If people were demanding gold, we would stop gold convertibility. If businesses were not producing because they could not sell at a profit, we would organize businesses to hold the prices up. That they would not be able to sell at the higher prices was a step of analysis beyond the interest of the decision makers.

If farmers could not sell their product at profitable prices, we would establish regulation limiting production to get the prices up. If workers did not get high enough wages to buy the product, we would pass legislation protecting their right to organize and get higher wages. If people were unemployed, we would put them to work for the government. (This simple notion received a more sophisticated elaboration and rationalization after 1936 in the form of Keynesianism.) If there was not enough money, we would print greenbacks. If old people had insufficient incomes and, perhaps more serious, kept on working when younger people would like their jobs, we would establish social insurance to pay them benefits if they would stop working. If Wall Street had been found to be full of crooks, we would establish regulations and an agency to monitor financial transactions.

And if the Supreme Court did not like this—so much the worse for the Supreme Court.

To none of this list of changes was there any significant objection on the ground that it violated the rules of capitalism, or free enterprise, or the free market—until later, after the danger had passed, when objection did arise, as we shall see. The list, interestingly, did not include any significant moves toward public ownership of what had been private enterprise—not because there would have been much objection if anyone had seriously proposed it. There was just no point: it would have been like nationalizing a burning building.

We came to the end of the New Deal, then, with a quite different capitalism from what we had in 1929. We now had an embryonic welfare state. We had accepted federal responsibility for the maintenance of high employment by monetary and fiscal means. We had initiated a major increase in the power of labor unions. Agriculture, housing, transportation, communications, banking, and other aspects of finance had been brought under heavy federal influence. We had a progressive tax system. And we had left behind, probably forever, reliance on the wisdom and responsibility of "business."

One can argue that all this was unnecessary and a mistake. A kind of horseshoe nail theory of the depression says that if the Federal Reserve had behaved differently in 1931 and 1932, the whole thing would have passed away, and we would never have gotten into the New Deal, which in any case delayed rather than advanced recovery. That may all be true. In fact, I believe much of it may be so. But it is irrelevant to my main point. If we look around the world today and say that capitalism has survived and succeeded, we have to recognize it as the capitalism as altered by the New Deal, not the capitalism of 1929. Perhaps the triumph of capitalism would have been even greater if we had never had the New Deal. That is something that cannot be read from the historical record. A more precise and reliable general theory of economic development would be needed to affirm or deny that.

Postwar Economic Theory

The story of capitalism did not end in 1939. After we came out of the depression and the war, questions abounded about whether the system as it then existed, or was tending, could survive. These questions came from two directions. First were those who thought that the system would come to disaster as a result of the changes made during the depression or the forecast continuation of policy in the same direction, notably the increasing influence of government in the economy. Later would come others who thought that in America, at least, the degree of government involvement and responsibility was still too small for successful functioning and that more planning was needed.

The worries from what I may call the free market side took several forms and expressions. Predictably, the business community made what we would later call a supply-side argument against the tax system as it was left by the New Deal and the war: the high marginal rates would seriously retard economic growth.

The notion of using fiscal management to maintain high employment that had begun to take hold in the later days of the New Deal after Keynes's *General Theory* and that had been elaborated and exaggerated by his more zealous followers, came to be seen as a serious threat. In his initial review of Keynes, Jacob Viner warned

that the Keynesian analysis and prescription could lead to an inflationary race between the wage demands of trade unions and the
creation of money by the printing press. This kind of warning became
more widespread as the ambitions of the Keynesians became clearer.
At the end of the war, many Keynesian economists predicted a
severe recession and recommended an increase of government
spending to avert it. When the prediction proved false, the incident
was taken as evidence of the willingness of some to use the
Keynesian argument as a cover for the real objective of increasing
the scope of government. In 1947, the Committee for Economic
Development, in words that I wrote myself, said that the policy of
managed compensatory finance would lead to an endless escalation
of government expenditures and deficits.[4]

The increased pervasiveness and strength of trade unionism
was also a cause of fear for the future of capitalism. This fear was,
naturally, most common among businessmen but was shared by
others. It was, for example, well expressed in one of the last
writings of Henry Simons, "Some Reflections on Syndicalism."[5] The
argument was that the power of the unions would make private
investment excessively risky and also create a continuous pressure
toward inflation, requiring the intervention of the government to
invest the nation's savings to maintain full employment and economic
growth and also to control prices and wages directly to prevent
inflation. The most powerful warning about the future of the American economic and political system was Friedrich Hayek's *The Road
to Serfdom,* published in 1944.[6] Written in England during the war,
and reflecting mainly British developments, the book was considered
both by its author and by its readers in the United States to be
applicable to American conditions. Hayek's thesis was that the trend
of economic thinking and policy, which he considered to be forty to
fifty years old in Britain but arose only with the New Deal in the
United States, was leading to a degree of government control
incompatible with personal freedom and democracy. The disease
was "social planning," and the end of the road was totalitarianism on

---

4. Committee for Economic Development, Taxes and the Budget, "A Program for Prosperity in a Free Economy" (New York: 1947).

5. Henry Simons, *Journal of Political Economy* (March 1944), pp. 1–25.

6. Friedrich Hayek, *The Road to Serfdom* (Chicago: University of Chicago
Press, 1944; reprinted 1974).

the style of Hitler's Germany or Stalin's Soviet Union. Hayek's book had a tremendous circulation in the United States. A short version of it was published in the *Reader's Digest,* at the time the American magazine with the widest readership.

A more moderate and also more provocative and durable analysis of the future of capitalism was presented by Joseph Schumpeter in *Capitalism, Socialism and Democracy,*[7] published in 1942. He foresaw the possibility that capitalism would be undermined by its own success. Output would become so large and the process of managing production would become so routinized that there would be no further need for the entrepreneur-owner. Society would lose its deference to such people, who would also have outgrown their earlier connection with a traditional aristocracy to which respect was paid. Business would be managed by bureaucrats, who could just as well be employed by the government as by the absentee institutional investors who would otherwise be their nominal masters. The degradation of the position of the entrepreneur-capitalists would be accelerated by the hostility of the intellectuals, who would resent their inferior position in the society and would promote an ideology that demeaned the capitalist achievement. The transition from high capitalism, which had already passed its peak at the beginning of the twentieth century, would be gradual and possibly not noticeable. As he said in his *Encyclopaedia Britannica* article on capitalism in 1945:

> Government control of the capital and labour markets, of price policies and, by means of taxation, of income distribution is already established and needs only to be complemented systematically by government initiative in indicating the general lines of production (housing programs, foreign investments) in order to transform, even without extensive nationalization of industry, regulated, or fettered, capitalism into a guided capitalism that might, with almost equal justice, be called socialism. Thus, prediction of whether or not the capitalist order will survive is, in part a matter of terminology.[8]

Schumpeter did not think that this system, whether called capitalism or socialism, would necessarily be undemocratic or repres-

---

7. Joseph Schumpeter, *Capitalism, Socialism and Democracy* (New York: Harper and Row, 1942).

8. *Encyclopaedia Britannica,* 1957, vol. 4, p. 807.

sive of personal liberty. Moreover, he thought that it could manage existing economic resources in existing modes of production efficiently. He did not, however, believe that it would be as dynamic and innovative as the earlier and purer form of capitalism.

With both Hayek and Schumpeter, there is question about the degree to which they were making forecasts. Admirers of both tend now to stress the conditionality of their forecasts and the value of their writings as warnings that helped avert the undesired future. But no doubt they foresaw the decline of capitalism as highly probable, even if not inevitable, and their view was highly credible to many people who thought about such things at all. Surely neither Hayek nor Schumpeter or their numerous followers would have made a big bet that in 1989 we would have celebrated the triumph of capitalism.

Clearly, the conditions that worried these people in the 1930s were moderated, the trends they foresaw did not turn out to be irreversible, and the disastrous results they feared did not occur. In saying this, I leave aside for the moment Schumpeter's prognosis, which was much more ambiguous than the others.

The tax system that worried the businessmen so much was substantially corrected from their standpoint, in part by the Revenue Act of 1948, passed by a Republican Congress over the third of President Truman's vetoes. Also, the businessmen learned that they could live with a tax system that in, say, 1935, they found shocking. The Taft-Hartley Act of 1948 reduced the danger that had been seen from the growing strength of trade unions. In addition, business learned that it had considerable ability to move out from under the power of the unions. Keynesian fiscal policy was, as I called it in *The Fiscal Revolution in America,* "domesticated."[9] It was no longer an engine for the wild escalation of budget deficits. We got really large budget deficits only much later, in the regime of Ronald Reagan, our most pre-Keynesian president since Calvin Coolidge.

The Role of Government in the Economy

The idea of government planning never had an important influence on government policy in America, except possibly in 1933 when the

---

9. Herbert Stein, *The Fiscal Revolution in America* (Chicago: University of Chicago Press, 1969).

National Recovery Administration was established. Hayek seems to have given too much weight to the fact that during the 1930s we had the National Planning Board, an entirely insignificant agency. The wartime controls, which some had thought might be the way into a more planned peacetime system, were totally dismantled. The industrial plants that the government had built for war production were gotten into private hands as quickly as possible. Federal expenditures remained higher after the war than they had been earlier, but this was entirely because of defense expenditures and expenditures for interest on the debt, mainly accumulated during World War II, and for veterans' benefits. Moreover, the course of federal spending was not frightening. Nondefense spending as a fraction of GNP was only slightly higher in 1960 than in 1948 (8.76 percent as compared with 8.34 percent) and nondefense spending for purposes other than social security declined significantly as a fraction of GNP during those two years. The rise in social security outlays was due to the increase in the number of beneficiaries and in their average benefits under the system as set up in the 1930s, not to any expansion of the program thereafter. No new regulatory systems were established between the end of World War II and 1960, except for the temporary measures associated with the Korean War.

The policy of the Truman-Eisenhower years did not return the government's role in the economy to what it had been in the 1920s or anything like it. Only a little of the New Deal had been undone. But the great fears that had been expressed about the future of capitalism were based more on the extrapolation of trends believed to be visible than upon the conditions actually in effect in 1939 or 1945. The experience of the postwar years suggested that this extrapolation was not inevitable or even highly probable. Moreover, the experience suggested something else: what had seemed so frightening about the New Deal was not really so suffocating of freedom and enterprise as had been thought. The economy was expanding, and if there were now some things that could not be done because of government regulations, the range of things that could be done in that expanding economy was very large and growing.

Of course, the expansion of government's role in the economy between 1933 and 1945 had been in response to the depression and the war. The fact that these conditions had passed was probably the main reason why this expansion did not continue. But those concerned for the future of capitalism had known that the depression and the war would end. They believed that forces had been set in motion—and might indeed have existed even before the depression—that would continue to work to the breakdown of capitalism after the war and depression were past. Their worries and warnings themselves probably contributed to averting the feared developments. But to a considerable extent, these worries and warnings, like many that reappeared later from the conservative side, reflected an overly simple view of the American political lineup. They visualized a homogeneous and omnipotent majority, liberated by the depression from its respect for authority, provided with an ideological justification by a disaffected intelligentsia, on a one-directional course to kill the goose that laid the golden eggs of freedom and prosperity. But this pessimistic view overlooked important realities in the American situation.

We are a nation of minorities with diverse interests. As the public choice theorists have emphasized, a minority with a strong concentrated interest can often get its way against the more diffused interest of the majority. Thus, a minority can enlist the power of the government to exploit the majority, as programs to aid an agricultural minority exploit a majority of consumers. But it can also enable a minority to keep itself from being taxed or controlled by a majority, as a minority of upper-income people have resisted taxation or a minority of employers have been able to get labor legislation amended in their favor.

Political Entrepreneurship

Schumpeter might have called this process entrepreneurship, which goes on in the political and intellectual world as well as in the commercial world. Politicians seeking office try to create and identify themselves with a new product to offer to the American public in exchange for their support. Life being imperfect, there are always possibilities for change that will be looked on as improvement. This can give rise to an alternation of periods of government activism and periods of stability and slowdown or even some reversal in the government's economic role. Thus, after almost twenty years of economic activism in depression and war, the Republicans created a new product (stability and predictability), found the perfect representative for it (Dwight Eisenhower), and found the American people ready for it. We can see this political entrepreneurship at work even more clearly later in the Kennedy-Johnson era and in the Reagan era.

Similarly, intellectuals respond to the market. They seek to differentiate their product and to find a niche in the world of ideas where they can sell their product in exchange for attention and, possibly, power. Thus, as "liberalism" or "anticapitalism" became the mainstream of the intellectuals, other intellectuals found a rewarding niche in being "conservative" or "anti–anti-capitalist." The possibilities for intellectual entrepreneurship are especially strong when active forces in the community are prepared to support the dissenters, and it does not take much in the way of resources to support a dissenting intellectual. So, the force of the intellectuals was less one directional than Schumpeter and his followers believed. In any event, the influence of the intellectuals was probably exaggerated in their analysis. Intellectuals tend to think that the opinions of other intellectuals are the *Zeitgeist* or a clue to the wave of the future, which they are bound to join or resist. But to a considerable extent, these joinings and resistings are a private fight, irrelevant to the actual course of events.

In an interesting essay, "The Cycles of American Politics," Arthur Schlesinger, Jr., calls attention to the alternation of periods of government activism and passivity in relation to the economy and to other aspects of life.[10] His attempts to find a regular periodicity in these alternations is not very convincing, and the search for a general explanation is not satisfactory. But the alternations seem real enough. One possible explanation, although Schlesinger does not put it that way, is boredom—the tendency of the populace to take the status quo for granted and ask if that's all there is. Then the political and intellectual entrepreneurs have a market for change, and they develop programs, arguments, and postures to meet that market. That may help to explain the period of passivity in the government's relation to the economy after World War II and is even more obviously relevant to the ending of that period.

By the late 1950s, the worries of a decade or so earlier that the capitalist system was endangered by an excess of government activism—of controls, planning, spending, and taxing—had

10. Reprinted in Arthur Schlesinger, Jr., *The Cycles of American History* (Boston: Houghton Mifflin, 1986).

faded.[11] A new anxiety arose. More people argued that the American economy was failing because the government was insufficiently active, using its powers too little to solve the nation's economic problems. Of course, all through the Truman and Eisenhower administrations people had thought that, but the idea became common and politically significant only as the 1960 election approached. To a considerable degree, this idea was the creation of political and intellectual entrepreneurs who needed a new product to sell to the American people. Although they could point to certain objective facts in support of their argument, that is always more or less true. Actually, the economic performance of the Eisenhower years had been extraordinarily good. The need for a change was not evident to the naked eye, as it had been in 1932. It had to be explained to the American people.

The American versus the Soviet Economy

This new feeling of doubt about the American economic system—or renewed feeling since the recovery from the depression—was stimulated by the launching of the Soviet Sputnik in 1957. This event raised the possibility that the Soviet system might be capable of more technological advance than ours. This concern grew to the more general concern over economic growth. For the first time, I think, the possibility was raised that communism might generate more rapid economic growth than capitalism. Khrushchev boasted that he would "bury" us—in output (he apparently had meat in mind). Previously, the Marxist position had been that although total growth might be larger under capitalism, that system would suffer from extreme instability and unfairness, as well as other evils, mainly

11. Note should be taken of Milton Friedman's book, *Capitalism and Freedom* (Chicago: University of Chicago Press, 1962, based on lectures he first gave in 1956 and published in 1962. This was a strong statement of the importance of capitalism—really, free markets—for political and personal freedom as well as for efficiency and other goals. But the actual conditions and trends to which he pointed did not, even then, seem very frightening. If that was the tip of the iceberg, it was probably a pretty small iceberg. On the whole, the tone of the book, while a warning against some possibilities, was hopeful. It was certainly much less apocalyptic than *The Road to Serfdom*, for example.

cultural. Now, the Soviets were threatening to beat us at our own game, and Americans were worried.[12]

It was not only the USSR that seemed to be gaining on us but also the countries of Western Europe. From 1950 to 1962, the annual growth rate of real income per capita in the United States was 1.6 percent; the comparable figures for Western Europe ranged from 6.1 percent in Germany and 5.3 percent in Italy to a low of 1.8 percent in the United Kingdom.[13]

This "lag" of the U.S. growth rate was claimed by many to result from a deficiency of the American economic system—namely, the absence of any "plan." This was the period of the French indicative planning, of the National Economic Development Council in Britain, and of new forms of cooperation among government, business, and labor in Germany. A leading expression of the idea that the United States was suffering from a deficiency of planning was a popular book of the period, *Modern Capitalism,* by Andrew Shonfield.[14] The precise content of the "planning" that the United States needed was never clear. For that matter, neither was the precise content of the planning that was supposed to be responsible for the superior performance of Western Europe.[15] Although the

12. I can illustrate this worry from my own experience. In 1959, Anastas Mikoyan, then deputy prime minister of the USSR, visited the United States and was entertained by, among others, the Committee for Economic Development, for which I was then working. The chairman of the CED had been primed by the State Department to suggest to Mikoyan that there should be an exchange of economists. Mikoyan agreed, and in 1960, I went with five other men for the first visit of U.S. economists to the Soviet Union, at least since World War II. The main question we took with us was whether the Soviets had some superior method for guiding research and development. Not only did we not get any answer, but we also did not find anyone who understood the question. The Soviet production system looked terribly backward to us. I did think that as long as they could commit a large part of the national output to investment, including research and education, they would grow. In retrospect, I probably underestimated how inefficient that investment would be.

13. Edward Denison, *Why Growth Rates Differ* (Washington, D.C.: Brookings Institution, 1967).

14. Andrew Shonfield, *Modern Capitalism* (London: Oxford University Press, 1965).

15. Another personal experience will illustrate the fascination with the idea of planning and its vacuity. In 1962, the trustees of CED visited President Kennedy in the Rose Garden of the White House. He advised them to study the French plan, to see what made it work. Accordingly, a group of CED trustees and I went to Paris to meet with government officials and businessmen and learn what was going on.

idea that we needed a national plan never bore any fruit—as it failed to bear fruit when it became a fad again around 1975—the idea that we needed to grow more rapidly and that it was the responsibility of government to make that happen, somehow, did have general acceptance. In the 1960 presidential election, candidates on both sides competed in promising how high a growth rate they would achieve. But inadequate growth was only one of the problems that were "discovered" in the 1960s and made the occasion for more active economic policy by government. Unemployment was too high, even in "good" times. We were suffering from "public squalor and private opulence." The environment was deteriorating. There were many poor people in parts of the country, such as Appalachia. There were altogether too many poor people in the country. Old people could not pay for medical care. Minorities, especially blacks, were suffering discrimination in their economic lives as well as in other respects.

Some of these were real problems. Some, as I said at the time, were not, or at least not serious ones. Some were getting better. Poverty was declining and so was discrimination. Probably the environmental problem was getting worse. But there was surely no radical deterioration in our condition that called for major changes of policy, as there had been in 1933. The idea that conditions were terrible and needed drastic action was in large part created by the political and intellectual entrepreneurs.

Activist Government

In any case, the country adapted to these real and perceived problems by entering into another period of activism in economic policy. Both fiscal and monetary policies became more vigorous in pursuit of the ambitious goal of reducing the unemployment rate. The inflationary consequences of that were at first resisted by "incomes" policy, an attempt to hold down particular wages and prices by informal and superficially voluntary means. This metamorphosed in time into President Nixon's comprehensive, mandatory wage and price controls. A war on poverty was launched, with federal money and direction. New federally financed medical care

---

Upon our return, I summarized our findings with the sentence, "Le Plan français n'existe pas."

programs for the elderly and the needy were initiated. Programs were started to spur development in economically backward areas. New regulatory systems for the environment, for health and safety in the workplace, and for the protection of consumers' safety were set up. Detailed controls were established over the energy industry. The social security system was made more generous. Legislation was enacted to end discrimination against minorities and women in economic life, and agencies were created to enforce that legislation. As a fraction of the GNP, government expenditures other than for defense rose from 8.8 percent in 1960 to 11.5 percent in 1970 and 17.1 percent in 1980.

Movement was not entirely in one direction. Although total receipts rose as a percentage of GNP from 18.3 in 1960 to 19.4 in 1980, there was a reduction in the marginal rates of income tax and in the corporate tax burden, while the burden of payroll taxes increased. Control of international capital movements, which existed early in the period, was abolished, and the dollar was allowed to float. The draft was replaced by volunteer armed forces. Restrictions on international trade were relaxed. Beginnings were made on deregulating interest rates and the transportation industries. But on balance there is no doubt that the years 1960 to 1980, or perhaps more accurately to 1978, were years of a great expansion of the government's influence on the economy.

This trend was, during most of its duration, warmly received by the public. Barry Goldwater offered the most clear-cut opposition to this trend of any Republican candidate for the presidency since Alf Landon, and he suffered a defeat worse than any other candidate since Landon. In 1971, when Richard Nixon imposed the wage and price controls, the greatest affront to the idea of a free market since the time of slavery, his action was praised by almost everyone except a few economists of the Chicago school, and the stock market soared. Fifteen months later, while these controls were still in full force, he received an enormous electoral victory.

In December 1965, five years after the country had been bemoaning the lags and inadequacies of the American economy, *Time* magazine ran a cover story celebrating the triumph of the American economy. The portrait on the cover was not of Adam Smith or of some captain of American industry: it was a portrait of John Maynard Keynes.

It is important to note, as we shall describe later, that most of what happened to the economy in the Kennedy, Johnson, and Nixon years remains. If capitalism has triumphed, it is capitalism as modified in those years as well as in the years of Roosevelt.

Reaction to Activism

A reaction to this trend set in around the middle of the 1970s for several objective reasons. The rate of economic growth declined after 1973, for reasons that are still not entirely clear. Inflation accelerated, raising tax burdens. High taxes became a subject of great concern to a large majority of middle-income Americans and not only to the well-to-do. The irritation with high taxes was intensified by the feeling that the taxes were going to support many shiftless and unworthy poor people, an attitude that probably contained an element of racism.

The idea that a change was needed found intellectual support. To some extent this was a revival, in diluted form, of the arguments about the planned economy and the cradle-to-the-grave welfare state that had been popular in the early postwar period. A representation of the argument is found in the new foreword that Hayek wrote for *The Road to Serfdom,* when it was reprinted in the 1970s:

> If few people in the Western world now want to remake society from the bottom according to some ideal blueprint, a great many still believe in measures which, although not designed completely to remodel the economy, in their aggregate effect may well unintentionally produce this result. And, even more than at the time when I wrote this book, the advocacy of policies which can no longer be reconciled with the preservation of a free society is no longer a party matter. That hodge-podge of ill-assembled and often inconsistent ideals which under the name of the Welfare State has largely replaced socialism as the goal of the reformers needs very careful sorting-out if its results are not to be very similar to those of full-fledged socialism.[16]

But there was a more popular version of the intellectual case for a change of policies. The traditional argument for "conservative" economic policy had an austere sound. It was the case for tight

---

16. Hayek, *Road to Serfdom,* p. ix.

money, low government spending, balanced budgets, and letting the market grind out its long-run solutions. Associated with the overwhelming defeat of Barry Goldwater, it came to be called "deep root-canal economics." The more popular argument was what, in my book *Presidential Economics,* I called "the economics of joy."[17] It promised tax reductions for all—not just reduction of those high marginal rates that were traditionally thought to be serious obstacles to economic efficiency. The tax reductions would greatly stimulate economic growth. In common understanding, this stimulus would be great enough to keep the revenue from falling when tax rates were cut, although there is now some disagreement about whether Ronald Reagan really meant that. There would be a cut in expenditures for welfare, but this would not increase poverty because the new argument was that welfare expenditures caused, and did not cure, poverty. Another ingredient in the new case for change was that with sufficient "credibility," inflation would be sharply reduced without even a temporary increase of unemployment.

This approach, called "supply-side economics," could be interpreted to mean economics supplied to meet the demand of politicians to rationalize what they intended to do. How far this argument influenced the elections or policies of the 1980s, I do not know. In any case, these policies, as it turned out, did not reverse the policies of the previous two decades or substantially change the system those policies left. Some of the trends of the previous decades were slowed down, a process that had already begun between 1975 and 1980. The growth of expenditures as a percentage of GNP was stopped, although that conclusion is somewhat clouded by the recent discovery of claims not previously recognized—for obligations to depositors in failed savings and loans, for cleaning up atomic plants, and for neglected infrastructure, among other things.

As a fraction of GNP, federal expenditures were higher in 1988 than in any year between the end of World War II and 1980. The growth of receipts relative to GNP was also stopped but not reversed. Here too there remain possible claims on the future as the result of the cumulative budget deficits of the 1980s. There was a considerable restructuring of the tax system, shifting some burden from income taxes to payroll taxes, and reforming the income taxes

---

17. Herbert Stein, *Presidential Economics* (New York: Simon and Schuster, 1984).

in ways that probably reduce distortions of economic decisions. Some regulations were eliminated, especially in the field of energy, and some were made more rational. But new regulations also were imposed, especially over international trade. It would be difficult to say whether there was more or less regulation in 1988 than in 1980. The money and personnel devoted to regulation were little changed. With the memory of the inflation of the 1970s still fairly fresh, monetary policy had a more anti-inflationary cast in the 1980s than in the previous decades. The dollar exchange rate, which was freely floating in 1980, came under coordinated international management, the implications of which are still unclear.

Although the intrinsic worth of what has happened or not happened during these years may be questioned, there seems no doubt that the policy, and even more the attitudes, was an adaptation to a serious situation in the country: the feeling by the middle class, which is the great majority, that it was being ignored and mistreated.[18]

It is worth comparing the behavior of the economy under the system we are now celebrating with the behavior of the economy under the New Economics of Kennedy and Johnson. From 1980 to 1988, real GNP rose by 26 percent; from 1960 to 1968, real GNP rose by 42 percent. From 1980 to 1988, civilian employment rose by 15.8 percent; from 1960 to 1968, it rose by 15.4 percent. As is implied by these two figures, output per worker hour rose much less in the later period than in the earlier one—13 percent compared with 30 percent. The proportion of the population living in poverty declined during the earlier period, while it did not in the later period. Also more progress seems to have been made in reducing inequality between the wages of whites and blacks in the earlier period than in the later one. Of course, we now know that the sequel to the Kennedy-Johnson period was not happy. But we do not know the sequel to the Reagan period.

I do not recite these facts to show that the economic system and policy of the Kennedy-Johnson period were superior to those of the Reagan period. Indeed, I do not think that the systems were

---

18. Sometime in the early 1980s, a Soviet economist asked whether I was not afraid that there would be a social revolution in America because President Reagan was reducing programs for assistance to the poor. I explained to him that we had already had our social revolution in 1980—the revolution of the middle class.

very different, and I do not think that the earlier policy was superior. I do want to suggest, however, that the performance of the economy is influenced by much other than the contemporary policy and that the superiority of systems or policies cannot be demonstrated by such numbers.

The Triumph of a Free Economic System

So, what is this system like? Whose triumph are we celebrating? It is a free economic system. It is a system in which almost all decisions about what gets produced, how, and for whom are the outcome of decisions by private individuals in voluntary exchange with other private individuals, each of whom has enough options to be substantially independent of any other. Despite the growth of government and government regulation, it is not only still a free system but also more free than it has ever been. The list of things that cannot be done at all or cannot be done without permission from the government or must be done because government requires it may be longer than ever. But the list of things that can be freely done is also much longer than ever before. The economic freedom of private individuals has been greatly expanded by the transition from local markets to the national market and then to the world market, by the increased availability of information, by the increased income, assets, education, and mobility of the labor force, and by the lessening of discrimination against women and minorities.

The American economy is a welfare state. About 15 percent of personal income comes from transfer payments from government, mainly for old people but also for the poor. In 1929, this figure was less than 2 percent—mainly for veterans. Today, as for a long time in the past, government programs in one way or another support farm incomes. That may be considered part of the welfare state also, even though it is not reflected in transfer payments. In that sense, we also have welfare programs for the automobile industry, the steel industry, the textile industry, and others that receive government protection.

Federal government expenditures are large—about 23 percent of the GNP. The government is essentially a consumer and transferrer of income. As a producer, the government is small. Federal government product is about 3 percent of GNP.

The government takes responsibility for stabilizing the economy. Its chief instrument for doing this is discretionary monetary policy, with fiscal policy playing an uncertain but subordinate role. Through its fiscal, credit, and regulatory policies, the federal government profoundly influences, but does not firmly control, the allocation of the national output among consumption, housing, other investment, medical care, and research. To a considerable extent, this influence is intended, but there is no comprehensive plan for this allocation. There is no national economic plan.

This is certainly not, to repeat, the capitalist economy of 1929 or the laissez-faire system of some textbooks or caricatures. But neither is it the centrally planned and controlled system that many feared we were headed for forty years ago or that some thought we needed at intervals in the past sixty years. The quotation from Schumpeter, cited above, is relevant here. He foresaw developments that would "transform, even without extensive nationalization of industry, regulated, or fettered capitalism into a guided capitalism that might, with almost equal justice, be called socialism. Thus, prediction of whether or not the capitalist order will survive is, in part, a matter of terminology."

Has the question whether it is capitalism or socialism that has survived become a matter of terminology? That is an interesting but not an important question. The fact that it is a puzzle indicates that we should not spend much time or heat in arguing about "systems" at that level of generality.

Although I have concentrated here on developments in the United States, an appraisal of what has survived and triumphed is assisted by looking outside our borders. For the triumph of whatever it is that has triumphed is not only the triumph of Reagan America, or even that plus Thatcher Britain, but the triumph of the non-Communist industrial world, from Singapore to Sweden. When the Estonians, Lithuanians, and Latvians look for a country to emulate, they look to their neighbors, Sweden and Finland. The Hungarians look to Austrians. These societies that have triumphed differ substantially in many respects. Government expenditures range from about 60 percent of GNP in the Netherlands to about 17 percent in Japan. Transfer payments as a percentage of household income range from 29 percent in the Netherlands to 13 percent in the United States. The degree and character of government regulation and detailed control of the economy are hard to measure but obviously vary greatly from country to country. Japan seems to be one of the most highly controlled and is also one of the leading examples of capitalist "success," whether because of or in spite of the controls is a subject of debate among students of the subject.

Even the countries that we used to think of as "Socialist" no longer have any interest in national ownership of industry and are trying to "privatize." As we have seen, Schumpeter already foresaw the possibility of socialism without nationalization. A country that has a progressive tax system, a developed welfare system, and ad hoc regulations has no need for national ownership and can find it only a distraction. Even countries that once had a national plan, or claimed to, have abandoned that as impossible. In contrast, what seemed the most capitalist and free market systems, now have large governments, major welfare programs, active stabilization programs, and a good deal of ad hoc regulation.

This general system—the free enterprise, welfare state, managed stabilization, and ad hoc regulation system—is what has triumphed. It has triumphed in the sense that there is no serious alternative in the countries that have it and that it is envied in all the countries that do not. While some would measure the triumph of this system by the rate of growth of real output per capita, I think this is a narrow measure and explanation of what has happened. With rare exceptions, it has been thought that capitalist countries would excel in the long-run growth of output. The alleged superiority of other systems lay in other dimensions, including security, stability, and fairness.

It is not at all clear that our system would have triumphed over others solely by virtue of superior long-run growth, but it had much more to offer. We not only produce more, as conventionally measured, but what we produce is closer to what the consumer wants. It has more style, variety, and ingenuity. Significantly, when a Soviet cabinet member went on a buying trip to the West recently, he did not come back with $150,000,000 worth of housedresses from the 1928 Sears, Roebuck catalog. He came back with pantyhose and lipsticks. That adaptation to the consumers' desires is a great contribution of the free market and a value that national planners constantly overlook.

But at the same time, it is doubtful that our system would have triumphed so surely if it had not been able to moderate its instability, to provide a safety net for its disadvantaged, and to make a start on dealing with its environmental problems. These are functions that government has performed. The systems that we are proud of and that the Communist world envies have done these things, as well as raised per capita output at a good pace. I am not suggesting that the particular combination of measures—the precise levels of expenditures or taxes, the specific kind of monetary policy, the kinds and extent of regulations—now found in the United States or elsewhere in the industrial world is ideal. This system has major problems to solve.

In the United States, for example, we need to learn to deal with the stubborn persistence of a tragic amount of poverty. We need to learn how to make better decisions about the distribution of resources between the present and the future. We need to learn how to deal better with the rest of the world—to avoid getting into economic warfare with our friends, to help the poor countries move along the path of development, and to encourage our adversaries to turn their resources to productive and pacific uses. Undoubtedly, we shall encounter other problems. What underlies confidence in our system is not that it is ideal—not that it has reached the end of history, as someone has recently declared—but that it has shown the capacity to adapt.

The Lessons of the Past Sixty Years

Sixty years ago, Americans were supremely confident of the new era, believing that they had entered a period of endlessly growing and widely shared prosperity. Twenty-five years ago, we were celebrating the triumph of the New Economics of Kennedy and Johnson, which had similarly conquered all economic problems. Each of these episodes was followed by a severe disillusionment. In the early 1930s, the end of capitalism was commonly predicted because of its failure in the depression. In the mid-1940s, the end of capitalism and indeed of the free society was predicted because of the trends toward government economic management then seen to be under way. By the late 1950s, the American economy was seen to be lagging behind the rest of the world because of its failure to adopt national economic planning. All of this foreboding turned out to be unjustified.

In the course of sixty years, we have seen that government could take on major powers over the economy and still leave it as free as it had ever been, or even more free. Looking at the story from the other direction, we have seen that the economy could remain free and greatly reduce instability, poverty, insecurity, and the feeling of unfairness. There are important lessons in this experience. It is a warning against absolutism, despair, and pride. Do not judge every turn of the economy as if it would go on forever and every policy as if it would be carried to what seems its logical conclusion. Every step to increase government expenditure or government regulation is not to be judged as if it meant the end of the free economy. Every step in the other direction is not to be judged as if it meant a return to the law of the jungle.

Very few of the policy choices that confront us can be answered by deciding whether one supports socialism or capitalism or is a conservative or a liberal. We should beware of slippery-slope arguments. The point was well made by Jacob Viner thirty years ago. Speaking of the genre of writing symbolized by *The Road to Serfdom,* which he suggested should also include roads to tyranny and anarchy, he said:

> Route 1, a great national highway which connects Boston, New York, Philadelphia, Baltimore and Washington, begins at Fort Kent in Maine and ends in a sand dune at the southern tip of Florida. Except on the arbitrary assumption that travel on this road, in either direction, is totally without benefit of brakes, the terminal points of our metaphorical road are often assigned an extravagant degree of practical significance in discourse in this field. Until quite recent years, actual and vital discussion in the public forum has turned mainly on the comparative merits of resting places along our highway of points not greatly distant from each other, or perhaps more accurately, as between no movement at all and a limited amount of movement, sometimes in both directions simultaneously, from the existing resting place.[19]

And what Viner says was true until quite recent years continues to be true in the United States.

When I was younger, I was fascinated by John Jewkes's epigram: "To consider every case on its merits is not to consider the merits of the case." I now think of that as a narrowly one-sided

---

19. Jacob Viner, "The Intellectual History of Laissez Faire," *Journal of Law and Economics* (October 1960), p. 46.

dictum. We should say that to consider every case only by reference to universal principles, without regard to the particulars of the case, is not to consider the merits of the case.

The main lesson of the past is, Be not proud. Previous beliefs that we have found the final answer to economic problems have been disappointed. Some people think the answer has now been found, in the varieties of capitalism that exist today. The disillusionment this time may be less painful than in the earlier cases. But we will discover—I believe we have already discovered—problems for which this formula is inadequate. We will have to adapt, and will. We will adapt better, though, if we are not too inflated with the idea that we already live in the Golden Age. *(September 1989)*

5

Will, War, and Bureaucrats

It was a glorious victory, the Gulf War of 1991. It was a victory conceived and executed by a government agency, the Department of Defense. The leading figures were old bureaucrats, Richard Cheney, Colin Powell, and Norman Schwartzkopf. Their combined annual salary is less than one-thousandth of Michael Milken's in his best year. Two of the three got their advanced training in the government. I don't think that any one of them ever met a payroll, to recall a test from my youth. The subordinate actors were also government bureaucrats. None of them got profit sharing or stock options. They were all part of a system that bought $600 toilet seat covers and armored personnel carriers that capsized in two inches of water.

What are we to make of that? Not too much, surely. But something. It does not mean that the Department of Defense can or should do everything, or that bureaucrats more generally can or should do everything. But the time is ripe for rethinking attitudes toward the administrative agencies of government and the career employees of government.

Perhaps for a time we will not hear Ronald Reagan's favorite story about the clerk in the Bureau of Indian Affairs who was seen to be weeping bitterly and explained it was because his Indian had died. That clerk has his counterpart in the DOD shuffling the paperwork for the production of the Patriot missile, the driver of the tank-truck that supplies tanks, and the man inside the tank.

Perhaps for a time we will not hear as a presumed stopper to any argument about any possible government functions, "Do you want it performed by the same people who run the Post Office?"—as if that proved that government operations are ipso facto inefficient and ineffective. Now we have seen a government operation that was efficient and effective.

One may say that the analogy is inappropriate and that the military departments are fundamentally different from the civilian ones. But people do not become efficient and innovative by putting on government-issue clothing. We surely thought that the cliché characteristics of bureaucrats applied to the DOD when they bought the $600 toilet seat covers. And we thought it was just another example of bureaucratic ineptitude when, during the invasion of Granada, the navy and the air force had to communicate with each other by a credit card phone call through Baltimore. If the test of bureaucracy is distance from the profit motive, the military forces qualify.

How did this bureaucratic government agency perform so well? One explanation was that a lot of money was spent on it. The Gulf War is the answer to the proposition that you cannot solve problems by throwing money at them. It proved Stein's Law, that if an agency wastes one-fourth of its budget, you should give it one-third more money than it would need if it was optimally efficient. Or, if 30 percent of the bombs hit their target, as has been said about the Gulf War, you have to drop 3⅓ times as many bombs—as we did.

The "incremental" cost of the war was small, possibly in the range of $50 billion. But the incremental cost was small because from 1981 to 1990 we had spent $2,800 billion (1990 prices) in training forces and developing and acquiring equipment. This expenditure was not mainly for fighting Iraq. It was for deterring the USSR and for meeting contingencies, of which Iraq turned out to be one. When the contingency arrived, the resources to meet it were ample.

Much has been said about the "smart weapons" the United States employed in the gulf. But the smartest weapon turned out to be the Reagan defense budgets. What was smart was the recognition that for a country with a gross national product of $5,000 billion, $300 billion is not too much to spend in defense of vital interests or even in reducing the risks and casualties of that defense. Many thought the spending was excessive when it was made. Few will now say they would have preferred less defense spending in the 1980s and more casualties in the gulf.

We have learned something about waste. I was a member of

the Packard Commission, and I have heard a lot about waste in the DOD. But I now have to wonder whether there is not a basic conflict between economy in the small and effectiveness in the large. Would an institution so organized and so motivated that it never bought a $600 toilet seat cover be sufficiently audacious and imaginative to fight a successful war? Or, to change the venue, would a system so organized and circumscribed that it never paid money to Mr. Reagan's favorite welfare queen ever do much good for many people?

People will say that warfare is a unique problem, unlike poverty or education or crime, so that although a government agency may be excellent at warfare, that government agency cannot contribute much to the solution of the problems of other agencies. They think of warfare as a linear problem, with known, or at least knowable, quantitative relations between inputs and outputs, so that a good mathematician could figure out the optimum strategy. Anyone who believes that has not read *War and Peace*. War is an intensely human activity. It requires the recruitment, training, and motivation of large numbers of people, the reconciliation of many conflicting interests, and excruciatingly difficult choices, involving life or death for thousands of people. It is conducted in an atmosphere of uncertainty and ignorance and requires constant adaptation to unforeseen developments.

War is not just like other problems. But it has similarities to other problems. In a recent article, Daniel Bell pointed out, correctly, that "waging war is not like fixing schools." He gives an example of a problem in education that would not yield to the techniques that succeed in war: "Should schools teach tradition or great books or multicultural schemes?" But the question, "Does c-a-t spell cat, and should every six-year old know that, and how do we get them to know that?" might be one that would yield to the application of money and intelligence through a government agency.

Our other problems do have many differences from the military problem. One of them is surely that they have never been elevated to the level of national will and attention that the war had. When speaking of the nation's problems in his inaugural address in 1989, Mr. Bush said, "We have more will than wallet." He emphasized the limits to what could be done. But when he spoke of the invasion of Kuwait, he said, "This will not stand." There was no reference to limits. He did not say, "This will not stand if we can undo it within the limits of existing appropriations." He said that there would not be another Vietnam. He never said that there would not be another failed war on illiteracy or poverty.

Before Iraq, there was a widespread feeling of the incompetence of our military forces, going back to Vietnam, the Iranian rescue attempt, Lebanon, and Granada. We have learned that this impression was mistaken or that the causes of it have been corrected. We should be considering whether similar impressions of the ineptitude of government in other fields are mistaken, or the reasons correctible, and whether other great national enterprises could be successfully pursued if backed by sufficient will.

My dream is to see the under secretary of education hold a daily briefing on the war on ignorance. He would stand before a blackboard and say, "Yesterday, 35,471 children learned that c-a-t spells cat; 64,283 did not learn it. We will go back to them tomorrow." *(March 1991)*

6

A Crypto-Liberal Takes the Cure

"So, Mr. Stein. You are back on the couch. I thought we straightened you out already."

"That was five or six years ago, when I was afraid that I might be a Keynesian."

"Then what happened?"

"With your help, I learned that we are all Keynesians now and there are no longer any Keynesians. That made me see that I couldn't be a Keynesian and that it didn't matter if I was."

"So why are you back here?"

"Well, I have this terrible fear that I may be a Liberal. I wake up at night in a cold sweat, after dreaming that I am a Liberal. And when I go into the dining room at the American Enterprise Institute I hear people whispering, 'Liberal,' 'Liberal.' "

"Is that so awful?"

"Oh, it really is. It's the L word. It stands for Left, Lewd, Lecherous, Libertine, Lazy, Lascivious, Loafer, Lenin, and Marx."

"Marx doesn't start with an L."

"I know, but it's close. Another important thing is this. Being a Liberal is not like being a Democrat. Being a Democrat or a Republican is like having the red pieces or the black pieces in a checkers game. It doesn't have any moral implications. But being a Liberal is Ba-a-ad. You can be a good Democrat if you're not Liberal and you can be a bad Republican if you are Liberal."

"Then what do you call people who are not Liberal?"

"That's interesting. Only the intelligentsia call themselves conservatives. A politician who says that his opponent is a Liberal doesn't say that he himself is a conservative. He usually says only that he himself is not Liberal. Sometimes he might say that he is American."

"What makes you think that you might be a Liberal?"

"I suppose it's mainly something about taxes. I seem to be soft on taxes."

"You mean that you love taxes, that you're a taxophiliac?"

"No, I don't love taxes, but when I say to myself, 'Taxes 20 percent of GNP, result bliss; taxes 21 percent of GNP, result misery,' I get mixed up. I forget how it goes and sometimes I get it backward."

"Have you been doing anything to try to correct this condition?"

"Yes, I've been trying to read my lips. I stand in front of a mirror trying to read my lips saying, 'No New Taxes!' "

"What happens when you do that?"

"All I see is a silly old man standing in front of a mirror saying 'No Nude Actress!' to himself."

"That hardly seems to be enough. After all, even President Reagan raised taxes."

"He's a special case. For ordinary folk, taxes are a litmus test. Anyway, that isn't all."

"Aha! So what else is there?"

"I'm worried about this 'card-carrying member' thing."

"You don't mean that you are a member of the ACLU!"

"Oh, no. But when this card-carrying business started I went through my wallet and found that I'm a card-carrying member of the AARP, the AAA, the Cosmos Club, and the D.C. Video Rental Club."

"That all seems safe enough to me."

"Oh, you can't be sure. I haven't studied all the things these organizations stand for and checked them out against the certified list of 'Liberal' positions. The AARP wants to spend more government money for old people. The AAA wants to spend more money for roads. The Cosmos Club has just voted to admit women after 100 years of segregation. And the video rental club has adult films in the back room. That's all pretty worrisome. You never know what they might find out."

"I have a feeling you're holding back. Is there something else you ought to tell me before we begin?"

"Doctor, can I count on you to keep this completely confidential?"

"Who can count on anything? But you can tell me."

"Well, there are two things. When I was a boy in school and learned the Pledge of Allegiance we didn't say 'under God' and that still doesn't sound natural to me. Also, I have to confess that I know only one stanza of the Star Spangled Banner. So, what do you advise, doctor?"

"It looks like a pretty clear case. So, you're a Liberal. You should come out of the closet and admit it. Then you could move to Sweden. There are many Liberals there and they are accepted in society."

"But I'm not a Liberal. I can't admit to being something I'm not. That's my whole problem. I feel guilty when I'm not."

"What makes you think that you're not a Liberal? Everything you've said today sounds like a Liberal."

"There are lots of things. I helped to raise money for Ronald Reagan's campaign in 1980. I'm for Bush this year. I'm for SDI and a big defense budget. I'm for aid to the Contras. I want not only to balance the budget but to run a surplus. I'm for a tight, anti-inflationary monetary policy. I'm against middle-class subsidies, like the farm program. I'm against 'industrial policy' and protectionism. I could give you a much longer list.

"And yet, when people divide the world into black and white, Liberals and Conservatives, I'm not sure where I belong and I'm afraid of where other people would put me."

"So, So! That makes the problem a little harder. Let me think for a minute."

"I'm waiting."

"All right. This is my advice. We wait until the day after the election. If Dukakis wins, I think you will quickly discover all by yourself that you are not a Liberal. If Bush wins, I'll see you three times a week starting Monday, November 14, at 11 o'clock."

"Thank you, doctor." *(October 1988)*

7

Lessons from Living with Economic Policy

A ll my writing and speaking these days consists of reminiscences. I have a lot to reminisce about: I have practiced Washington economics—observing and participating in the making of federal economic policy—for over fifty-six years. That is longer than any other economist in the history of the republic.

The recent death of Richard Nixon prompts me to recall my experience as one of his economic advisers. That experience illustrates two general points about economic policy: the lack of strategic thinking about economic policy and the limited consequences of policy mistakes. These points are supported by the whole history of the past fifty years; I use the Nixon experience only because I know it best.

Lack of Strategic Thinking

There is little strategic thinking about economic policy: that is, having clear and consistent goals, having plans for achieving them, and having a plan or policy for adapting when the plans are not working. This latter feature is almost always missing. Presidential administrations come into office with many goals, and with plans for achieving them, but often the world turns out different from what was assumed in the plans and the administration founders in an effort to deal with conditions it had not foreseen, even as possibilities.

Although I could say some positive things about what we did or tried to do in economic policy during the Nixon years, what stands out is the big gap between what was expected at the beginning and what turned out at the end. Two examples of this discrepancy come to mind.

At the time of Nixon's first inauguration in 1969, a dominant feature of his economics appeared to be a phobia about unemployment. At my first meeting with him, in December 1968, he asked me what I thought our main economic problem was. I said it was inflation, and he said, "Yes, but you must worry about unemployment."

A second dominant feature of Nixon's economics at the beginning of his term was opposition to price and wage controls. This was, for Nixon, more than conventional Republican paternoster or standard classical economics: it was a strong personal conviction. His brief tenure as a lawyer in the Office of Price Administration at the beginning of World War II had been a frustrating experience.

But the unemployment rate that had been 3.4 percent when we came into office was 9 percent in May 1975. That was nine months after Mr. Nixon's premature departure from office, but it would have been no lower if he had stayed. Insofar as the unemployment rate is ever the president's, that 9 percent rate was Nixon's.

And in August 1971, Mr. Nixon, the great enemy of price controls, inaugurated the only comprehensive, mandatory price and wage controls in America's peacetime history. These controls remained more or less in effect for two and a half years.

I could list a great many reasons for this big gap between our promises and expectations and the outcomes. We inherited what at the time seemed a high inflation rate. No one knew how much slowdown of the economy would be required to curb that inflation or what monetary policy would be necessary to bring about the disinflation. In any case, the administration did not control monetary policy. The course of the economy in 1970 was disturbed by a major strike at General Motors. The Nixon administration had to deal with a Democratic Congress that was much less averse to price controls than the administration was and, moreover, wanted to embarrass the administration for its reluctance to use controls. Later, in 1972 and 1973, there were major disruptions of the world supply situation—Soviet crop failures, the departure of the anchovies from the Pacific coast of South America, and, most severe, the oil shock.

These conditions and developments ensured that the course of economic policy during the Nixon administration would not run smoothly, no matter what we did. But my point is that in our decisions and statements we did not take much account of these possible obstacles and uncertainties. Some of these conditions—such as the presence of a Democratic Congress—were obvious from the outset, but the possible consequences of that fact were not explored and given adequate attention. Some of these developments—such as the oil embargo—were probably not foreseeable, but the possibility of some kind of external shock, even if not that particular one, could have been recognized. The implications of that possibility were not given attention either.

We had a view of what we called the optimum feasible path of the economy. It would bring us to 1972 with low inflation, without price controls, and after having passed through a brief period of only moderately high unemployment. We also had a view of the combination of fiscal and monetary measures that would make the economy move along that path. Every few months, when we recognized that we were off the path, we would revise the path and the necessary policy, always to reach the same goals. But we never prepared ourselves or the public for the very likely possibility that reality would turn out to be as far from the new path as it had been from the old one.

As a result, we were constantly revising our policy to catch up with events, and the public was continuously losing confidence in our policy and our forecasts. That made it impossible finally to convince the country that gradualism would end inflation and that price controls were unnecessary, even dangerous. The condition of the economy at the time we imposed the controls was not terribly bad by any standard except one: the standard of our own promises. Both inflation and unemployment were higher than we had been promising for two years. We could no longer convince people, probably including the president, that our policy of avoiding price controls was working. If we had recognized and insisted on the inevitable uncertainties from the outset, we would have been in a better position to argue for patience.

Moreover, our own conception of the bad consequences of price controls was abstract and academic. If we had been more conscious of the way price controls might work out, we might have been even more reluctant than we were to impose them and more successful in explaining to the public why we did not want to use them.

As I look back to that weekend some twenty years ago when we decided to impose the ninety-day freeze on prices and wages, I am amazed to recall how unconcerned and ignorant we were about what would happen next. We had a vague idea that after ninety days we would get down to a system of essentially voluntary exhortation to large businesses and unions about their price and wage behavior. We did not foresee that the public would love the ninety-day freeze so much that we could not retreat from it very quickly. We did not foresee that we would be living with the system for two and a half years. We did not foresee that the initial apparent success of the controls would seduce us into excessively expansionary fiscal and monetary policy. We did not count on the possibility of shocks to the world food and energy supplies that would end the system in an explosion of inflation followed by the worst recession of the postwar period up to that time.

If we had visualized that course of events, not as most probable but as possible, we might have resisted the imposition of the controls more and have explained more successfully to the public why we did that. We suffered from a tendency to regard the most probable scenario as the only possible scenario and to neglect the implications of the uncertainties of our condition.

This deficiency, of course, was not peculiar to the administration in which I served. The Kennedy-Johnson administration failed to recognize the possible consequences of its policy of fine-tuning fiscal measures combined with arm-twisting businesses and unions to prevent inflation. Members of the Reagan team had various assumptions of what the consequences of the initial big tax cut would be and found themselves struggling for seven years with the fact that none of these assumptions turned out to be true. The Bush administration found itself seriously embarrassed for having failed to recognize and prepare for the possibility that its pledge of no new taxes might be inconsistent with its pledge to balance the budget in five years.

Consequences of Policy Mistakes

This history illustrates my first point, which is the common lack of strategic thinking. My second point is more comforting: like hurricanes in Hartford, Hereford, and Hampshire, terrible things hardly ever happen, at least as a result of mistakes of economic policy. The story of the follies of economic policy is the story of irony, of the gap between pretensions and outcomes, not a story of tragedy.

Most people would probably agree that the imposition of price controls in 1971 was one of the great mistakes of economic policy of the postwar period. Some generally sensible observers thought that the American economy would never be the same and that we would never get back to free markets. But that did not turn out to be the case. We did go through some foolish experiences, like the drowning of baby chicks allegedly because of the price controls, and having to wait in line for gasoline. We did end up with a recession, but recessions are a common part of our economic history. The 1974– 1975 recession was not much worse than our average. And we did have an exceptional rise of output and employment in 1972, which we might not have had without the controls.

Many people would agree that the deficits of the Reagan and Bush administrations were a major mistake of economic policy. But it is hard now to point to any substantial damage they did. Economists will say that the deficits depressed private investment and slowed down long-term growth, but when we try to estimate the size of this effect, it seems to be quite small.

How do we explain this apparent fact that we can have so much folly with so little resulting damage? I will suggest an explanation by referring to three quotations.

Adam Smith, the fount of all wisdom, said, "There is a great deal of ruin in a nation." He meant, I believe, that a nation is a sturdy, flexible institution, reflecting the private decisions of millions of individuals, and that the follies of government do not much disturb the national condition unless the follies are exceptionally great.

A second quotation is less elegant but more pointed: "Economic policy is random with respect to the performance of the American economy, but thank God there isn't much of it." That revelation did not come from the fount of all wisdom but from me; it suddenly came to me ten years ago as a summary of my experience in forty-six years of Washington economics. The fact is that most of the things that we regard as big issues are really small relative to the size of the American economy.

The third quotation is, to me, the most interesting. Axel Oxenstiern, chancellor of Sweden 350 years ago, said: "Behold, my son, with how little wisdom the world is governed." For a long time, I thought he was saying that the world is governed badly because it is governed with so little wisdom. I now believe that he may have been saying that even a little wisdom is sufficient to govern the world—that the world can be well governed without much wisdom.

That idea should be familiar to economists. Thanks to Adam Smith, we believe that good performance of the economy does not depend on the wisdom of the individual actors in the economy. We have an institution, the market, that produces good results even though the individuals may not be very wise. The institution winnows out the follies of the participants. That, we suppose, is what Adam Smith meant by reference to the Invisible Hand, although since he put the initials of those words in capital letters he may also have been speaking of God.

But we generally reject, or at least overlook, the possibility that an Invisible Hand controls government to prevent the follies of our governors from resulting in tragedy. I recently read the First Inaugural Address of George Washington and was surprised to find him saying this: "No people can be bound to acknowledge and adore the Invisible Hand which conducts the affairs of men more than those of the United States."

I do not know whether George Washington ever read *The Wealth of Nations*. Alexander Hamilton, who helped Washington as a speech writer, may have done so, and that may be the connection between Smith's Invisible Hand and Washington's. Clearly, Washington was referring to God, as Smith probably was also. But Washington like Smith was probably also referring to institutional arrangements that yielded good results without great demands on either the wisdom or the virtue of individuals. In Smith's case, the institution was the free market. In Washington's case, it may have been the structure of government, starting with the Constitution in which he and his contemporaries placed so much faith. The Invisible Hand may have been the guidance and limitation placed on the policies of government by the division of functions among the federal government, the states, and the citizens; the balance of powers among the branches of the federal government; the room left for the play of diverse factions and interests; and the assurance of freedom of discussion and the competition of ideas. This may be the Invisible Hand that despite the lack of strategic thinking about which I have complained saves us from extreme and persistent errors of government. *(June 1994)*

PART TWO

White House Economics

8

What Economic Policy Advisers Do

I have now had more than fifty-two years of experience as an inside-the-beltway adviser on economic policy. I believe that I have played that role longer than anyone else now even slightly active, and probably longer than anyone else there has ever been. I would like to offer some thoughts on what people serving in that capacity do. But I must warn that my observations are personal and that one might get different views from other people with Washington experience. I should also say that of my fifty-two years in Washington, only thirteen were in the government, so my views should not be identified with an inside-the-government perspective.

The Economics Industry

I will start with a description of the economics industry as I see it, to show where the part in which I have worked fits into the industry as a whole. The industry has three main segments—the raw-material–production part, the teaching part, and the advising part.

Many economists are at work producing raw economics, in the form of papers. These papers flow into a journal mill, where they are revolved and grated against each other. This process has several products. It is an exercise for economists to develop their skills. It is a way of demonstrating ability to produce a paper, which has a certain symbolic value in the industry. Much of the raw economics is ejected from the mill as waste, after having served its purposes as demonstration of practice. Some remains in the mill for a long time, as pure, refined economics. Some is siphoned off in small streams, adding to the stocks of teachable economics and advisable economics.

The teachable economics is made available to students, some of whom later become part of the raw-material–producing process and the teaching process, some of whom retain what they have learned as part of their general education, and some of whom soon forget the whole thing. I shall have nothing to say about that part of the industry.

In the advising part of the industry, there is a stock of advisable economics—that is, economics usable for giving advice to people who are going to do things other than teaching economics. This stock is mostly quite old. Much of it is probably two hundred years old, some of it is about fifty years old, and some accretions have been added to the stock in the past generation. This stock does not include much of what is in the journal mill, and it is only slowly replenished by the product of the journal mill.

The stock of advisable economics consists, in my opinion, of a few elemental concepts and propositions. It consists of a few general ideas about the microorganization of a market economy, about demand curves and supply curves and their elasticities, and about the significance of an economy being organized in this way. It consists of a few basic propositions about the macroeconomy— mainly identities derived from the equality of income, output, and expenditure—with various notions about what are the most important and stable relationships. It consists of a theory of economic growth, and some ideas about what are the most important determinants of that.

This may seem a shocking thing to say, but most of the economics that is usable for advising on public policy is at the level of the introductory undergraduate course. One might think that is a confession of my own limitations and failure to understand what is going on in the journal circle of economics, a failure I may share with others who have been primarily engaged in Washington advising on public policy. That is not the main factor, however, limiting the utility of "advanced" economics.

The Gap between Writing and Public Policy Advising

It is true that the people who have been concerned mainly with public-policy advising have not been the people at the forefront of the advance of economics and have not been regular participants in the writing of journal papers. This is a condition that has changed since fifty, or possibly even thirty, years ago. Then, a substantial part of the writing in journals and especially of the papers given at meetings of the economic societies was done by Washington practitioners. It is much less so today. The gap between the paper-writers and the practitioners has widened. One may note that there have been forty-eight members of the President's Council of Economic Advisers (CEA) who were economists, three chairmen of the Federal Reserve and probably about ten members who were economists, and about five cabinet members who were economists. Only one of these, James Tobin, has received a Nobel Prize in economics. Of course, some of the younger ones may yet do so.

But the most sophisticated economists, the ones who are probably totally abreast of the latest journal articles, use only the most elementary notions when they come to advise officials or the public about economic policy. The first thing that happens when a new Nobel Prize winner in economics is named is that the press asks him what we should do about the budget, or about the trade deficit, or about the possibility of a recession. And the answer he gives has no relation to the advanced theories for which he got the prize but is the same answer that could be given by a student who had had the sophomore course, or at most the junior course—an A student, to be sure, but a novice nonetheless.

I can give many examples. I think of one at the moment. In the fall of 1971, when the economy was very weak, President Richard Nixon announced a program for cutting government expenditures and taxes equally. This was presented as a policy for stimulating the economy. At once there came a reply from Professor Paul Samuelson that an equal reduction of taxes and expenditures would not stimulate but would depress the economy. This was an application of the balanced-budget theorem out of the elementary textbook. But of course, if he had been writing a journal article he would have recognized that much depended on the nature of the taxes and of the expenditures, and that without knowing more he could not predict the outcome.

In that case, the advisers within the government were at least a little more discriminating than the most advanced of economic theorists. The leaders of our profession, the producers of new theories of greater and greater complexity and delicacy, lead at least two lives. There is the life they lead as scientists and the life they lead when they venture into the policy-advising arena—as witnesses before congressional committees, as members of advisory panels, or as authors of op-ed pieces in the newspapers. In this second life, they leave most of their scientific apparatus behind them and rely on the elementary principles plus, like everyone else, the usual mixture of hunch, anecdote, politics, and rhetoric.

Why is this flow of journal writing so little used and, I believe, so little usable, in forming advice on public policy? There are several reasons.

Establishing the truth of any proposition in economics is difficult. The experimental method is not generally available, and the history is always ambiguous. Ideas in economics deserve confidence only after they have been chewed over for a long time, been the subject of controversy, and exposed to whatever tests may be available. For an economic adviser to rely on the latest and still-undigested ideas from the journals would be as irresponsible as for a medical doctor to try out on his patients the latest ideas from the medical journals, before they have been tried out on mice.

Much of the writing in journals is timeless and placeless, and abstract not only from any actual facts but even conceptually, from any potentially measurable variables. An interesting reflection of this condition is contained in the *New Palgrave Dictionary of Economics*, probably as good a representation of the current state of economic knowledge as we have. In the preface, the editors say that it deals in economics "mainly in its theoretical and applied aspects rather than in descriptive and institutional detail. The latter becomes outdated within a very few years, depreciating too rapidly for a publication meant for a longer shelf life than that." In reviewing the *Dictionary*, I said, "Thus, the article 'Profit and Profit Theory' does not contain a single number for what profits are or ever have been, in the United States or any other country, or any reference to any source that might provide such a number."

In the article on economic laws in the *Palgrave Dictionary*, the author, Stephen Zamagna, says: "Since no scientific law, in the natural scientific sense, has been established in economics, on which economists can base predictions, what are used, to explain or predict, are tendencies or patterns expressed in empirical or historical generalizations of less than universal validity, restricted by local and temporal limits."

To the Washington policy adviser, the local and temporal limits are all-important, and they may be very narrow limits. He must arrive at conclusions relevant to his local and temporal limits, and he gets little help in that from the body of economics in the journal mill. Generally, he must "roll his own" conclusions from his observations and experience.

A third factor limiting the usefulness of much current economic writing to the policy adviser is that he needs to convey the lesson to someone else, either an official or the general public. The audience will accept the lesson only if it understand it. A nuclear physicist may advise the secretary of energy, and the secretary will not believe that he needs to understand how the physicist reached his conclusion. Economics does not have that status. If an economist tells the secretary of the Treasury something, the secretary will want to be shown why it is true. Thus, even if the adviser himself understands current writing in economics, he will not be able to use it unless he can explain it to lay people in a way that commands confidence. That rules out much "scientific" writing in economics, at least until its essential gist has been distilled into understandable terms.

In saying that most of the economics used by economic policy advisers is that of the elementary course, I am not belittling all the work and study that go on beyond the elementary course. From the standpoint of economic policy advice, that work and study make it possible really to learn what is in the elementary course. It is practice in thinking like an economist, which means being able to keep several variables in mind at once, looking for indirect effects, and recognizing the difference between the long run and the short.

Probably a person who has learned the French taught in the first-year French course knows enough to read, write, and talk in French. He knows the grammatical rules, some vocabulary, and where to find more if he needs it. But he cannot really read, write, and talk in French, and he cannot think in French, until he has had much more study and practice. Economics is similar. What is taught in the elementary course will go a long way if one really knows it, but one does not really know it until he has lived with it for some time.

I saw the value of this when I was on the Council of Economic Advisers. We always had on our staff a few young economists, associate or assistant professors from one place or another, who were spending a year or two in Washington. One of their functions was to make sure that we were not missing anything from the recent flow of academic economics that might be useful. Their main contribution was not their knowledge of advanced economics, however, but their mastery of elementary economics. They were accustomed to using the basic concepts of economics. When a new problem arose that they had never encountered before, like the energy problem or the law of the sea problem, they could combine these old concepts with new data and generate a useful product. This elementary economics may seem to outsiders a trivial contribution to the decision-making process, but really it is not. However general, simple, even obvious and tautological it may seem, the fact is that few people who are not economists are accustomed to it or would arrive at it without the advice of economists.

The Lessons of Washington Experience

In the preface to a book of mine called *Washington Bedtime Stories,* I summed up two main lessons of fifty years as a Washington economist:

- Economists do not know very much.
- Other people, including the politicians who make economic policy, know even less about economics than economists do.

So the Washington economic policy adviser operates with a little stock of basic ideas that I call advisable economics, a stock that is slowly replenished and refreshed with an inflow of ideas from the journal mill. But this stock of basic ideas is only part of the material that the adviser works with and that enters into his product. I would identify six other elements that enter into the adviser's product:

- knowledge of the institutions in the field of his concern
- a body of relevant statistical information
- a set of ideas about how government works
- a political calculus of several kinds
- judgment
- communication skills

The policy adviser has a body of knowledge about some institutions involved in making and implementing policy. If he is an adviser at the Federal Reserve, for example, he knows a great deal about how the Federal Reserve system and the banking system work.

Most of this knowledge he has probably acquired on the job. I am frequently impressed with what Washington economists know about the particular subjects of their concern. In my earlier years, I learned a great deal about the federal budget, about the character of the various expenditure and revenue programs, about the amounts involved and their likely changes, and about the processes by which the decisions were made. I learned this in the process of writing an annual policy statement about the budget for a private organization.

The policy adviser has familiarity with a certain body of statistical data, a familiarity that he is unlikely to acquire in the academic world. This means not only knowing what is purported to be measured and what the numbers are but also something about the reliability and stability of the estimates and the reasonably expectable changes in the numbers. My own first education in this field came with learning about the national income statistics, which did not exist in anything like their present form when I was a graduate student. My ability to manipulate this body of data was enhanced by the experience of working for some time with Edward Denison, one of the pioneers of growth accounting. Incidentally, I learned from Denison one of the most important and least understood facts about economics, which is that the difference between 2 percent and 3 percent is not 1 percent but 50 percent.

Later, when I was on the Council of Economic Advisers, I acquired familiarity with a much broader range of statistics. This was partly because we wrote a memo to the president almost every day about the economic statistics being reported that day, explaining their significance. I was assisted in understanding these statistics by having available a staff of people who had spent many years with them. That is important to note. Within the government, and in many private settings, giving economic advice is a team project. What the chairman of the CEA says, for example, reflects the effort, especially the data inputs, of many expert people, not only on his own staff but also from other branches of the government. He and a few other officials are able to bring to bear upon a subject a much greater body of knowledge, although not necessarily of wisdom, than almost anybody operating on his own. I certainly know much less about many things now than I did when I was on the CEA.

In addition to some stock of institutional and statistical knowledge, the policy adviser operates with a few notions or basic attitudes about government. He must take account of how governments will operate in certain economic policy regimes. If I am in favor of a tax increase and Milton Friedman is opposed, for example, the difference between us is not about economic effects. It is about political effects. Friedman believes in Parkinson's law, that expenditures rise to equal the revenues. I do not, at least not dollar-for-dollar.

But Parkinson's law is not a proposition in economics, although most of the efforts to test it empirically have been made by economists. The division of opinion among economists between reliance on rules for policy and reliance on the discretion of policy makers also relates to ideas about how government works, more than to ideas about how the economy works. Even more generally, economists differ about the extent to which one can reasonably rely on rationality in the making of economic policy.

These are matters on which political science, if there were such a science, could provide guidance for economists. But I have sought such guidance from political scientists and have been assured that there is none to give. So economists have had to "roll their own," on the basis of what some would call casual empiricism.

The Political Calculus

Political calculations of another, more immediate kind, as distinguished from theories about how governments work, also enter into the process by which economists arrive at advice. I divide this political calculus into three kinds:

- calculus of the political feasibility of implementing a proposed policy
- calculus of the political effect of proposing the policy on the person whom the adviser is advising
- calculus of the political effect of the advice on the adviser

The economic adviser is an amateur on the first and second of these matters and possibly also on the third. This need not prevent him from having and expressing opinions about them, especially since there are no certified, expert professionals about them. But his amateur status does impose certain requirements on him in different contexts. If he is advising the public at large, through op-ed pieces, for example, he should not conceal certain options on the ground that they are politically unacceptable. A main purpose of his talking to the public is to change what is politically acceptable.

If the adviser is dealing with a politician—the president or a cabinet secretary or a congressman, for example—he may give his principal his ideas of the political feasibility or consequences of a policy, but he should not allow this to be confused with the ideas that arise out of his economics. In fact, there is little danger of this, because the politician will know how much or how little weight to give the political ideas of his economists.

The role of the adviser's calculus of his own gains and losses in the advisory process is a perplexing and interesting one. We have recently seen the rise of a school of economics that explains all public policy as the consequence of self-maximizing behavior of decision makers. Presumably, this theory should hold for economic advisers also. I once had occasion to plan the annual meetings of the Southern Economic Association, and I arranged for a session at which leading public choice economists in the government would speak on the question, "What do public choice economists maximize when they are in the government?" They came and spoke, all right, but only about what other people were maximizing, not about what they themselves were maximizing.

In my observation, people who accept the role of economic adviser consult their own interests in doing so. But I also believe that having accepted this role, they have gone on to live up to their responsibility to their principal, which is to give him the advice that is in the principal's interest, not necessarily their own. I am aware that in both the private and the public sectors there are people who put their own interests over their responsibilities. There have been people who awarded procurement contracts with an eye to their possible future employment with the contractors. But I have never heard any suspicion of this about economic advisers. Of course, an adviser may serve a private interest in less pecuniary ways—to curry favor with his principal, to show loyalty to some team or school, to differentiate himself from competitors, or only to show off. But my observation is that people in positions of serious responsibility behave responsibly.

This is probably a good point at which to explain what responsible economic advice is like. One might think of an economic adviser in his study, like the mad scientist in his laboratory, cooking up the ideal prescription and giving it to his principal. It is really not like that at all. Any responsible economist will recognize that in most cases there is no objective and certain way to determine the ideal policy. There are several options for which some reasonable case can be made, and for which respectable economists do make a case. The adviser may have a preference among these options. He usually does. But it is not his business to make the decision for his principal. His business is to inform his principal of the eligible options and of what can be said for and against each.

I concluded when I was at the CEA that the highest product and best test of an adviser was the options paper. This is not an easy thing to produce. It requires an ability to understand other people's arguments and a high degree of objectivity to present them fairly.

No one, however diligent, could possibly include in his advice all possible options and all possible arguments for and against each. The adviser has to make some selection of what he considers the most eligible options and the most weighty arguments. He will have no scientific, objective basis finally for making this selection. The adviser has to use something called "judgment." I think we do not know exactly what that is. It seems to be a sense of what is plausible and what is not, of what conforms to the way the world works and what does not. It is sometimes called "common sense."

Finally, the adviser must communicate his advice, his presentation of the options, to someone else, who will in turn decide what to do with it. The advice, however cogent, will not be useful unless it can be communicated.

So we have the picture of the adviser using his judgment to select what seem to him the most eligible options revealed by his advisable economics, his statistical and institutional knowledge, his view of how government works, and his political calculus and communicating these options and the relevant arguments to his principal.

I have used the word *principal* several times here. Of course, advising is a two-sided process. It requires an adviser and an advisee. The nature and quality of the advice depend very much on the advisee. President Harry Truman is quoted as saying that he wanted a one-armed economist who would not say "on the one hand and on the other hand." A person who thinks that way cannot get good economic advice, because the essence of the matter is uncertainty and the need to consider different possibilities. I had the impression, when I served on President Ronald Reagan's economic policy advisory board, that some questions such as the desirability of raising taxes, were taboo, although perhaps in more private sessions he might have been willing to listen to talk on those subjects. To get good advice, an advisee must want it.

I feel that I have been fortunate in the advisees with whom I have worked, especially Richard Nixon. He wanted to hear from his advisers, and not only from the highest-ranking ones. He wanted to have competing views presented to him. He understood the fallibility of economics, did not complain about its errors, and appreciated its insights. Without any background in economic theory, he had a quick grasp of arguments and a retentive memory for data.

Of course, he did not always follow the preferred options of his economic advisers. But that is not a good test of an advisory relationship. What the advisee can expect is a clear, objective evaluation of the options, and what the adviser can expect in return is that the advisee listen. Beyond that, the advisee must make decisions, and the adviser must recognize that there are more things in heaven and earth than his economics. *(March 1991)*

9

Presidents and Economics

I n 1994, the American Enterprise Institute published a new edition of my book, *Presidential Economics,* which now extends the story of the making of economic policy in the White House from the time of Franklin Roosevelt to the first impression given by Bill Clinton. This book draws upon my observations in Washington since 1938 as well as upon my earlier book, *The Fiscal Revolution in America,* which covered the administration of Herbert Hoover as well.

I would like here to draw some generalizations from this history. I am an admirer of Vladimir Nabokov, who once said of himself, "I make no general observations; I am not a general." I will depart from his example only a little. My generalizations will not be at a high level. They will be only one-star generalizations, not four-star ones.

Presidents are not economists. Presidents have little comprehension of economics in the sense of a scientific, academic discipline, and little interest in it. Economists who have served as advisers to presidents like to claim that "their" president was different, but that is mostly self-serving fantasy.

Herbert Hoover was probably the president who was most up on the scientific economics of his time. He had been secretary of commerce, which creates a certain connection with economics; he was aware of the work on economic fluctuations going on at the National Bureau of Economic Research; and he sometimes consulted with Wesley Mitchell, the great expert on business cycles. We have the picture of Hoover alone at night in the Oval Office poring over charts and tables, trying to figure out when the depression would end. Unfortunately, the economics of his time was inadequate and, anyway, circumstances gave Hoover little latitude.

Franklin Delano Roosevelt was more cavalier about economics. At an early press conference, he said that he was for "sound money," but when a reporter asked him what he meant by that he replied, "I don't intend to write a book about it."

Roosevelt was a coconspirator in letting the Keynesian virus into the American body politic, but the only meeting between what many consider the greatest American president of the twentieth century and the greatest economist of that time was not a happy one. After their meeting, in June 1934, Keynes told Frances Perkins, secretary of labor, that he had "supposed the President was more literate, economically speaking." Roosevelt for his part said: "He left a whole rigmarole of figures. He must be a mathematician rather than a political economist."

The most memorable statement by Harry Truman on the subject of economics was his wishing for a one-armed economist who would not say "on the one hand and on the other hand" all the time. This shows a deep misunderstanding of economics, which too often is shared by economists. Leon Keyserling, who was chairman of the Council of Economic Advisers, describes himself as being constantly at Truman's elbow. But it is interesting that McCullough's comprehensive biography of Truman finds no place for Keyserling.

No one ever accused Eisenhower of being an economist, although his policy showed considerable sophistication. He was used to the military system of delegating responsibility, and he once told Arthur Burns that Burns would have made a good chief of staff in the army. Eisenhower had a certain facility in translating economic ideas into homely language, as when he said there was no need to balance the budget in the particular length of time it takes the earth to revolve around the sun. But there is no evidence of any interest in economics as a science.

John F. Kennedy was the president most credited by his advisers with having had a personal interest in economics. I believe, however, that this claim is part of the whole mythology that developed around his personality. He once said he could never remember the difference between fiscal and monetary policy, but he remembered that William McChesney Martin was chairman of the Federal

Reserve, that Martin started with an *M,* as did money, so he knew that the Federal Reserve was responsible for monetary policy. I have always wondered why he did not tell himself that Federal Reserve started with an *F* and therefore the Fed was in charge of fiscal policy. But the story does not sound to me like evidence of John Kennedy's proficiency in economics.

I once asked Richard Nixon whether he had studied economics in college. He told me he had had a course at Whittier College, taught by the college preacher. According to Nixon, the preacher "didn't know his —— from first base about economics," and Nixon finished the course not knowing any more than that.

Nixon knew the names of the players in the field of economics—as he did in many other sports. He also liked the idea of being identified as sophisticated and modern about economics. That is why he was proud to say, after presenting the budget in 1971, "Now I am a Keynesian."[1] But that only meant that he had found a rationalization for proposing an unbalanced budget. With all due respect, the most that can be said for Nixon and economic science is that he was tolerant of it and its practitioners.

Ronald Reagan majored in economics at Eureka College. He was also, more than any other president, associated with a unique brand of economics, "supply-side economics." But I believe he came to the supply side out of political necessity before the 1980 campaign rather than, or at least prior to, intellectual conversion. Moreover, there is still a question about what Reagan meant by it. Did he mean that cutting taxes would raise the revenue, or that cutting taxes would reduce the revenue less than would occur if there were no positive effect on taxable incomes? I once had the occasion to say that I hoped he would not oppose a tax increase on ideological grounds. He replied that his reason was not ideological, but that he knew what the Muslim philosopher of the Middle Ages had said: the king came into office with high taxes and left with low revenue. That suggested to me a lack of awareness of the basis of his own economic philosophy.

George Bush majored in economics at Yale. I attribute to his education there the most significant thing he ever said about economics, namely his 1980 statement that the Reagan plan for tax reduction was "voodoo economics." He did not attain that height again.

---

1. He is almost always misquoted as saying, "We are all Keynesians now," but that was something Milton Friedman said in 1965.

To draw any conclusions at this time about Bill Clinton would be premature. We have not yet had the memoirs of his devoted advisers, who will tell of pleasant conversations with the president about the theory of factor price equalization while jogging around the south lawn. But one can say that up to this point Clinton's public discussions of economic policy, which are abundant, do not reveal consciousness of any economic theory.

Most presidents have had little experience in the private economy. Almost all have spent most of their adult lives in government. Ronald Reagan was the exception, partly because his adult life before coming into the presidency was unusually long. His experience was in a peculiar industry, motion pictures. The main lesson he derived from that experience was that if the tax rates were steeply progressive the stars would not make more than one picture a year.

The closest we have come to having a businessman in the White House recently was Ross Perot. Thinking about that possibility suggests why, although business experience may be useful, having someone who is *only* a businessman may be dangerous. A businessman has a single, clear, and objective goal—profits. His standard of performance is effectiveness in achieving that goal. That is exemplified by Perot's idea that what the president has to do is to lift up the hood, presumably of the society, and fix it. The goal is known—to get the vehicle running. But the president has to exercise judgment about the priority to be given to each of a large number of competing goals. That calls for a person whose sense of values we can trust, and business success is no indication of that.

Many presidents know a great deal about the nuts and bolts of economic policy. To know economics is not to know all that needs to be known about economic policy. Most economists know little about the specific legislation that prescribes economic policy or about the administrative processes that carry it out. Many presidents know a great deal about that. This is especially true of presidents who have spent a good deal of time in Congress. My own observation of Nixon and of Gerald Ford confirms that. Experience as governor has something, but less, to contribute. Roosevelt, of course, dealt mainly with new programs that he had created himself, so his prior experience as governor of New York was of little value. Since Hoover, we have had no president with much experience in the executive branch, unless Eisenhower's military experience is counted.

Presidents are intelligent and capable people. They have won in a tough competition. Most show considerable ability in absorbing the part of an economic argument that is essential for their purposes, making decisions about it, and rearticulating the argument in a way that will be understandable and acceptable to the audience they care about—if not to the readers of the *American Economic Review.* I was always impressed by the ability of Richard Nixon to listen to a discussion among the quadriad, which included three professional economists—George Shultz, Arthur Burns, and Herbert Stein—as well as Treasury secretary John Connally, and at the end synthesize the discussion accurately and come at least to a tentative conclusion about it. I do not have such first-hand observation of others, but I believe that many of them had ability like that.

Presidents who come into office with specific promises are likely to be disappointed and disappointing. Preparation for office does not expose them to reality, and campaigning encourages unrealistic and irresponsible promises.

We tend to forget that Roosevelt campaigned in 1932 on the promise to balance the budget. Nixon, Reagan, and Bush failed on the same promise. Kennedy came into office with a list of expenditure programs he was going to initiate or enlarge. He could not get much of it through Congress, and then he turned to tax reduction, which had not been part of his original plan. Nixon's turn to price and wage controls was, of course, diametrically opposite to his campaign talk about the free market. Clinton found that he had to raise taxes on the middle class, rather than cut them as he had promised. Probably the most famous reversal, because the promise had been made so emphatically, was Bush's abandonment of his "No new taxes!" pledge.

Presidents have come increasingly to rely on members of their own administration for economic advice. Roosevelt, Truman, and Eisenhower looked to other political leaders, especially members of Congress, to businessmen, and to officials of labor unions. Kennedy sought the advice of Paul Samuelson, who was not in the government, and he received but did not seek the advice of John Kenneth Galbraith, who was far enough away as ambassador to India to be called an outsider. But thereafter reliance on outside advice became less frequent.

The most formal effort to arrange outside advice was the establishment in 1981 under Reagan of the President's Economic Policy Advisory Board (PEPAB). This body consisted of about a dozen people, all of whom had been officials of previous Republican administrations, and most of whom had been advisers in Reagan's 1980 campaign. The PEPAB turned out to be mainly a claque telling the president how well he was doing.

The dominance of insiders in advising a president is perfectly natural. They see the president much more frequently than any outsiders could. The president has confidence that they share his interests; he chose them with that in mind, and they have linked their futures with his. And on most subjects they have more information, or at least more up-to-date information, than outsiders have.

Still, outside advisers have something to contribute. The insiders have an inescapable tendency to believe that the policies they helped formulate are working, or will work, long after they have become doubtful. Outsiders are more likely to be objective in this regard.

The president usually gets his economic advice from a small special committee. On every major issue, there are many officials who have something to say. Some presidents have tried to work with each of these officials separately and to synthesize their advice independently. This is said to have been Jimmy Carter's intention. But it is an unworkable procedure, because it wastes the president's time and does not give him the benefit of a confrontation among the positions held by different officials.

At the opposite extreme is the effort to involve all the economic officials at once in all the big issues. Nixon tried that at the beginning of his administration. He established a body called the Cabinet Committee on Economic Policy (CABCOMMECOPOL, as dubbed by William Safire) that included about a dozen people—about ten cabinet secretaries, plus the director of the budget, plus the chairman of the Council of Economic Advisers. That also turned out to be unworkable. On any given subject, it invited endless talk by people who were ignorant and had no responsibility.

Generally, the advice-giving body has dwindled down to a small group that has as its core the three agencies whose advice the president wants on almost every economic matter—the Treasury, the Office of Management and Budget, and the Council of Economic Advisers. This group of three (the troika) is supplemented as the occasion requires. During the Nixon administration, for example, when we had both the price and wage controls and the energy crisis, officials responsible for those two areas usually joined the troika. Umbrella organizations with more members often existed, but in those cases the work was done by subcommittees of the people most directly concerned with particular problems. The secretary of the Treasury, as the senior economic official, usually served as chairman of the advisory group. There were exceptions, however, as when Kenneth Rush, Nixon's own former law professor, served as leader in the final days of the Nixon administration, and William Seidman, Ford's old friend from Michigan, served in the Ford administration.

The Clinton administration has established a National Economic Council and advertises it as evidence of the elevation of economic policy and coordination in the president's list of priorities. But this is evidence only of a characteristic that is common to most administrations—ignorance of historical precedents.

A final generalization is that economists do not make economic policy, presidents do. That is not to say that presidents reject the advice of their economists. It means two things.

First, the president has chosen his advisers. As Paul Samuelson once said, "The leaders of this world may seem to be led around through the nose by their economic advisers. But who is pulling and who is pushing? And note this: he who picks his own doctor from an array of competing doctors is in a real sense his own doctor. The prince often gets what he wants to hear."

Presidents tend to choose advisers who share their own values and views. When Nixon appointed Paul McCracken, Hendrik Houthakker, and me to his Council of Economic Advisers, McCracken said that the president had no choice, since we were the only three Republican economists in existence. That was a joke for several reasons, one being that at the time I was a registered Democrat. But Nixon knew that we were opposed to fine-tuning and in favor of budget balancing and free markets. So he chose the kind of advice he got, although we tried conscientiously to evaluate his options.

Second, even on the president's own team, among the advisers most sympathetic to him, there will be differences, and he will have to use his own judgment to choose among them. In fact, in most cases any single adviser, if he is behaving responsibly, will recognize that economics does not point unequivocally to one policy as being best. Then the president has to choose.

If well used, economics can serve a valuable function for a president. It can help him to see what his policy options are—both broadening and narrowing the list of options. That is, it may reveal some options that he might not have considered or rule out some options that are beyond the pale of eligibility. Economics can, up to a point, help the president to visualize the consequences of following different options. Beyond that, it is up to the president. *(November 1993)*

10

O, Weep for the White House Mess!

As part of his grand strategy for solving America's economic, social, and moral problems, President Clinton is going to convert the White House mess into a cafeteria, open to all, and charging break-even prices. I am saddened to learn that. Another memorial of a happy day, gone! And not only gone but besmirched. Now the world and I are told that in all those years when I was eating subsidized hamburgers for lunch, except on Thursdays when there was Mexican food, I was robbing the taxpayer.

I suppose I should feel guilty, but I cannot. I feel only sorry. I'm sorry for myself that the memory has been clouded. I'm sorry for my successors, who will not have the privilege I had. And I'm sorry for those small-minded people, knowing the price of everything but the value of nothing, who decided to plow under this one oasis of romance in a desert of bookkeeping.

My love affair with the White House mess began in December 1968. This was shortly after Nixon's first election as president, and I had been invited to become a member of his Council of Economic Advisers (CEA). I sought advice from Kermit Gordon, who was then the president of the Brookings Institution, where I was working. He was a wise and experienced man, who had been a member of the CEA in the Kennedy years. He said I should take the appointment, but only if I would be made a member of the White House mess. In some earlier administrations, only the chairman, not the other two members, of the CEA had mess privileges.

Admission to the mess must have seemed to me a peculiar requirement, and I do not recall that I ever mentioned it to anyone. But I took the job and found that I was to have mess privileges. I soon learned the significance of Gordon's advice.

Being a member of the mess meant being a member of the team. The concept of *team* is central to the significance of the mess. The team is a group of people devoted to a common objective, who recognize that devotion in each other, who will help each other and share information with each other in the pursuit of the objective, who will comfort each other in difficulties and share each other's successes. I found such a team at the White House, and as far as the team had a geographic locale it was the White House mess.

It was in the mess that I met the press people, the speech writers, the congressional liaisons, the legal counsels, the advance men, and others who were part of the team. We were very different people, with different training, personalities, and agendas. But we accepted each other as members of the team, and being members of the mess was our certificate of membership. The mess was the place where we could communicate freely with each other without having to demonstrate any "need to know." How many there were on the team I do not know—perhaps forty or fifty, all the people on the staff that the president would know and know something about.

The essence of the team and of the mess as its symbol and home was exclusivity. If anyone, or even anyone with a White House pass, could have walked in for lunch, there would have been nothing special about it, nothing to distinguish members from nonmembers.

Clearly, the mess was extremely satisfying and encouraging to those who belonged to it. Was it of any value to the White House, the government, and the country? I believe the answer is yes. Every large enterprise, especially one as embattled as the White House is likely to be, needs a cadre of devoted people. It cannot be run by people whose test of every issue is, What's in it for me? It cannot be run by a gaggle of pundits who will decide every Tuesday and Friday whether they are for the administration or against it. The value of devotion and team spirit is recognized in every walk of life, from the high school football team to the marine combat platoon. It is also important in the White House. If present, it can deliver a degree of loyalty, effort, attentiveness, and diligence that cannot be obtained in any other way. And the mess was one of the ways in which this team spirit was fostered.

But what about the subsidy? That is not so clear a question. The mess subsidy was part of a total pay package. If the total pay package is too large—which I do not believe it is—that can be corrected by means other than eliminating the mess subsidy. The relevant question is whether, given the size of the total pay package, it is better to provide it entirely in cash or partly in a smaller amount of cash and a mess subsidy. Any economist will tell you that all cash is better. It leads the staff member to make a more efficient choice between eating in the mess and eating at, say McDonald's, based on the true costs of each. But that is one of the things that is wrong with economics. The subsidy was a constant, small, subliminal reminder that we were being treated as something special. It did not create the feeling, as demagogues like to say, that we were the masters of the people. We knew that we were the servants of the people. But the special treatment made us think that we were valued, honored servants of the people. That was good for us. It was also good for the White House and the country—and it did not cost very much.

Probably I am not a good witness on this subject. Clearly, I was and am in love with the White House mess. Management consultants can tell you how to organize the White House efficiently, without emotion. But emotion is what the White House is all about. It exists to create a certain atmosphere. By its furnishings, its paintings, and its protocol, it serves to remind the present incumbents that they are in a line stretching back to Washington, Jefferson, and Lincoln and to inspire them with the feeling that they can be better than they have ever been. If the White House does not do that, we might as well move the presidency to offices in Crystal City and lease the White House to Walt Disney Enterprises. Like closing the mess, that would be a way to reduce the budget deficit. *(February 1993)*

11

Richard Nixon, Economics, and Me

I had not met Richard Nixon before the day, December 18, 1968, when he announced his intention to name me to his Council of Economic Advisers. I had, of course, seen him on television many times and had once seen him in person, when, as vice president, he addressed the Board of Trustees of the Council on Economic Development at lunch in the Mayflower Hotel in Washington. My impression of him from these early observations was summed up in one word—*wooden.* His gestures and his manner of speech seemed to me unnatural. Moreover, although I thought of myself as a conservative, I did not think that I was his kind of conservative.

Early in 1968, when I decided that I would like to participate in the political process rather than only observing it from the outside, I offered my services to Nelson Rockefeller, who was then a candidate for the Republican nomination. I had known Rockefeller somewhat through the CED and otherwise. But he was not to be the nominee.

After the Miami convention at which Nixon was nominated, Arthur Burns and Milton Friedman called to ask me if I would work on a task force to prepare position papers that a Nixon administration could use if it came into office. I agreed to head a task force on the budget, and we did write two papers that were duly submitted to Mr. Nixon after he was elected. I could never see that these papers had any effect on the policy of the administration. This work did, I suppose, help establish my eligibility for appointment to something in the Nixon administration. But I was really appointed on the recommendation of Paul McCracken, who had known Mr. Nixon when he was vice president and who would be the chairman of his Council of Economic Advisers. I later learned that McCracken selected me because he knew that the CEA had to do a lot of writing and that I was a writer.

So, on the afternoon of December 18, 1968, I visited Mr. Nixon in the Pierre Hotel in New York, where he had his transition headquarters. For him to meet me, before such a minor appointment, was not really necessary. But I suppose that his managers thought it might look careless for him to name someone he had not met. Perhaps the meeting was part of a plan to have a news story of some kind for every day.

The First Meeting with Nixon

Two things stick with me from that meeting with Richard Nixon. First, I felt comfortable with him. I felt that I could tell him anything I wanted to say. That may not seem so surprising because I was almost as old as he was and had been in Washington for thirty years and seen a lot of presidents. I had also worked at the CED with the heads of America's biggest businesses. But I had never been in conversation with any president or president-elect and had never been in a room alone with one. I could have been nervous or overawed, but I was not, and I attribute that ease to Mr. Nixon's manner toward me, which was not of one hiring a subordinate but of one welcoming me to his team.

The second lasting impression of that interview had more to do with economics. When Mr. Nixon asked me what I thought the country's biggest economic problem was, I replied with some discussion of inflation. He nodded but then said that we must never forget unemployment. I should have been prepared for that, for I knew that he had thought the rise of unemployment was one of the reasons he had lost the 1960 election, moderate though that rise was. At the time we were talking in the Pierre, however, the unemployment rate was only 3.4 percent, the lowest since World War II. Still, unemployment was very much on his mind and would remain so throughout his administration.

The Cabinet Committee

That brief encounter was not enough by itself to make a Nixonite out of me, although it helped. A more significant event came shortly after we took office. Mr. Nixon established a body called the Cabinet Committee on Economic Policy, consisting of every member of the Cabinet except the secretary of defense, plus the director of the budget and the chairman of the Council of Economic Advisers. Hendrik Houthakker and I, the two members of the CEA, also sat in. What impressed me was that the president always wanted to know what we thought too, even though we were the lowest-ranking people in a room full of Cabinet members. I thought that interest showed either unusual considerateness or unusual desire to learn, or possibly both, and I appreciated it a great deal.

Also, at the first meeting of this committee the president expressed some thoughts about the public relations aspects of our work. When he came to us, the CEA, he said that we, unlike the other officials present, should not speak at political occasions but should speak only at meetings of economists and, possibly, businessmen. He seemed to regard us as having an expert, nonpolitical status, and I thought that attitude was also considerate. It was also, strange to say, naive. As long as we were his advisers, anything we said would be "political," and if I had wanted to be nonpolitical, I would have stayed at Brookings.

In fact, as member and then as chairman of the CEA, I made a great many speeches, trying to explain and, of course, to sell the administration's economic policy but also with the hope of describing a general philosophy of economic policy that would influence the administration. I used to send copies of these speeches to the president, and they would come back with notations indicating that he had read and approved them. I think he recognized that I was a writer, with some wit, and he liked that. He believed that he had in me a polemicist who could compete with the Op-Ed writers who regularly criticized him.

Mr. Nixon soon found that meeting with the Committee on Economic Policy was not an efficient use of his time. It enabled too many people to spend too much time talking about subjects on which they had neither knowledge nor responsibility. Before the year was out, he turned the chairmanship of that body over to the vice president, which soon led to its end, because Cabinet secretaries would not take seriously a committee chaired by the vice president.

I believed that the president would have liked to abandon the Cabinet in the same way that he abandoned the committee. In the Nixon years, the chairman of the CEA, or his representative, did not sit at the Cabinet table unless economics was on the agenda. I used to sit against the wall, behind the vice president and facing the president, whom I wanted to watch. It seemed to me that he enjoyed being there but was also bored. Some members of the Cabinet spoke endlessly, I thought for no reason other than to bring themselves to the attention of the president. I cannot recall any decision being made at a Cabinet meeting. The president was either announcing a decision he had already made or taking in some information that he might use in making a decision later.

Experience on the CEA

A member of the CEA other than the chairman does not have much contact with the president. The chairman of the CEA is the president's economic adviser. The other members assist the chairman and also represent the CEA in dealings with lesser officials than the president. When the chairman is away, he designates one of the members as acting chairman, and in that capacity in April 1969 I received a memo from the White House asking that the CEA provide an estimate of the effect of repealing the investment tax credit. One of our staff members ran through his econometric exercise and produced an estimate of the effect on economic growth (to two decimal places, which in retrospect seems ridiculous). I incorporated that estimate in a memo to the president. My memo also said that I did not think that promoting business investment was as high a priority for us as financing assistance for the poor or sharing revenue with the states so that they could perform their functions better.

The next day I received my memo back from the White House with "Very good, RN" in the president's handwriting at the bottom. That naturally endeared him to me, partly, of course, because of the praise but also because it indicated that he shared my priorities. In a discussion of the issue in the Cabinet Room, chaired by the president, I found myself in opposition to the redoubtable Arthur Burns, then counselor to the president, who did not want the investment tax credit repealed. The president decided to recommend repeal of the

ITC. How much, if any, influence my memo had on his decision I do not know. He had been told that if he would agree to repeal of the ITC he would pick up 100 votes in the House in support of his proposal to extend the Vietnam War tax surcharge. Surely that had a part, probably the major part, in his decision. But I was still pleased by the decision.

I was pleased that he seemed to endorse my view that concern for the disadvantaged should be a high priority of our administration. He later showed that concern in more important ways—the Family Assistance Program, supplementary security income, his health care reform proposal, the Philadelphia Plan to break down discrimination against minorities by the construction workers' unions, and the effort to support minority business enterprises. I have only recently learned that as vice president under Eisenhower, he was one of the strongest supporters for social programs within the administration.

Although Mr. Nixon knew that economics was important, both to the country and to him as a politician, he did not want to manage economic policy in detail himself. He wanted to have a manager of economic policy whom he could trust to bring the relevant economic officials of government together, to bring about consensus on the decisions that did not require the involvement of the president, to keep the president informed of the big decisions that he had to make himself, and to serve as public spokesman for the administration on economic matters. He found the person he wanted, first in John Connally, who became secretary of the Treasury in December 1970, and then in George Shultz, who succeeded to that position in May 1972. (Connally was stronger in the public spokesman part of the job and Shultz in the consensus formation part of it.)

Although Nixon delegated much of economics to others, he nevertheless displayed an attitude toward economics that I found impressive, for several reasons. The CEA used to send Mr. Nixon memos almost every day informing him of newly appearing economic statistics and of other economic news. The president not only read all this but also remembered it and was able thereafter spontaneously to integrate this information in, for example, an informal talk to a group of congressmen.

The Nixon Style

The president met regularly with the quadriad—the heads of the Treasury, the OMB, the CEA, and the Federal Reserve. He would

listen and to some degree participate in a discussion of the economic
situation and key policy issues. The discussion was not particularly
structured, and conflicting views would be aired. At the end, the
president would sum up with a well-organized synthesis of the
information and the options. I always thought this ability in a field
with which he was not thoroughly familiar showed a high degree
of intelligence.

As one of Mr. Nixon's economists, I appreciated the fact that
he never, as far as I know, complained that our forecasts were
wrong, as they sometimes were. He seemed to understand the
inevitable fallibility of such forecasts. He also seemed to regard
economics as being something of a science. I remember him kidding
Daniel Patrick Moynihan about the "softness" of sociology as a
science. And once when he was awarding the Medal of Science, he
remarked that perhaps there is no political science. But he did not
make such remarks about economics.

Richard Nixon knew the *style* of economic policy he wanted. He
wanted to be modern, innovative, and dramatic. He did not want to
have a conventional, "know-nothing," Republican kind of economics.
He used to say, wistfully, that the policy of gradualism his advisers
produced for him was, in the football language he loved, a policy of
"three yards and a cloud of dust." He would have preferred to throw
the long bomb. But he was also cautious and did not want to throw
the long bomb all by himself. After all, he could have told us, his
officials, to develop a more dramatic program, and we would have
done so. He wanted company and encouragement.

A Balanced Budget

The first innovation of the Nixon administration, in the field of
macroeconomics, was his espousal of the idea that the budget should
be balanced at high employment, and not all the time. That was not
a new idea, having been in circulation at least since 1947, but his
adoption of it in the summer of 1970 was its first official use by a
president. I had been more involved in the development and exposition of the high-employment budget than anyone else in the country,
but it was not I who introduced the idea to the president. That was
done by George Shultz, then the director of OMB. By that time, I
was aware of several inadequacies in the rule of balancing the budget
at high employment, and we at the CEA were working with a more

sophisticated and complicated version of that rule. Shultz was, however, probably wise to stick with the simple version, because the more complicated version could not have been explained to the president or the public.

The high-employment-balance idea met the president's needs. It enabled him, or so he thought, to maintain faith with his conventional supporters to whom balancing the budget was a totem. At the same time, it relieved him of the need to try to balance the budget in a recession. And it aligned him with the "modern" idea that the budget should be used as an economic stabilizer.

Although this idea did not get much public attention during the second half of 1970 when the president was using it in speeches and press conferences, it did get attention in January 1971 when he highlighted it in his State of the Union and budget messages. In connection with these messages, he said to a journalist, "Now I am a Keynesian in economics." None of his economists had told him that he was a Keynesian, and they would not have done so. It was only his way of saying, proudly, that he was a modern thinker about economic policy. Calling himself a Keynesian won him no praise from Keynesian economists, but it did rouse complaints from outraged Republicans. Answering their letters and explaining that *Keynesian* did not mean *Red atheist* became my responsibility.

Wage and Price Controls

By the spring of 1971, we were in the preliminary stages of what would be Richard Nixon's real economic long bomb—the imposition of comprehensive, mandatory price and wage controls. Many reasons can be adduced for this step, seemingly so foreign to Mr. Nixon's philosophy. But surely one critical factor was the presence of John Connally. I doubt that Mr. Nixon would have taken the step without the encouragement of someone he trusted, and John Connally, whose reservations about daring, dramatic action were less than the president's, was just the man for that.

In the spring of 1971, the economy was clearly not on the track we had hoped for and forecast—both unemployment and the inflation rate being too high. The question naturally arose of what to do. Stories about disagreements within the administration began to appear in the press. The CEA wanted a more stimulative fiscal policy—a tax cut or expenditure increase or both. The Office of

Management and Budget wanted to stick with the budget we had. The president called a meeting of his economic chiefs—McCracken, Connally, and Shultz—at Camp David on June 21. After their return from the mountain, Connally announced the Four Noes—no expenditure increase, no tax cut, no price and wage controls, and no devaluation of the dollar. Within two months, we were to do all but the first of these.

This situation gave rise to the only occasion on which the president was, even by implication, critical of his economic advisers. The three of us—McCracken, Houthakker, and I—were summoned to a meeting in the Cabinet Room at which Connally, Shultz, and some others were also present. Mr. Nixon said that he was announcing publicly that John Connally would be his spokesman on economics. Then, turning to us, he said that we could write him any memos we wanted to, to be used in our future memoirs, but that nothing was to be leaked. I have a picture of the three of us, huddled together at one end of the Cabinet table like chastened schoolboys, receiving this news.

About a month later, the three of us were together with the president again, this time in the Oval Office. He wanted to talk about options with respect to price-wage control. After some discussion, he asked us to prepare plans for two options. One would be the "soft" option, a wage-price review board that would make nonbinding recommendations affecting the largest corporations and unions. The "hard" option would be comprehensive, mandatory controls. Although he asked us to study the two options, as we were leaving he said, "If I do this I'm going to leap-frog them all, so no one can say we didn't go far enough"—which made it clear that he had already opted for the long bomb.

The president announced his decision to impose mandatory, comprehensive wage and price controls in a TV address on August 15, 1971. The next day my son said to me, "Ideologically you should fall on your sword, but existentially it's great." He could have said that just as well to the president. The existentially great period lasted longer than one might have expected—through the end of 1972. Inflation and unemployment both came down, output rose strongly, and controls were being phased out little by little. But the great period would not last forever.

When the decision was made at Camp David on the weekend of August 15 to impose a ninety-day freeze on prices and wages, hardly any thought was given to what we would do after the ninety days had expired. I asked for and received responsibility for planning phase two, in which we would begin to get out of the controls. In October, George Shultz and I briefed the president on the plans for phase two. He said, "It's a good thing we are doing this rather than the Democrats, because if the controls get to be too bad we can strangle them in the cradle."

Strangling the controls turned out, however, to be more difficult than we thought at the time. After a while, controls become impossible to live with but traumatic to do without. That time came early in 1973, for several reasons, including a worldwide food shortage. In March, as Ezra Solomon was leaving his position as member of the CEA, the president and Mrs. Nixon invited the three members of the council—Solomon, Marina Whitman, and me—with our spouses for breakfast at the White House.

The president raised the possibility of going back into the price-wage freeze, which had been such a hit in August 1971. I replied, in what I now think of as a smart-alecky way, quoting Heraclitus, "You cannot step in the same river twice." His rejoinder was the wittiest remark I ever heard from him. "Yes, you can, if it's frozen."

His interest in restoring the freeze persisted and grew stronger as the price control system unraveled further. It is clearer to me now than it was at the time that he felt increasing political pressure because of Watergate and thought that another dramatic move like imposing a new freeze would help restore his position in the country. As I look back on that period, I am amazed at how much self-control he showed in dealing with economic matters when he must have been in anguish about Watergate. The insistence on restoring the freeze is the only case I know in which his economic policy seemed to have been affected by his personal troubles.

During the spring, the economic team met over and over again to concoct a policy for dealing with the weakening control system. We kept coming up with a recommendation against restoring the freeze. The president would ask us to think again and write more option papers. He asked John Connally to return as special counselor, probably hoping that he could pull a rabbit out of the hat, but even he could not endorse a new freeze. Finally, the president found someone who would tell him to freeze prices and wages again. That was Melvin Laird, then secretary of defense, former member of Congress, and esteemed in Washington as a political sage. That was enough, and we began a new freeze. It was a disaster, especially from a public relations standpoint, and after two months we abandoned it and returned to the path of decontrol.

Departures

When I was first asked to join the CEA, I had intended to stay for only a year, just to see what life around the White House was like. An old Washington hand advised me to plan on two years, saying that I would not really learn much in one year, so I took a leave of two years from Brookings. But in the fall of 1971, near the end of the second year, I was offered a professorship at the University of Virginia, with the understanding that I would come down to Charlottesville for the fall term in 1972. This date was twice postponed, but by 1974 I was told that I had either to take up the chair or to vacate it. So I decided to leave the council. The president urged me to stay and offered to appoint me to a position with a long tenure. But I decided to go, to try something new, and August 31 was set as the date for my departure. I did not know then that he would be leaving before me, on August 9.

When Mr. Nixon said good-bye to his staff, on the morning of August 9, I wept. It was not because of the successes and failures of his economic policy—in which I had shared—that I wept. I wept, my wife wept, and my son wept because he had been invariably considerate and kind to us. This man, who had been so distant and so unlike us six years earlier, had become our friend. We grieved to see him leave in disgrace and for an unknowable future and regretted that he had to do so. *(May 1994)*

12

On Nixon Economics

It is early to make a definitive evaluation of the presidency of Richard Nixon, and I am certainly not the person to do it. He was my patron and my friend. But I would like to recall some economic aspects of his presidency, less dramatic than clinking glasses with Chou En-lai or waving farewell from the steps of a helicopter, that are certainly part of the story.

Nixon's economic policy cannot be encapsulated in a bumper sticker. It does not fit into the neat ideological boxes, "liberal" or "conservative," and is disdained by liberals and conservatives alike. That is not because Nixon lacked guiding principles or because, in the pundits' cliché, he was "complex." His policy was complex and seemingly inconsistent because the real world is like that.

Expanding Economic Freedom

I start a recital of Nixon's economics with what may seem an esoteric matter. On August 15, 1971, President Nixon "closed the gold window," as we used to say. He ended the commitment of the United States to pay gold to foreign treasuries and central banks in exchange for dollars at a fixed rate. In so doing, he ushered in the era of floating rates, in which the exchange rates among currencies were determined in markets and not by the commitments of governments. That relieved governments of the obligation either to manipulate their domestic policies or to control international movements of trade and capital in an effort to maintain the fixed rates. Contrary to some expectations at the time, the era of floating has been an era of greatly expanded international trade and investment, contributing to the prosperity of millions of people in America and elsewhere who never heard of the gold window. President Nixon further contributed to the world's prosperity by initiating the Tokyo Round of trade negotiations that, like the Kennedy Round earlier and the Uruguay Round more recently, helped reduce barriers to trade.

Ending the draft, and instituting the all-volunteer army, is not usually thought of as an economic measure. But the market for personal services is an important part of the market, and for millions of young men the end of the draft was the most important possible step toward the free market.

Expanding Government's Positive Role

Floating the dollar, liberalizing international trade, and ending the draft signaled his high value on freedom and his low confidence in the competence of government. Thirty years in government, starting as a junior lawyer in the Office of Price Administration in World War II, had left him with few illusions on that score. Steps taken during his administration to end ceilings on the interest paid on bank deposits, to remove federal limitations on agricultural production, and to move toward deregulation of trucking and airlines were further reflections of that attitude.

At the same time, he realized that government has positive functions and that these functions should respond to changes in social and technological conditions. Thus, he proposed and obtained the establishment of the Environmental Protection Agency and the Occupational Safety and Health Administration. Undoubtedly, as might have been expected, some of the regulations later issued by these agencies were extreme, even ridiculous. But even the most ardent deregulators during the succeeding twenty years have not proposed to return to the situation that existed before these agencies were created.

Just as he disliked government regulations but recognized the necessity of some, he disliked government spending but felt the need to increase it for some purposes. He was exceptionally rigorous in vetoing appropriations and impounding funds for programs on which he placed low priority. But he fought for the defense budget that undergirded his foreign policy and proposed new domestic expenditures to meet what he thought were national needs. He introduced general revenue sharing, for example, as a way of helping the states perform their legitimate functions without dictation by the federal government.

He was not a fundamentalist about balancing the budget and was happy at one point to say, "Now I am a Keynesian in economics." But the deficits of his time in office amounted to only about 1 percent of gross domestic product, compared with, say, 4 percent in the Reagan years. At the end of Nixon's presidency, the federal debt as a fraction of GDP was at the lowest point it has ever reached in the years since the beginning of World War II.

President Nixon tried to establish as a principle of fiscal policy that expenditures should not exceed the revenues that would be yielded when the economy was at high employment. He thought that benchmark would serve as a limit to spending and to the accumulation of debt while still leaving room for deficits in recessions when they would be stabilizing. But this idea was derided by conservatives and rejected by liberals, and we have sloshed around for the past twenty years without any visible standard of fiscal policy.

Other Policy Proposals

This problem of being too liberal for the conservatives and too conservative for the liberals was to doom other proposals of Nixon's. He worked hard to develop welfare reforms that would set a floor under incomes while preserving incentives to work and to maintain family cohesion. He proposed a plan of health care reform that would concentrate federal participation on the urgent needs, protection against the costs of catastrophic illness and assistance to the indigent, without involving the government in managing the whole health care system. Looking back from today, we can see how sensible these proposals were. But they were beyond the common perceptions of his time.

For many people, certainly for most economists, Nixon's economics will be identified with the mistaken policy of wage and price controls. Recognizing their economic irrationality, Mr. Nixon thought they were a political necessity. A large part of the country, including the Republicans in Congress, wanted "some kind" of controls, and the imposition of the controls was, at the time, the most popular thing President Nixon ever did. I am not sure that he was right even about the political necessity, but he was the expert on that. He comforted himself with the thought that we at least, unlike the Democratic opposition, would manage the controls to minimize their harm and to get out of them as fast as possible. While there was something to that, they were still a mistake. The best that can be said for them is that they may have drowned for some time the idea that controls could be an effective way of achieving simultaneously high employment and low inflation.

Mr. Nixon did not win any Nobel Prize for economics. I doubt that any president will ever win it. Making national economic policy is a much messier business than writing journal articles or newspaper columns. It is playing "on a cloth untrue with a twisted cue and elliptical billiard balls." Those who feel the need to give Mr. Nixon a grade for his performance should look at the record, which they will find is, like the world, more mixed and complicated than they may think. *(April 1994)*

PART THREE
The State of the American Economy

13

On Doubling per Capita Income

I n his economic speech on February 17, 1993, President Clinton warned the nation that the way things have been going, it would be a hundred years before per capita income, on the average, doubled in the United States. He obviously thought that was a shocking prospect and that the government should and would do something about it.

I have been brooding about that ever since. Only a minor part of my concern is that he chose a rather unrepresentative period to project—a period consisting mainly of a cyclical recession. If he had taken a longer period, say, from 1973 to 1993, he would have found that per capita income doubles in about sixty years. Moreover, my concern is not especially directed at Mr. Clinton. Almost everyone, Republicans as well as Democrats, seems to share this feeling that the rate of growth is quite low and that the government needs to do something about it. They differ only on what the government should do.

What perplexes me is the idea that doubling per capita income in a hundred years is shockingly slow. There must surely have been few centuries at any time or in any place when per capita income doubled in a century. If in the first year of the Christian era in Rome per capita income had been $400, about like today's Bangladesh, and had doubled every hundred years, per capita income today would be about $400,000,000, whereas it is "only" $20,000. If per capita income doubles every century from today, in twenty more centuries it will be $20,000,000,000. Is that too little?

What Is Enough?

If doubling per capita income in a century is too little, what is enough? Saying "more" is not helpful. Obviously, neither as individuals nor as a society do we mean that we want to double income as fast as possible. Raising the rate of growth is not free. Basically, it requires diverting some present income from uses that do not promote growth, which we call consumption, to uses that do promote growth, which we call investment. No one thinks that consumption should be held down to the subsistence level so that investment and growth can be maximized. The questions are how much to restrain consumption and who should decide.

Of course, individuals and families make decisions about that every day. They decide how much of their income to consume and how much to save, including saving in the form of investment in the education of their children. And what they invest is not only money but their time and attention in increasing their own earning power and that of their children. These individual decisions added together are the major factor determining the rate of national economic growth.

A little arithmetic will illustrate how important these decisions are. Suppose a family earns an income from wages of $30,000, all of which it spends on consumption. If that income grows at the rate that distresses Mr. Clinton, the family's income will double in a hundred years. Suppose that instead of consuming all its income, the family saves 10 percent of it each year and invests the savings where they will yield 5 percent annual interest. Now instead of taking a hundred years, doubling its income will take only about sixty. That is a big difference. And the more families make that decision, the bigger will be the increase in national growth.

The Government's Role

To say that shortening the period required to double per capita income is a major objective of *government* policy is to say that these private decisions are not adequate. It says that the government should restrain consumption, by restraining its own consumption, by restraining the private consumption it supports through transfer payments, and by raising taxes. The government should then either directly invest the resources released from consumption or leave them available for private investment by the reduction of its budget deficit. People differ strenuously about the combination of measures to be used. Some prefer more taxes and more government investment. Others prefer less government consumption and government-financed consumption and less budget deficit. But in brief, all sides agree that the government should force the society to save and invest more.

Why should the government do that? The reason probably offered most often is that by running the big budget deficit, the government is now keeping the society from saving more, since the deficit offsets some of the private saving. At least, it is said, the government should stop doing that. But if private individuals were disturbed by the fact that the government is using up the private saving and thus retarding the rate of growth, they could save more. If people wanted the incomes of their children and grandchildren to double in less than a hundred years, they could accomplish that in spite of the budget deficit by saving more—as the example given above illustrates. Apparently, people do not care in their private behavior. Why should they care in their public behavior, as citizens?

Maybe the government has access to more productive investments than private individuals have. There would be a case for government investment in those instances. I suppose that the Louisiana Purchase was an example of such an investment, and the purchase of Alaska may have finally turned out to be a good investment also. But the desirability of such investments does not depend on the rate of aggregate growth in the economy.

While accelerating aggregate growth may have benefits of a kind that private individuals are unlikely to take into account, these benefits are not easy to identify. Per capita national income doubled in the past thirty-five years, and one can ask what benefits that yielded aside from the increase in private consumption and assets that motivated the private effort. Some real gains occurred in that period—the end of the cold war, for example, and the reduction of discrimination against women and minorities. But the rapid growth of average incomes was not essential for those gains. There was also a deterioration of the quality of life in some respects, which the rapid growth of incomes did not prevent.

Some people say that accelerating the growth of the income of the average American may not be as important an objective of national policy as accelerating the growth of the income of the poorest, most disadvantaged part of the American population. I agree. The question is whether accelerating the growth of average incomes is the most efficient way to accelerate the growth of the income of the poorest people. Is it more efficient to raise the tide in the hope of lifting all boats, including the submerged ones, than to do something specific about the submerged ones? Is it more important to reduce the deficit or to invest in a high-speed train and a fiber-optic network, the Clintonian prescription for growth, than to improve the education and training of the disadvantaged? I doubt it.

Our Critical Needs

In 1960, Edward Denison and I wrote "Economic Growth and High Employment," an essay for the Commission on National Goals. We said in conclusion:

> The number of goals calling for our attention is large—to help set the underdeveloped world on the path of economic progress, to reduce the barriers of nationalism and racialism, to strengthen our national security, to improve the lives we lead with our immense flow of goods and services, to set a floor of economic security and welfare for all. We need not feel guilty of negativism or passivity if we decide that accelerating growth is not one of our most critical needs.

I am of the same opinion still. Of course, many things have changed. Real per capita income is now twice as high as it was, but the rate of growth is much less than it was then. Perhaps our conclusion of 1960 is not valid today. But what does seem to me undeniable is that we ought to have more explicit discussion than we do of the priority to be attached to aggregate growth. *(March 1993)*

14

Adventures with Exchange Rates

I was traumatized by exchange rates long ago. It was in 1936, to be exact, when I had a course in international finance with the redoubtable Jacob Viner. I could never understand why the exchange rate on the British pound was $4.88, whereas the rate on the French franc was 20 to the dollar. If the pound was $4.88, why wasn't the franc $.05? Or if the franc was 20 to the dollar, why wasn't the pound .205 to the dollar? I didn't know which country was up. So I gave up thinking about the subject for a long, long time.

When I can't avoid the subject, it still baffles me. I do some work, for example, on the Israeli economy. Now, when Americans say that the exchange rate went up, they mean that the dollar rose relative to other currencies. But when the Israelis say that the exchange rate went up, they mean that other currencies rose relative to the shekel. Baffling! Maybe it's because they read from right to left.

My allergy to exchange rates really hurts when I travel abroad and have to meet a foreign currency hand to hand, as was seen on a recent trip to Israel and France. Leaving Israel to fly to Paris, I had a handful of leftover Israeli shekels. I decided to exchange them at Ben Gurion Airport for French francs. Going from the exotic shekel to the romantic franc without passing through the humdrum dollar made me feel like a sophisticated jet-setter.

I received 279 francs, which somehow seemed enough for taxi fare from Charles de Gaulle Airport to my Paris hotel. I also got a printout saying that the rate was .39. Since I thought that the shekel was worth about fifty cents and the franc about twenty, it seemed reasonable enough that a figure like .39 should appear somewhere, although I wouldn't have bet on doing the algebra right the first time.

Five hours later, I am speeding along in a French taxi at a furious pace and the taxi meter is clicking off 2 francs at an even more furious pace, along side a sign saying, "No checks accepted." I worry about whether my 279 francs will survive this race, at the same time trying to remember whether I should multiply the francs by .2 or by 5 to get them into my native currency.

To my relief, the taxi and the meter slow down as we enter the XVI Arondissement, and the meter only says 132 when we stop in front of the hotel. "One hundred and sixty," says the driver. (All this is a blur in my mind now, and I'm not sure what language we were using. I suppose English.) "Why?" I ask. "Luggage," he explains. I am so annoyed and angry about this, as well as by his general manner, that I determine to stand on my rights and give him no tip, but count out exactly 160 francs. I had barely reached the sidewalk, however, when I realized that I had only 19 francs left. I had given the driver 260. But he assured me that I was mistaken. He showed me that in one pocket he had a lot of money, which was his, and in the other pocket he had a little, which was what had been mine. Somehow, I didn't find the evidence convincing, but before we could pursue the subject, he drove off.

The receptionist in the hotel was philosophical. She explained that the event was not uncommon and there was nothing I could do about it.

So there we were (my wife and I) on a Sunday afternoon, Ascension Day to boot, in a small hotel, sans restaurant, in a quiet part of Paris, having had no dinner and with about $2.00 worth of francs, after tipping the bellman. I humbly asked the receptionist, who for some reason reminded me of Madame Defarge in *A Tale of Two Cities,* whether she could cash a traveler's check. Indeed she could, and the rate was 4.9. She saw my surprise and explained that the rate had gone down (this was three days after the invasion of Kuwait) but maybe it would go up next week. She was still philosophical. "It's only a few centimes," she said. Later, in a calmer mood I figured out that 4.9 is 2 percent less than 5.

All the money amounts in this story are trivial. The story is not about amounts of money; it is about confusion, mental anguish, humiliation. It is about states of mind, which is, after all, what economics is all about.

Armed with $50 worth of francs, we set out to find a light supper. Fortunately, French restaurants, brasseries, and bistros all have menus with prices posted outside, so we could review our options before committing ourselves. This review showed that even with $50 my options were not great. But the second time around, I realized that the solution to my problem was the brasserie whose menu welcomed credit cards. There I would not have to worry about running out of francs and someone else would have to figure out how much my bill was in dollars. (I should report that when I did get my credit card bill after I returned to the United States, my franc expenditures had been translated into dollars at a rate more favorable to me than any I encountered in Paris.)

The next morning we went to the bank to change money. There was the usual bulletin board with exchange rates in two columns—*Vente* and *Achat.* Which was I, buying or selling? I was selling dollars and buying francs. The bank was selling francs and buying dollars. I never got that cleared up, but I knew that whichever it was, I would get the smaller amount. And even the smaller amount was 5.2 with some more decimals, much more than La Tricoteuse at the hotel had paid. In fact, the rate was 5.27719 francs to the dollar. I cashed only $50 because I still had the money I had exchanged at the hotel. Also, hadn't I learned that when the price of oil went up, the dollar also went up, because people had to pay for oil in dollars? Probably I would get a better rate the next day.

The net I received for my $50 dollars was 234.21. The commission and the value-added tax had eaten up 29.61 francs. Later, at my leisure I figured that my net rate had been 4.6842, almost 5 percent less than I had gotten from La Tricoteuse, whom I had unjustly maligned.

We now had almost 500 francs and started out to spend them. Our first stop, as usual with us in Paris, was a fruit stand. Have you ever tried to calculate in your head what the price is in cents of two oranges when they cost 35.75 francs per kilo and you do not have access to scales for weighing them? Or how much money you should give the cashier when you are not immediately sure whether *quinze* is fifteen or fifty? You hold out a handful of change and let her pick what she wants. She seems honest.

Having managed to get rid of quite a few francs, we undertook to get more the next morning. I proposed to La Tricoteuse that she should sell me some, but she declined. I think she had an agreement with the bank next door not to do any banking during hours when the bank was open. At the bank, I discovered that, contrary to my speculation about the price of oil, the dollar had declined from 5.27719 francs to 5.22027. But we had learned about the commission, which was a constant, so by buying $200 worth we reduced (raised?) the net price to 5.072.

Now we were really flush with francs, and I had a sudden insight into the truth of monetarism. The idea is that individual behavior is significantly governed by the possession of a certain kind of asset, called "money." Here I was with dollar currency, traveler's checks, credit cards, and checks on an account in an internationally known bank. With a call to my broker in Washington, I could get a telegraphic transfer of a large amount of money from a money-market fund. Compared with my total liquid assets, the amounts of French currency I held were minute. But the difference between feeling that I had little French currency and feeling that I had much was significant. When I felt that I had little, I tried to hold on to it, fearing to find myself in a place or time when it would be indispensable to me. When I felt that I had much, I was quite prepared to get rid of it, lest I have it "left over" at some point, or have to trade it in at a great loss. I had demonstrated that money matters. How much it matters is a question that I leave to econometricians.

Feeling flush with francs, we presented ourselves on the day before we were to leave Paris at a very expensive restaurant for lunch. As soon as I looked at the menu, my franc anxiety returned. I had never seen such prices. I began a hasty and not reassuring estimate of how many francs were in my wallet and my wife's pocketbook. There was nothing on the menu to indicate that credit cards were accepted. This restaurant's style antedated the credit card. I couldn't see any money passing at other tables or even anyone signing checks. Presumably the waiter knew without being told whose lunch was to be charged to the Duc de Guermantes. But he would know that I wasn't the *duc* of anything. For one thing, I had had to borrow a coat and tie from the checkroom to get admitted in the first place. I wondered how many hours of dishwashing it would take to work off 500 francs. When the check came, I inquired, appearing as confident as I could, whether they took credit cards. The answer was affirmative, and I was rich again.

That left us with an unexpectedly large number of francs. Even after some splurging, I had some to turn in at the bank at the airport, where I sold at 5.77 to the dollar francs that I had bought at an average price of 4.9787. I was glad to get rid of them. Now I could stop thinking about centimes and resume thinking about trillions of dollars in the budget or the GNP. *(August 1990)*

15

The Balance of Payments

F
ew subjects in economics have caused so much confusion—
and so much groundless fear—in the past 400 years as the
thought that a country might have a deficit in its balance of
payments. This fear is groundless for two reasons: (1) there never
is a deficit, and (2) it wouldn't necessarily hurt if there were.

The balance of payments accounts of a country record the
payments and receipts of the residents of the country in their
transactions with residents of other countries. If all transactions are
included, the payments and receipts of each country are, and must
be, equal. Any apparent inequality simply leaves one country acquiring assets in the others. If Americans buy automobiles from Japan,
for example, and have no other transactions with Japan, the Japanese
must end up holding dollars, which they may hold in the form of bank
deposits in the United States or in some other U.S. investment. The
payments of Americans to Japan for automobiles are balanced by the
payments of Japanese to U.S. individuals and institutions, including
banks, for the acquisition of dollar assets. Put another way, Japan
sold the United States automobiles, and the United States sold Japan
dollars or dollar-denominated assets such as Treasury bills and New
York office buildings.

Although the totals of payments and receipts are necesarily
equal, there will be inequalities—excesses of payments or receipts,
called deficits or surpluses—in particular kinds of transactions. Thus,
there can be a deficit or surplus in any of the following: merchandise
trade (goods), services trade, foreign investment income, unilateral
transfers (foreign aid), private investment, the flow of gold and

TABLE 15–1

THE U.S. BALANCE OF PAYMENTS, 1991
(billions of dollars)

Merchandise trade	− 73.4
Services	+ 45.3
Investment income	+ 16.4
Balance on goods, services, and income	− 11.7
Unilateral transfers	+ 8.0
Balance on current account	− 3.7
Nonofficial capital[a]	− 20.5
Official reserve assets	+ 24.2
Balance on capital account	+ 3.7
Total balance	0

NOTE: + = surplus; − = deficit.
a. Includes statistical discrepancy.
SOURCE: U.S. Department of Commerce, *Survey of Current Business.*

money between central banks and treasuries, or any combination of these or other international transactions. The statement that a country has a deficit or surplus in its "balance of payments" must refer to some particular class of transactions. As table 15–1 shows, in 1991 the United States had a deficit in goods of $73.4 billion but a surplus in services of $45.3 billion.

Many different definitions of the balance of payments deficit or surplus have been used in the past. Each definition has different implications and purposes. Until about 1973, attention was focused on a definition of the balance of payments intended to measure a country's ability to meet its obligation to exchange its currency for other currencies or for gold at fixed exchange rates. To meet this obligation, countries maintained a stock of official reserves, in the form of gold or foreign currencies, that they could use to support their own currencies. A decline in this stock was considered an important balance of payments deficit because it threatened the ability of the country to meet its obligations. But that particular kind of deficit, by itself, was never a good indication of the country's financial position. The reason is that it ignored the likelihood that the country would be called upon to meet its obligation, and the willing-

ness of foreign or international monetary institutions to provide
support.

Interest in official reserve positions as a measure of balance of
payments greatly diminished after 1973 as the major countries gave
up their commitment to convert their currencies at fixed exchange
rates. This reduced the need for reserves and lessened concern
about changes in the size of reserves. Since 1973, discussions of
"the" balance of payments deficit or surplus usually refer to what is
called the current account. This account contains trade in goods and
services, investment income earned abroad, and unilateral transfers.
It excludes the capital account, which includes the acquisition or sale
of securities or other property.

Because the current account and the capital account add up to
the total account, which is necessarily balanced, a deficit in the
current account is always accompanied by an equal surplus in the
capital account, and vice versa. A deficit or surplus in the current
account cannot be explained or evaluated without simultaneous
explanation and evaluation of an equal surplus or deficit in the
capital account.

A country is more likely to have a deficit in its current account
the higher its price level, the higher its gross national product, the
higher its interest rates, the lower its barriers to imports, and the
more attractive its investment opportunities—all compared with
conditions in other countries—and the higher its exchange rate. The
effects of a change in one of these factors upon the current account
balance cannot be predicted without considering the effect on the
other causal factors. If the U.S. government increases tariffs, for
example, Americans will buy fewer imports, thus reducing the
current account deficit. But economic theory indicates that this
reduction will occur only if one of the other factors changes to bring
about a decrease in the capital account surplus. If none of these
other factors changes, the reduced imports from the tariff increase
will cause a decline in the demand for foreign currency (yen, deut-
sche marks, etc.), which in turn will raise the value of the U.S.
dollar. The increase in the value of the dollar will make U.S. exports
more expensive and imports cheaper, offsetting the effect of the
tariff increase. The net result is that the tariff increase brings no
change in the current account balance.

Contrary to the general perception, the existence of a current
account deficit is not, in itself, a sign of bad economic policy or of

bad economic conditions. If the United States has a current account deficit, all this means is that the United States is importing capital. And importing capital is no more unnatural or dangerous than importing coffee. The deficit is a response to conditions in the country. It may be a response to excessive inflation, to low productivity, or to inadequate saving. It may just as easily occur because investments in the United States are secure and profitable. Furthermore, the conditions to which the deficit responds may be good or bad and may be the results of good or bad policy, but if there is a problem, it is in the underlying conditions and not in the deficit per se.

During the 1980s, there was a great deal of concern about the shift of the U.S. current account balance from a surplus of $8 billion in 1981 to a deficit of $147 billion in 1987. This shift was accompanied by an increase of about the same amount in the U.S. deficit in goods. A common claim was that this shift in the international position was causing a loss of employment in the United States. But that was not true. In fact, between 1981 to 1987, the number of people employed rose by over 12 million, and employment as a percentage of population rose from 60 percent to 62.5 percent.

Anxiety was also expressed over the other side of the accounts, the inflow of foreign capital that accompanied the current account deficit. Many people feared that the United States was becoming owned by foreigners. The inflow of foreign capital did not, however, reduce the assets owned by Americans. Instead, it added to the capital within the country. In any event, the amount was small relative to the U.S. capital stock. Measurement of the net amount of foreign-owned assets in the United States (the excess of foreign assets in the United States over U.S. assets abroad) is very uncertain. At the end of 1988, however, it was surely much less than 4 percent of the U.S. capital stock and possibly even zero. Later, there was fear of what would happen when the capital inflow slowed down or stopped. But after 1987 it did slow down and the economy adjusted, just as it had adjusted to the big capital inflow earlier, by a decline in the current account and trade deficits. *(1992)*

16

The Generational Transfer

I read a lot about the generational transfer going on these days, with the coming to office of Bill Clinton and Al Gore. (I suppose it is part of that transfer that we don't call them William and Albert. Also, have we ever before had a vice president with a "Jr." after his name?) I recognize that this transfer has happened, now that we have a president younger than my son. I don't mind. Actually, it is something of a relief not to have to get up every morning and think about how to manage the economy. I do rather resent the implicit notion that the next generation, just because it is next, is better in some sense than mine. This projection is not clear to me. I don't suppose that my generation is better than that of 1776, a generation that included Thomas Jefferson, Adam Smith, Edward Gibbon, and Wolfgang Amadeus Mozart.

Of course, the notion of a generational transfer occurring on January 20, 1993, or on any other day is artificial. Every day some actors leave the stage of life and new ones enter it. But still the notion has a certain gravity: it highlights our interest not only in what Mr. Clinton will do in his years in office but even more in what will be done in twenty-five or thirty years, beginning now. It also calls attention to the fact that the new generation comprises not only Mr. Clinton and his successors in the White House, or even they plus all the bright new faces in the Congress, but all the private people who are making decisions about educating their children, saving, investing, starting new businesses, and doing all the other things that more than any presidential actions will determine economic life in America in the next thirty years.

I think that my generation ought to get a receipt from this new one for the economy we are handing on to them. Then, thirty years from now my grandson Tommy and his cohort can ask the people of the Clinton-Gore generation, the public and private people who will then be leaving the stage, what they have done with the economy they inherited.

As it happens, my colleague, Murray Foss (also over seventy) and I have recently produced a book, *An Illustrated Guide to the American Economy,* that provides a good basis for an audit of the economy that we are bequeathing to the new generation. I will summarize the main assets and liabilities.

The United States is rich in total output and in output per capita, by comparison with any earlier period and any other country. This output is basically produced and used by private individuals who have great freedom in deciding how to use their labor, capital, and income. The United States has a large stock of capital per person and per worker and a highly educated work force, at least as measured by years of schooling. Since 1973, output per capita has been growing less rapidly than in the earlier postwar years and output per hour of work much less rapidly. Output per capita has been growing faster than output per hour mainly because of the increase in employment relative to the population, owing to the increased employment of women outside the home.

As the rise of output per capita and per work hour have slowed down, so has the rise of incomes, necessarily. For the average family, and for most families, the rise has yet remained significant, even if less than in the exceptional period right after World War II. But for the people with the least income, the rise of income, and presumably the rise in the value of their work per hour, has risen little and even been negative. This development occurred partly because of the slow growth or decline of the value of the output of persons with little education, which fell greatly relative to the value of the output of more educated people.

Thus, we have an economy in which the distribution of income by size has been becoming somewhat more unequal. But in some other respects, the distribution has become less unequal. The gap between the wages of black males and white males with the same amount of schooling has declined substantially. The gap between male and female earnings has also declined. The difference between

income in the poorer and income in the richer parts of the country
fell in the postwar period, although it rose a little again in the 1980s.

By official measurements, the proportion of the population in
poverty has remained in the range of 10 to 13 percent for about
twenty years after having fallen sharply in previous decades. Different definitions of poverty would give either higher or lower figures
for the rate of poverty, but they would not dispute the facts that the
rate has not been declining, that the rate is much higher for blacks
than for whites, and that the proportion of the poverty population in
female-headed families has increased greatly.

The rate of inflation has been running around 3 percent per
annum. That is less than half as high as in the years 1969 to
1982 but still quite high in comparison with our earlier peacetime
experience. Inflation at the rate of 3 percent per annum would double
the price level in twenty-three years.

Real output in the United States fluctuates around its rising
trend. Since the end of World War II, there have been nine episodes
of decline, or recessions, the most recent having begun in 1990. The
average period of these declines has been about eleven months, and
the two longest were of sixteen-month duration. In none of these
declines did nonfarm employment fall by more than 5 percent, and
the average was about 2.7 percent. The postwar recessions have
been very much milder than the Great Depression of the 1930s.

The United States is a member of a club of rich countries,
extending geographically from Germany to Japan. The size of this
club is a source of strength. As David Hume said in 1787, "I will
venture to assert, that the increase of riches and commerce in any
one nation, instead of hurting, commonly promotes the riches and
commerce of all its neighbors." The United States also lives in a
world of very poor countries. Two-thirds of the world's population
lives in countries with average incomes of 20 percent of U.S. per
capita income or less.

In bare summary, this is the economy that the new generation
is inheriting. Thirty years from now, the next generation will be
entitled to ask them many questions about the stewardship of today's
new generation, including both public officials and private citizens.
Among the most obvious questions, as it seems from here, will be:

• Have you preserved the freedom and openness of the economy
that make it adapt to the wishes of the private individuals who
live here?

• Have you raised the rate of increase of output per hour of work, above the recent rate of 1 percent a year? That will be necessary if recent rates of increase of output per capita are to be sustained, or even prevented from turning into a decline, since the increase of workers per capita cannot be expected to continue for long, partly because of the aging of the population.

• Have you accelerated the growth of productivity and incomes of the least advantaged part of the population, which has been languishing?

• Have you resumed the decline of the national poverty rate and continued the decline of inequality among races, genders, and regions of the country?

• Have you sustained at least the degree of economic stability that has been achieved in the postwar period? Specifically, have you avoided a recurrence of rapid inflation followed by fairly severe recessions like those of 1974–1975 and 1981–1982?

• Have you maintained a mutually beneficial economic relation with the other rich countries and avoided conflicts over economic matters that would disrupt political harmony with them?

• Have you contributed to accelerating the economic advance of the poorest parts of the world's population?

Of course, I cannot foresee all the questions that will be active thirty years from now, but these are the kinds of questions that the new generation should have in mind as it takes on its responsibilities. *(November 1992)*

17

Letters of a Father and Son about a Grandson and Son

Dear Ben:

A term that is heard more and more around Washington is *intergenerational equity*. Suddenly, people are becoming concerned about the possibility that policies followed in this generation are unfair to the next one or even later ones. Since you and I and your son Tommy are three generations, I want to share with you some thoughts about all that.

The intergenerational question is usually raised in connection with social security. People of my generation, who are now old enough to collect their social security benefits, are on the average drawing more out of the social security reserves than the value of the payments made for them by themselves or their employers. (I do not think that is true of me personally, because I have continued to work and pay social security taxes longer than most people.) Some of what your generation is paying in social security taxes is not being saved to pay your future benefits but is being used to pay excess benefits to my generation.

At the same time, the reserves that your generation is presumably building up out of your social security taxes are not being invested in productive ways that will yield income to pay your benefits when you retire. Because the rest of the government, other than social security, is running a deficit, these social security reserves are used to finance the deficit rather than being returned to the capital markets where they would finance productive investment. So, when you retire, there will be a tax burden on Tommy to pay your benefits, and there will not be the income out of which to pay those taxes that there would have been if the reserves had been productively invested. This burden will be particularly heavy because the workers of Tommy's generation will have to support an unusually large number of retired people.

One possibility is that Tommy's generation will resist bearing this burden and will cut back on the benefits that are now promised to you. This does not seem to me very likely because the old people will be even more numerous, and presumably even more powerful politically, than they are now. You and I, recognizing the burden we are storing up for Tommy, could save to pass on to him some earning assets that would help him meet this burden. I hope that we are doing that to some extent. But the fact is that Americans on the whole are not doing that. Our rate of saving is exceptionally low.

That is the heart of the problem, insofar as it is an income problem at all. My generation and yours, the people who are now earning and voting, are not saving as much as preceding generations did. We are not saving as much privately, and we are using more of the private saving to finance the budget deficit. Therefore, we are adding to the stock of productive capital less rapidly than we did and reducing the income that Tommy will have to enjoy. The way we handle social security and the prospect of an increasing proportion of retired persons intensify this problem but do not create it.

But I do not think that income is the critical matter in the relation among our generations. Over the past 120 years for which some estimates exist, real per capita income in the United States rose by about 1¾ percent per annum. If that rate were to prevail for another generation—say, thirty years—Tommy's income then would be 68 percent higher than yours was at the same age. If the deficiency of our saving were to reduce that growth rate to 1½ percent, which seems to me a high estimate, or 1¼ percent, which is probably an extreme estimate, his income in thirty years would be 56 percent, or, in the extreme case, 45 percent higher than yours. I do not believe that any critical aspect of Tommy's life will depend on whether his income is 68 percent or 56 percent or 45 percent higher than yours. The important matter will, I believe, not be Tommy's income or the nation's income but will be the kind of country and world in which Tommy will live. That may be where your generation and mine are not doing right by him.

One key value we should be guarding for him is freedom. Probably the main thing my generation can be proud of is that we paid the price of defending the free world against the Nazis and, for forty years, against the Communists. Perhaps the threat has passed, and the price no longer has to be paid. But that is not clear. What I sense in your generation is a rush to believe that the threat has passed, mainly because you are tired and unwilling to bear the cost any longer. You could be leaving a terrible legacy to the next generation.

Even if the cold war is receding, I wonder whether Tommy can expect to live in a secure and stable world while hundreds of millions, perhaps billions, of people in Africa, Asia, and parts of Latin America are in miserable poverty. However poor, they will not be too poor to know of the disparity between their lives and life in the developed world. They will be a threat and a burden, at least on the consciences of humane and civilized people everywhere.

Love,
Pop

Dear Pop:

When I was a child of fifteen, in 1959, we never once had a bottle of imported bottled water in our refrigerator. Now, I have both Vittel and Evian cramming the shelves. In 1959, we had a Chevrolet and a Ford in the driveway. I was sorry about it, but we got by. Now, my wife and I have a BMW and a Mercedes. When I was a child, I would never have even considered flying first class. Now, I fly only first class, except on the briefest flights.

There is something going on here that is more than pure pretension, although that's part of it, and it has to do with intergenerational equity.

When I was a child, back in the now-gilded 1950s, we lived extremely modestly. I now know that within our little family, we lived more modestly than we really had to, in large part so that you and Mom could accumulate savings sufficient to educate me and my sister, which is to say to provide us with human capital; to assure a

---

Ben Stein is a lawyer, economist, and writer who lives in Los Angeles.

secure retirement for you and Mom, and presumably to pass on some financial capital to my sister and me.

All of this was meant to defer pleasure, to lessen consumption, to provide greater security down the road for you and Mom as well as for me and my sister. I am not sure that you calculated all of this explicitly (although you might have), but you certainly did it instinctively.

Back in those modest 1950s, as far as I can tell, the society in general did what you and Mom did. As families, parents lived with some added measure of frugality so that their children could rise up on the platform of human and financial capital that was provided. As a nation, we built vast superhighways and rebuilt cities out of current tax revenue to provide added capital for future prosperity. President Dwight Eisenhower had as his stated goal (as you have often told me) to reduce the deficit and not add to it, so as not to burden his grandchildren with his generation's expenses.

I believe, based on a general knowledge of history, that this kind of sacrifice by the older generation for the younger has been a basic factor in the growth of prosperity since the Middle Ages.

With it came an attitude of discipline, both self-discipline and social discipline. Human beings behaved with some kind of self-restraint because they knew that if they did not do so, basic harm would come to them and to the society as a whole. As you so aptly said, we had safe streets then. In the almost two decades that our family lived on our little street in Silver Spring, Maryland, a decidedly unchic suburb of Washington, not one crime against life or property ever took place. There were no car alarms, no house alarms, and no need for them.

At some time in the middle and late 1960s, a fundamental rip in the social fabric took place. Perhaps the world finally allowed itself to realize the horror of what Nazism had done in Europe and that simply tore off the mask of civilization.

Perhaps American society was thrown into self-doubt by the civil rights movement and the Vietnam War.

Perhaps it had to do with a natural process that all societies undergo.

But after a decade of seemingly altruistic demonstrations for peace and justice, the whole mood of America became "me first and devil take the hindmost." Or perhaps the mood might better be summarized by what I always thought was Ronald Reagan's real message: *Après moi le déluge.*

Parents stopped saving for their children either as individuals or as a nation. The generation that was alive and in political power said that it would burden its children by borrowing from them, spend the money on Mercedes and BMWs and Vittel and Evian, and let the unborn and immature pay the piper. The body politic said that it would no longer set aside reserves to replace the depreciation in our roads and bridges and schools and airports and factories, but would instead just use up what had been left to it and let someone else worry about it.

As a nation, we stopped worrying about educating our children, giving the poor a chance to become middle class, or keeping even minimum safety on our streets. We would live it up, spend all we could as fast as we could, and not think about tomorrow.

This was Reaganism with its tax cuts and its huge deficits. This is Bushism, with its adamant head-in-the-sand approach to every real problem. This is the leveraged-buyout decade, which sought to replace any real investment in the future by simply looting existing piles of cash. (And it is interesting that the LBO, like the Reagan-Bush budget policy, relies largely on making money by simply using up what's already there without any provision for replacement and adding debt to collect huge profits right now.) For about twenty years now, as a nation, we have been living it up within the middle class and upper class as if there were no tomorrow.

Now it is tomorrow. Our cities are civil war zones. Our public education is a dim memory in most urban areas. We face a rapidly growing incurable plague, AIDS, and an even more rapidly growing curable plague, crack and ice. Our industrial competitiveness tracks our education level and our capital spending level. In other words, it is a joke.

As individuals, we can correct much of the national effort to rob Tommy to pay Benjy. We can save, teach, sacrifice within the family. But we cannot correct all of it except through the political process. People like you and me, Dad, can begin by putting little thoughts in the air, helping others by writing about what we have gained and lost. We have traded bottled water and BMWs and liposuction for making America into Brazil in all too many ways. We have to let people know. We have to know that decline is not inevitable. That a return to responsibility will pay dividends.

And if it seems hopeless, I am sure that's the way it seemed to Harriet Beecher Stowe and to Martin Luther King, Jr., and to your father when he first arrived here from Europe. And if it's bewildering where to start, we can always take the safest, surest course: "Dear God, let it begin with me."

Love,
Ben

(January 1990)

PART FOUR
The State of Economic Policy

18

Industrial Policy, The New Old Idea

T welve years ago, or possibly sixteen, presidential candidates
became taken with the thought that they needed Ideas,
preferably New Ideas. Incumbents did not have this need.
For a sitting president seeking reelection suddenly to come up with
New Ideas could be embarrassing. People might ask what he had
been doing during his first term.

I use the capital letter to distinguish Ideas from ideas. Ideas
have to have, or seem to have, a certain intellectual, even scientific,
background. If you say, for example, that we should promise to build
two nuclear submarines in Connecticut to carry the state in the
election, you have an idea. But if you say that the future of the
country depends on the promotion of advanced technology and
that nuclear submarines embody advanced technology and that,
therefore, we should build two nuclear submarines, you have an Idea.

The belief that Ideas are extremely useful to candidates seemed
to be confirmed by the experience of 1980, when the "supply-side"
Idea apparently helped Reagan to victory. In my opinion, voters
were more impressed by the prospect of getting their taxes down
than by any consideration of the slope of the Laffer curve. But, still,
proponents of Ideas took comfort from 1980 and hope to repeat it.

Industrial Policy Defined

One Idea that is being recycled into a New Idea is that the United
States needs a substantial change in the relation between govern-

ment and the economy, called "industrial policy." This thought is part of Governor Clinton's program, although, one must admit, not a very prominent part. It is being vigorously pushed by a little group of advocates, including Robert Kuttner, an economic journalist; Lester Thurow, an MIT economist; Clyde Prestowitz, a Washington promoter of protectionism; and a few businessmen. The idea received its greatest, and probably most revealing, exposure in an article by Kuttner in the *New York Times Magazine* of April 19, 1992, and it is mainly that article I have in mind in these comments.

To discuss industrial policy intelligently, we need to know what its proponents mean by the term. If it means that the federal government promotes and protects selected industries or economic projects when a national interest is clear or political pressures are strong, we have always had industrial policy and will continue to have it. Land grants for railroad construction, the Panama Canal, the interstate highway system, subsidies for getting oil out of shale, protection for automobile producers against Japanese competition, and innumerable provisions of the tax law are examples—some successful and some not. The plan now supported by both Republicans and Democrats for establishing "enterprise zones" could be described as an industrial policy in which the government selects not a list of industries but a list of areas for economic preferences.

But if industrial policy means that a government agency will exhaustively survey all industries and mark some for promotion and some for extinction, then nobody wants that. In previous discussions, industrial policy became tagged as a plan for having the government pick winners and losers. That suggestion quickly became the object of ridicule because of the common suspicion that government would, accidentally or intentionally, pick the losers for promotion.

Today's Industrial Policy

So, what do today's advocates of industrial policy want that is neither what we have nor what everyone rejects? I think that what they want is that the government, meaning a government agency, should more aggressively search for industrial projects that would make major contributions to national productivity and that would not, for one reason or another, be undertaken by private firms. Having found projects that meet the test, the government would promote them in a variety of ways. The basic premise is that such projects exist in substantial number and that the government agency would find them.

What is missing is any description of the agency, procedure, and funds with which this assignment would be carried out. The illustration to Kuttner's article in the *New York Times* reveals the way he and other proponents think about the process. We see two men with extremely high foreheads and opaque glasses, wearing suits that might almost be lab technicians' uniforms. They are either physics professors or visitors from another planet. One of them is holding in his very large hand a very small industrial plant, and they are making a high-science, objective, nonpolitical judgment about whether to foster the project.

My own vision, which I believe is more realistic, is of a new Industrial Policy Administration with temporary offices in the Department of Commerce building. It has an administrator who is a retired air force general, having racked up a record of $50 billion of cost overruns. It has a deputy administrator who is a defeated congressman from Indiana. It has several divisions, each headed by an associate professor from a leading business school, the full professors being unable to afford the government salary. And they have an appropriation of, say, $5 billion.

Every Monday morning this cast meets in the board room to select projects that though good for the country are not profitable enough to attract IBM or AT&T or Merck. They will find them, of course, but most will be dry holes. And no one will ever be able to prove that they were dry holes, because the criterion for success is not profitability in the private sense but contribution to national productivity through a very complicated chain of developments. Moreover, many of the dry holes will be in West Virginia, if Robert Byrd remains in power.

American politics and the American people do not dogmatically reject government interventions in the economy. But they accept such interventions reluctantly, as exceptions, and do not want to extend an invitation for the government to seek more of them. Proponents of industrial policy think that the American people and American politicians have been brainwashed by long-dead classical economists, such as David Ricardo (1772–1823), who seems to be Kuttner's pet peeve. I am sure that most Americans if they recognize the name David Ricardo at all think that he was Lucille Ball's husband. The American public, in my view, does not support industrial policy first because the whole thing sounds like an academic exercise—which it is—and second because they have little confidence in government agencies.

Except for Lester Thurow, I can't think of a professional economist who supports much of what proponents of industrial policy are talking about. Resistance to those ideas among economists is not a partisan matter. In fact, one of the most devastating critiques of industrial policy was written by a prominent Democratic economist, Charles Schultze.

An interesting case is that of Professor Paul Krugman of MIT, who has written several articles about strategic trade *theory,* showing that in some conditions protection of a particular industry might be highly advantageous to the country that extends it. Kuttner and other supporters of industrial policy like to cite these articles as supporting their case. But Krugman has never suggested that U.S. policy should be based on that theory. A few years ago, Krugman, Prestowitz, a few other people, and I were on a Twentieth Century Fund panel on trade policy. The panel was split down the middle on whether the United States should follow a policy of managed trade or a policy of trade liberalization. Krugman and I were on the same side, for trade liberalization. Prestowitz, who is supported by a number of firms seeking protection, was the leader of the other side, which included Kuttner.

Supporters of Industrial Policy

I am not impressed by the fact that a certain number of businessmen favor something called industrial policy. Businessmen have not been known for a particularly broad view of national economic policy. There have always been some businessmen who wanted the government to help them, and they have used whatever argument was handy. None of the major business organizations—the National Association of Manufacturers, the Chamber of Commerce, the Committee for Economic Development, the Business Round Table—has espoused industrial policy.

People like Kuttner try to frighten us by saying that the Japanese are getting ahead of us because they have an industrial policy. But the Japanese do a lot of other things as well: they save more, they study more, and many of them work harder. I have seen no evidence that industrial planning by government has been a major factor in

Japanese growth. We know too that their planners made several big mistakes.

Supporters of industrial policy have a problem. On the one hand, they want to show that it is indeed a New Idea and sufficiently different so that its adoption would have a big effect on the economy. On the other hand, they do not want to sound so radical that they frighten off the voters. So they use an argument like this:

• Everybody recognizes that certain micro or structural policies, such as education, regulation, antitrust policy, and tax policy, can have major effects on the performance of the economy and are proper concerns of government.
• Industrial policy is another structural policy.
• Therefore, there is no reason to reject industrial policy.

But what is at issue, of course, is not whether the government should pursue structural policies but whether it should pursue this particular one.

Interest in industrial policy is more realistically an interest in the quality of public discussion than in possible political or economic consequences. I do not think that there is much political mileage in the proposal. In my opinion, the American people don't understand it and don't care about it. In one speech, Governor Clinton gave an example of what an industrial policy might do for us: it would connect every telephone in America with every other telephone in America by fiber-optic cable by the year 2015. I can think of hardly any promise less likely to make voters pull the Democratic lever.

The Idea is not of much economic significance either. Even if Mr. Clinton were to be elected, he would probably not want to invest much money in this sort of thing. He might throw a few billion dollars down this particular rat hole, but that would not be the first few billion dollars in various rat holes and would not make much difference in a $6 trillion economy. Perhaps the danger is greater on the side of trade policy. There will be a temptation to protect certain industries, rationalized by the argument that they are the carriers of great technological advance and productivity growth. But the evidence suggests that, whatever their prior thoughts, American presidents, being responsible for foreign policy, will avoid trade measures that are seriously divisive and offensive to foreign countries.

The Idea of industrial policy will continue to be a prominent item in the stock of idea merchants, but the country will be safe from it because there will be little of it in practice. *(May 1992)*

19

Whose Growth?

E veryone is in favor of making the pie bigger. No one—or at least no politically ambitious person—is in favor of "just" redividing the existing pie. That is, we are all for growth and against redistribution. I use *growth* to mean a long-term increase in national income or income per capita and not a short-term recovery from a cyclically depressed condition. Failure to make this distinction is a source of much confusion. Measures whose effect will be felt only in the long run are proposed as means of expediting recovery and reducing unemployment in the short run.

The preference for growth is an understandable and, for some issues, a valid position. To be for growth is for making some people better off without necessarily making anyone worse off. To be for redistribution certainly implies that someone is to be made worse off.

But for many lively policy issues, the distinction between growth and redistribution is misleading. There is an implication that growth is an increase in some grand aggregate, like national income or national income per person, that falleth as the gentle rain from heaven upon the multitude below, among whom it is distributed equally or "fairly" or in a way about which we are indifferent. In this view, if we consider policies to increase growth, we do not need to be concerned with how that growth will be distributed. There is the further implication that measures to change the distribution of the national income—presumably in favor of the poor—are all and equally hostile to growth.

But these implications are wrong. The growth of the national income is simply the sum of the growth of the incomes of all the people in the nation. The distribution of that growth among individuals is largely determined in the process by which the growth is produced. That is, the increasing incomes are mainly distributed to the individuals who cause the increase by their saving, investment, and effort. But government policy, which affects growth, also affects the way in which the growth is distributed. Cutting the capital gains tax and increasing expenditure for Head Start may both be ways of increasing the growth of the national income, but the resulting additional income will be distributed differently depending on which policy is chosen.

Any measure to increase growth will have diffused effects beyond those persons who are its initial beneficiaries. Thus, although cutting the capital gains tax may initially benefit suppliers of capital, if it promotes an increase in the capital stock it will also benefit workers who work with the capital. Similarly, although increased expenditure for Head Start may initially benefit the children who go through the program, it will also benefit suppliers of capital if it produces an enlarged skilled labor force. But surely the proportions will be different in the two cases. Policy to affect growth requires a redistribution of the uses of the existing output and entails a redistribution of the income among persons. So it is not sufficient to be "for growth" without considering how the resulting growth is to be distributed.

Similarly, policies to affect the distribution of income, presumably for the benefit of the poor, have consequences not only for the distribution of income but also for economic growth. Some measures will do more than others to increase the productivity of the poor and so to contribute to the growth of the national income. As we have become increasingly aware, policy to help the poor must give great weight to improving their productivity, both for the sake of the poor and for the sake of the rest of the nation.

Measures to promote growth are not usually costless. In general, they involve some sacrifice of current consumption or some expenditure of current effort. Once upon a time—say, twelve years ago—there was a common belief in "free lunch" growth policy. The idea was that tax reduction would generate enough additional revenue plus enough additional saving to finance additional investment without sacrifice, or at least without enforced sacrifice, by anyone. Twelve years of experience have not served to validate this notion. A more plausible theory is that tax reduction would generate enough additional revenue plus additional saving plus additional capital from abroad to finance additional investment, without having to enforce any sacrifice of consumption at home. Whether this process works sufficiently to increase total investment is unclear, but even if it does, part of the additional income resulting from the additional investment would belong to foreigners rather than to Americans.

In general, then, it seems most realistic to think of a situation in which growth strategies implemented by government involve the enforced sacrifice of present consumption to finance an increase of some kind of investment. Different growth strategies have different distributional consequences, and these consequences should be considered in choosing a growth strategy.

Growth policy is sometimes described, and properly, as choosing a larger future income at some sacrifice of a present one, or choosing larger future income at some sacrifice of present consumption. But that present consumption that is sacrificed is somebody's, and the future income that is gained is also somebody's, usually somebody else's, so that there is a shift of benefits between people as well as between times. If this were not the case, and if growth policy involved only making people give up consumption now so that the same people would have higher incomes later, the wisdom or propriety of such a policy would be questionable. People can voluntarily give up present consumption to increase their future incomes, and if they choose not to do so, the justification for government intervention is unclear. The reasonable assumption is that in any growth strategy there are losers as well as winners, that these are not the same people, and it is relevant to ask who is which. The losers and winners in growth policy can be classified.

Losers

Primary Losers. These are the people whose consumption is restrained. If the amounts involved are large, this means the middle class, which does most of the consumption. Restraining their consumption requires increasing taxes on them or reducing benefits they receive from government, like subsidized medical care. Just which members of the middle class bear the burden of sacrificing present consumption depends on the method chosen, but the burden would probably be widely diffused and the choice of method is not a critical matter for choosing among growth strategies.

Suppliers of Consumption Goods. These are the workers and the owners of capital who are specialized to the production of consumption goods and services and who would lose as the market for their product is restrained.

Winners

Primary Winners. These are the people who would own the additional investment generated by the growth policy and who would be the primary recipients of the income that investment produces. Who these people are would depend on the growth strategy pursued and is a main basis for distinguishing among different strategies. This will be the subject of discussion below.

Suppliers of Investment Goods. The identity of these people also varies, in obvious ways, with the growth strategy. If the strategy emphasizes investment in infrastructure—roads, for example—the beneficiaries will be road builders, manufacturers of heavy construction equipment, and so forth. If the emphasis is on investment in education, the suppliers who benefit will include teachers and persons who aspire to be teachers. The suppliers involved are, of course, quite aware of their interests in the choice of growth strategies—cement manufacturers prefer roads, for example—and make these interests known.

Suppliers of Complementary Resources. Increasing investment of a particular kind will increase the productivity and therefore the incomes of the resources that work along with that kind of investment. If the investment is in plant and equipment, the suppliers of labor to work with the plant and equipment will gain. If the investment is in human capital, in the education and training of workers, the suppliers of the physical capital that goes with them will gain. This effect on the complementary resources are the main route by which the beneficial effects of higher investment are spread through the economy and the population.

Some effects of growth policy are so broadly diffused that they can hardly be traced, although we know that they exist. Other distributional effects are so obvious, like the effect of road building on cement manufacturers, that they need no discussion. The interesting question is how different strategies affect what I have called the

primary winners. Who will own the investment that any growth
strategy counts on?

Strategies for Investment

I would identify four different strategies, each of them involving the
same measures to restrain consumption but each using different
means of promoting investment.

Deficit Reduction. Reducing the budget deficit will reduce the
amount of private saving that is absorbed in financing it and will leave
more of the saving available for private investment. In ordinary
circumstances, that is, leaving recessions aside, this will increase
investment. To whom will the income generated by this investment
belong? At first glance, it might seem to belong to the private savers
who are now financing private investment rather than the budget
deficit. But that is incorrect. The private savers have no more assets
than they would otherwise have. Only the portfolio of their assets
has changed. They now own less government debt and more private
securities. The real beneficiaries of the deficit reduction are the
future taxpayers whose liability in the form of government debt and
whose burden of paying interest on that debt have been reduced.

**Reduction of Taxes on Upper-Income Individuals and Corpo-
rations.** The rationale for such a strategy is that it will increase
private saving and consequently increase private investment and
economic growth. Whether the increase in private saving would
occur is the subject of some disagreement, but for present purposes
that may be assumed. The point to be made here is that the
additional private investment, and the income it would generate,
would belong to the persons whose taxes had been reduced.

Increased Expenditure on Infrastructure. Roads, bridges, airports, high-speed rail systems, and the like fall into this category.
Superficially, it might seem that "the government" and therefore the
people at large would be the owners of this physical capital and the
primary beneficiary of the services it provides. But that is not
realistic. The beneficiaries, and therefore the owners, are the people
who are the primary users of the particular infrastructure investment. Thus, if the investment is in an airport in New York, people

who do business in the New York area will be the primary beneficiaries, and the residents of South Dakota will get little out of the increase in the national income that may result. The senators from South Dakota will be well aware of this fact.

Human Capital. Investment in human capital, mainly by education and training but also possibly by measures to improve health, will primarily benefit those people in whom the education, training, and improved health are embodied. They will have higher earnings as a consequence. Within this general category, the distribution of the benefits will depend on the specific means employed. Investment in Head Start will benefit a different group of people from general subsidization of higher education, for example.

A person's preferences among these strategies will depend on his private interests and social values. Upper-income people will have no difficulty seeing the advantages of a growth strategy that operates through reduction of their taxes. Residents of southern California will see the superior value of promoting growth by public construction of a high-speed rail line between Los Angeles and San Diego. Those who are most concerned with the status of the poor will easily appreciate a growth strategy that invests in educating and training the disadvantaged. Probably a growth strategy that promises benefits mainly to future taxpayers, by deficit reduction, has the fewest representatives, but even for that there are some advocates.

It is not my intention here to choose a preferred growth strategy or to suggest that distributional consequences are the only grounds for such a choice. But it is my intention to say that advocates of one strategy or another should not be allowed to wrap themselves in the flag of "growth" as if that was an equal good for all, whereas consideration of who gets what is to be ruled out as divisive promotion of class warfare. *(September 1992)*

20

A Long View of the American Economy

I n writing this essay, I had been asked to address macroeconomics and the consequences for the American standard of living of a continuation of the status quo in macroeconomic policy. But I don't think there is such a thing as macroeconomic policy, except for the part of the world governed by the Federal Reserve. Someone has said that all politics is local; I have come to the conclusion that all economics is micro, except for monetary policy. Even if macroeconomic policy means budget policy primarily, budget policy is primarily policy to affect the allocation of the national output and resources among competing uses; it is part of a group of policies that include regulation and selective credit measures.

I focus here on budget policy. The consequences of continuing the status quo in budget policy, as compared with changes in the policy that seem at all eligible or likely, would probably not make a big difference in the rate of growth of the American standard of living. Moreover, and more important in my own thinking, I do not place great value on a somewhat faster as compared with a somewhat slower rate of growth in the average American standard of living over the next decade—again within the range of differences that seem a possible result from differences in federal policy.

The Status Quo

In my opinion, the essential characteristic of the status quo in budget policy is its high priority on promoting and protecting the

148

consumption of the vast majority of the American population that is not poor, including expenditures for their medical care.

This priority on consumption became the status quo well before the administration of Ronald Reagan. It dates from about 1972 when a big increase was made in social security benefits. During the remainder of the 1970s, the budget promoted consumption mainly by increasing transfer payments to middle- and upper-income people, through social security and Medicare. Although taxes as a share of gross national product rose, mainly because of inflation, transfers rose faster, and taxes minus transfers fell as a share of GNP.

In the Reagan administration, the growth of revenues relative to GNP slowed down. The growth of transfers also slowed down, but not so much. The Reagan administration and Congress agreed in protecting the rise of social security and Medicare benefits, so that taxes minus transfers fell further.

An important aspect of this policy was the stimulus it provided to increasing the share of the national income devoted to medical care. That share would probably have increased anyway, given the rise of per capita incomes, but the budget policy aggravated this trend. It was not only the provision of Medicare that made the difference but also the deductibility of medical benefits from the taxable income of employers while they were not included in the taxable incomes of workers.

So that is what I consider the status quo in budget policy—high priority to the consumption of middle- and upper-income Americans. Of course, that is what one should expect in an unguided and undisciplined democracy—in a demagogic state—since the immediate beneficiaries are the vast majority of voters to whom all politicians appeal. But there is no free lunch, neither a Keynesian nor a supply-side free lunch. Priority on consumption meant less emphasis on other things. It meant less priority on investment. The policy involved large budget deficits, which absorbed private saving and limited private investment. It also limited government expenditures for infrastructure and other capital of kinds usually provided by government. It also meant lower priority on government expenditures addressed to such social or national purposes as national defense, foreign aid, education, law enforcement, and assistance to the very poor. As a byproduct of the budget deficits, we got an inflow of foreign capital and a corresponding trade deficit.

Thus, the budget policy of the 1970s and 1980s gave us a high rate of consumption, a low rate of investment owned by Americans (with a negative effect on economic growth), a skimping on assorted national and social objectives, and large trade deficits. Continuation of such a budget policy will continue those consequences. Now the question is how to value those effects.

The Value of the Effects

Some will say that those effects are perfectly acceptable. After all, the objective of economic activity is consumption. Anyway, we are talking about the use of the income that private people earned, and if they prefer to consume it, that is up to them. That is not my position. The amount of consumption is not simply the result of private decisions that are no one else's business. They are also in part the result of government decisions about taxes and transfer payments that are made in a constitutional process and that could just as legitimately be made differently. So I say without apology that the level of consumption is a proper subject of public policy.

Consumption has some value, but I cannot believe that the rapid increase of per capita consumption in America is a matter of high priority. Per capita consumption in America is now higher than it has ever been at any other place or time. It is almost three times as high as it was in 1929 and 50 percent higher than it was only twenty years ago. Since 1969, real per capita consumption has increased by 2 percent per annum, while real total output has increased by 1.7 percent per annum. This is, of course, a personal and subjective judgment, but as I look at these figures and more directly at life in America, continued rapid growth of per capita consumption does not seem very important.

At the same time, and for essentially the same reason, I do not think that speeding up total economic growth in America is very important. The main result of such a speedup would be more consumption. I cannot understand the "Economic Report of the President" when it says: "The primary economic goal of my Administration is to achieve the highest possible rate of sustainable economic growth." Surely the president cannot mean that literally.

Economic growth in America seems to have become something that we pursue not for the sake of the goods and services it provides but for the sake of winning a competition with other countries. That is a mean and trivial outlook. Nothing in the welfare of the American people depends on our getting richer faster than the Japanese—to name what is usually considered our main competitor.

Even though we are very rich, there is some value in becoming richer, because of the psychological value in the expectation of progress. But from that standpoint there is not much difference between per capita GNP growth of 1.8 percent per annum and growth of 2.2 percent per annum—which is probably a much bigger difference than might be expected to result from any of the policy choices before us.

While I think that more rapid growth is a plus, it is a mild plus, for which I would not be willing to sacrifice very much. I favor reducing the budget deficit, as probably the most useful step in public policy to speeding up growth, but I would not give up anything I valued very much to achieve the reduction of the deficit. My main object in writing about the deficit has not been the policy but the hypocrisy of people who claim to be stout champions of a balanced budget but are unwilling to do the simplest thing to achieve it.

The Budget Deficit

Some people worry about the budget deficit less because of its effect on national saving, investment, and growth than because of its effect on the balance of payments. The balance of payments is a mysterious subject, and it is not surprising that people fear a great evil lurking in a balance-of-payments deficit. But the fear is unjustified. The inflow of capital from abroad has helped Americans by raising the stock of capital with which they work and so raising their productivity and real incomes. The increase in the stock of capital came in the only real form it could come in, by an increase in our imports of goods relative to our exports. If for some reason the rest of the world does not want to invest here, we shall have to go back to living with our own savings. That will be too bad, but we can adjust to it and meanwhile we will have had the benefit of the foreign investment here. It is a shame that this perfectly natural and beneficial process should be a source of irritation between us and our allies.

The serious consequence of our budget policy of the past decade or more, and the serious consequence of continuing that policy, is that it severely limits our ability to use our vast national income to deal with national problems. Essentially, because we are unwilling to limit the growth of consumption, of which we have plenty, we are forced to limit the growth of other things of which we have too little. This misallocation of the national output was most obvious during the years from, say, 1983 to 1989 with respect to the defense program. The Reagan defense program was sharply cut for no reason other than that it seemed the easiest way out of a budget crunch that we had created ourselves. As it turned out, the economic incompetence of the Soviet system rescued us from the worst results of our political incompetence, but no one could have foreseen that eventuality when the defense budget was cut. And even now we are engaged in a premature rush to cut the defense program mainly because that will relieve us of making harder but more sensible choices.

But defense aside, a number of other national purposes are skimped in our public decision-making process. The list is well known. It includes education, uplifting the underclass, assisting the poor to escape poverty, fighting drugs and crime, aiding the development and stability of the newly democratizing countries of Eastern Europe, and relieving misery among the world's poorest populations. This list of objectives, and the associated programs, apparently has the support of almost everyone. But almost everyone says that we cannot afford to do what we would like to do. What that really means is that we prefer to devote another $10, 20, or 30 billion of the national income to the consumption of the vast not-poor majority of the American population rather than to these purposes.

The American Example

The situation is indeed ironic. We are holding out to the people of Eastern Europe the prospect that if they adopt free-market capitalist economic systems they will become rich. And we are the richest of all. But still we are too poor to educate our children, to get our homeless off the street, and to make our streets safe for ordinary citizens.

In my opinion, the status quo in budget policy for another decade will lead to fatter consumers but not to a good society. This is a personal, subjective valuation; others may find this development acceptable. I do not suppose that I could complain about the present policy if it appeared to be the outcome of explicit, well-informed decisions. But it is not. We have a tax policy arrived at without any awareness of the real consequences of taxes. The American people do not believe that they are expressing only ordinary shortsighted selfishness in not wanting to pay more taxes: they think that they are conforming to some higher economic or moral law. When they defend their social security benefits and Medicare benefits as untouchable, they do not regard themselves as the equivalent of the notorious welfare queen; they think they are getting only their just deserts. And they are encouraged in these attitudes by their political leaders who want to tell the public only what the public wants to hear.

Prospects for Change

How can this debilitating status quo of economic policy be changed, if it can be changed? I do not think we have to be defeatist. Those of us who live in Washington are used to the idea that government is shortsighted, narrow-minded, ignorant, and stalemated. But the government actually did some quite remarkable and admirable things over the past fifty years: it fought a great war, it maintained the defenses of the democracies for forty-five years, and it provided leadership for the establishment of a more open and efficient world economy than we had ever known before. At home, it developed institutions and policies that made the economy more stable. It carried through a revolution in the legal treatment of blacks. Given a vivid awareness of a problem, and moderately responsible leadership, government can act, even if the problem is a long-run and general one.

Moreover, I believe that the status quo will change. I believe that the American people will become, if nothing else, bored with a government that does nothing more than allow them to become richer and richer couch potatoes, watching bigger and bigger television screens and munching on fatter and fatter foods delivered to their homes faster and faster. They will want a more activist government that promises to make America better, and politicians will emerge to offer to meet that demand.

The question, then, is how to accelerate this process and improve it so that problems will be recognized when they are only serious but not yet critical and so that the solutions proposed will be efficient. I know only one way to do that, and that is to raise the level of public discussion. We need a discussion that starts with the fact that to govern is to choose; proponents of specific policies must be explicit about the choices they are urging upon us, not promising us more of everything but more of something at the expense of less of something. Leaders must explain why they make those particular choices and must defend the assumptions that get them from their particular objectives to their particular policies. I have tried in my book, *Governing the $5 Trillion Economy,* to describe a process of budget making that would meet this test. But, of course, before such a process can begin, there have to be people who want to do it. I do not look mainly to politicians to take the lead in improving public discussion of economic policy; they have too many incentives in the opposite direction. I look to people in the private sector to take the lead, as they have done at times in the past. *(March 1990)*

21

The Disintegration of Fiscal Policy

T he truism that if we knew better where we have been and where we are we would know better how to proceed applies to decisions that now have to be made about the federal budget.

Rummaging through my old files recently, I came across a speech that I gave in May 1967, in which I tried to appraise the state of budget policy as it then existed. These remarks of some twenty-five years ago are suggestive of where we have been and where we are.

The History of Budget Policy

In my 1967 speech, I outlined three stages in the history of budget policy:

• *The liberation of budget policy in 1933.* Herbert Hoover's budget policy in the depression had been inhibited by the gold standard and by lack of cooperation from the Federal Reserve. Roosevelt changed that. He took the country off gold and took control of the monetary system so that he did not have to fear that even large budget deficits would have unwanted monetary consequences. This change was permissive: it freed the budget from previous inhibitions but did not say what budget policy should be.

• *The adoption of a policy of functional finance in 1938.* The government would take positive fiscal action to achieve full employ-

ment, the scale of the action being flexibly adapted to the expected
state of the economy. This step was prepared by the wildfire spread
of Keynesianism, and precipitated by the fall of the economy into
recession in 1937.

• *The domestication of fiscal policy in the years 1947 to 1949.* This
was an attempt to establish some rules of budget policy as safeguards
against the dangers of unconstrained functional finance. First, the
policy of flexible adaptation might be destabilizing rather than stabilizing, because of the unreliability of economic forecasts. Second, as
implemented in the political process, the new policy might undermine
the discipline of requiring expenditures to be matched by taxes. As
a result, expenditures and deficits would rise excessively, with
damaging effects on economic growth in the long run.

In the rule that emerged, taxes would be high enough to balance
the budget, or yield a moderate surplus, when the economy was
operating at high employment. This policy would leave room for
deficits when the economy was in recession but would restrain the
long-run rise of spending and deficits. The argument for this policy
acknowledged the emotional appeal of balancing the budget, and
relied on the belief that even in the watered-down form of balancing
at high employment, the budget-balancing rule might resist political
pressures. The fiscal policies of the Eisenhower and Kennedy administrations conformed to this kind of rule.

When I made my speech in 1967, which was three years after
the Kennedy-Johnson tax cut, we appeared to be shedding the
constraints of even this watered-down budget rule. The economists
of that time, in and out of government, did not really like the rule of
balancing the budget at high employment. They had appealed to it to
rationalize the 1964 tax cut, but they believed that the rule unduly
limited their ability to manage the economy. Walter Heller, President
Kennedy's economic adviser, dismissed the balanced-budget rule as
"the Puritan ethic." As soon as the rule began to bind, the Johnson
administration abandoned it. But the Congress and other active
forces in the country were not prepared to have their fiscal decisions
dictated by econometric calculations from the Council of Economic
Advisers.

So we were left, as I said in 1967, with "the specter of
disintegration of fiscal policy. . . . It is not simply that we have
abandoned what little was left of budget-balancing, but that we have

abandoned it without having accepted anything in its place." I then tried to foresee the long-run consequences of this development:

> One would expect that if fiscal decisions are freed of overall restraints within some range, the decisions will gradually move to the edge of the range where expenditures are high, taxes low and the deficit is big. Decisions will be dominated by the political attractiveness of taxing less and spending more, until the deficit reaches the size which the public considers shocking or until the economy reaches the rate of inflation that the country finds intolerable. These are both moving limits, mainly matters of habituation, so one could visualize continuously growing deficits and infla-tion as the result of the process. Or monetary restraint might not permit endless inflation, so this curb on rising deficits would not exist, but the consequences of the deficits would still be felt in the absorption of private saving to finance public spending and the consequent restraint of private investment.

This forecast has surely come true. The deficits have risen to levels that would once have been shocking. But the public's percep-tion of what is a shockingly large deficit has risen in step, so that we are always shocked somewhat but never enough to prevent a further rise of the deficit, which accustoms us to a further rise and so on. Monetary restraint has been sufficient to prevent the rate of inflation from accelerating, although not to stabilize the price level. We now think that an inflation rate of 3 percent per annum, doubling the price level in twenty-four years, is price stability. Perhaps more important, the deficit has become a significant drain on private saving, and thereby on private investment, contributing to the dreary prospect for income growth that now confronts the nation.

Fiscal Policy under Reagan and Bush

The Reagan-Bush experience contributed much to this disintegration of fiscal policy, in several ways. It was, of course, in this period that we became habituated to larger and larger deficits. The Reagan years were a laboratory demonstration of the ability of the country to live with large deficits and still avoid the evils usually forecast—accelerating inflation, persistent stagnation, or both.

In 1990, the economy did run into trouble, and many people

associated that with the deficit. But we did not know whether the problem was that the deficit was too large or too small.

Before the Reagan presidency, it seemed that the president was the guardian of the fisc, as against the free-spending, tax-cutting Congress. Ronald Reagan decided in 1980 to give up that hair-shirt approach to the presidency by making a big tax cut the centerpiece of his policy. That this shift in the role of the president occurred with Ronald Reagan was especially significant because it made overt what had previously been less obvious—that the attachment of conservatives to balancing the budget was only skin-deep.

The Reagan-Bush team could not make a forceful case against budget deficits because they were so allergic to taxes. If deficits per se were really terrible, an increase in taxes to reduce the deficit might be an eligible option, which they could not admit. So the Reagan-Bush formulation of the fiscal objective was "deficit reduction through restraint of expenditures." This approach, however, was not economically logical because there is no general difference in economic effect between a tax increase and an expenditure reduction. Although *particular* tax increases have effects that will be different, perhaps better or perhaps worse, from some standpoint, than *particular* expenditure reductions, nothing valid can be said about that without specification of the taxes and the expenditures.

Politically, the proposition was unsalable because it looked like insistence on reducing the deficit by cutting the benefits of the poor and the middle class while protecting the rich from sharing the pain as they would if taxes were raised.

Congress shares the blame for the degradation of budget policy after 1980. But irresponsible fiscal behavior has been a characteristic of Congress for a long time. What happened after 1980 was that the president joined in this behavior.

The Present Situation

The past, however, is water over the dam. What is the present situation?

• The budget deficit for fiscal 1993 will apparently be the largest ever.

• Although with present policies the deficit may decline for a year or two, according to the best estimates the deficit will rise again thereafter and without strong measures will become much larger relative to gross domestic product than it now is. The idea that a combination of economic growth, reductions of defense spending, and the end of the savings and loan bailout will solve the deficit problem has faded.

• Although balancing the budget seems impossibly remote, it retains appeal in the minds of many people. The positive response to Ross Perot is some evidence that the appeal remains if the promise is taken to be sincere. Mr. Perot's apparent willingness to specify and support painful measures to reduce the budget deficit attracted many people, whereas Mr. Bush's attempt to exploit the sentiment for balancing the budget by calling for a constitutional amendment was unpersuasive. Mr. Bush did not support visible, strong, and balanced measures to eliminate the deficit, and his support of the constitutional amendment was therefore seen as hypocritical.

• We seem to be groping our way to a better understanding of the real economic significance of large, continued budget deficits. While people no longer talk much about the inflationary consequences or about the obstacle such deficits may place to the achievement of high employment, the deficits are seen as a critical element in the national choice between present national consumption and future national income—sometimes called the intergenerational equity problem. This view of the significance of deficits is not new; indeed, it is very old. But it is more broadly recognized among those who make national decisions and influence national opinion than it has been in a long time.

But we are still far from knowing just how to translate that view into policy. We do not know what is the most relevant measure of the deficit from this standpoint, how to calculate the quantitative trade-off between present deficits and future national income, and how to get such calculations heeded in the decision-making process.

• President Clinton is less inhibited by prior commitments or ideology against raising taxes and therefore has more flexibility in developing a package of measures to reduce the deficit.

• For the first time in twelve years, we have a president and a Congress of the same party, and it may be the first time in twenty-four years that we have had a Congress with some inclination to follow the president's lead.

In this year, 1993, the need to stop the disintegration of budget policy that I foresaw in 1967 and the opportunity to do so are both greater than at any time in many years. If this opportunity is not taken now, it will not soon come again; we will drift farther and farther from a desirable path, and the effort to get onto the path will be more difficult and potentially more disruptive.

The Clinton Plan

Mr. Clinton has revealed the outlines of his proposal for reducing the budget deficit substantially over the next four years. The president's plan would take the most essential but most unpopular step: it would impose sacrifice on the middle class through an energy tax, increased taxation of social security benefits, and reduction of the Medicare subsidy. Without some step in this direction, no substantial deficit-reduction plan can be devised. Without strong political leadership, this step will not be taken, because the political risks for its proponents are great. The president has now described the terms on which he will exercise this leadership—the character of the total package within which he will not only propose but also fight for this middle-class sacrifice. If his terms are rejected, no other leadership is in sight that can develop an alternative package and bring the country to accept it.

I would object to many parts of the program. The combination of taxes on business—raising the corporate tax rate, taxing energy use by business, giving a credit for investment in excess of some base, and providing a preference for capital gains earned in new businesses—violates principles of equity and promises little of value in economic efficiency or growth. The caps on charges by hospitals and doctors under Medicare are unlikely to yield real saving. Many expenditures ripe for cutting—farm price supports, the super collider, manned-space exploration—have been spared. I could write a better deficit reduction program; so could you, dear reader. But neither of us could get our program adopted.

That the Clinton deficit-reduction program conforms to the priorities, values, and constituencies of the Democratic party should be no surprise, since he is a Democrat, working with a Democratic Congress. If there is a Republican alternative, it evidently could not be adopted under a Republican president and surely could not be adopted under a Democratic president.

What Mr. Clinton has announced so far is a step, but by itself does not constitute the budget policy we need. At some point, he will have to go further.

What Clinton Must Do

To initiate an effective budget policy, President Clinton will have to invoke both what remains of the "Puritan ethic" about budget balancing and an economic calculus of the consequences of continued deficits. He will have to demonstrate that he considers balancing the budget imperative by being willing to subordinate other, highly attractive, objectives. And he will have to show that balancing the budget serves an important economic objective and is not *only* obeisance to a traditional rule.

The following steps will be necessary:

• Mr. Clinton should make a dramatic announcement of the new program, preferably to a special session of Congress.

• The program should spell out a path to a balanced budget, not just to cutting the deficit in half or reducing it to 2 percent of gross national product, or some other plausible goal. No size of the deficit will intuitively strike a majority of people as "right" other than zero. Zero does not have to be reached in four years; it could be reached in eight years. But it should be the destination.

• The program should incorporate specific scheduled steps for reaching the goal. The time for flexible freezes, caps, Gramm-Rudman sequesters, and constitutional amendments is over. These are all seen as dodges, devices for willing the end, or seeming to do so, without willing the means.

• The program should include tax increases as well as expenditure reductions. No other program will be accepted as a serious attempt to address a problem of national concern. A program that includes only one side of the equation will be seen as pursuit of a hidden agenda.

• The tax increases and expenditure reductions should be aimed at reducing consumption, public and private. That is the purpose of the effort—to reduce the share of the national output that is consumed, making room for more investment and promoting future economic growth. This does not necessarily mean that the taxes should be "consumption taxes"; income taxes also reduce consumption.

• A credible program will have to deal with federal government health care costs, because the prospective rise of these costs is a major element in the prospective rise of budget deficits. The distinction between federal government health care costs and national health care costs, which include private costs, is important. It is the federal costs, through Medicare, Medicaid, and the deductibility of health insurance premiums from taxable income, that affect the budget, the deficit, and, therefore, investment. Ways to cut the federal costs, by reducing the subsidy in Medicare and by eliminating or capping the deductibility of health insurance premiums, are clear, although politically difficult. Ways to cut the national costs, by limiting fees paid to doctors and hospitals, restricting services, eliminating red tape, and so on, are harder to specify.

• The program should be accompanied by the best estimate the administration can produce of its likely effects on investment and future national income. Such an estimate cannot prove that the proposed program is the best of all possible programs, both because the estimates will be uncertain and because the definition of *best* is not an objective matter. But the estimate can indicate that the program has a rational, pragmatic basis and that it lies within the range of programs that can be defended on strictly economic grounds, aside from what remains of the intuitive appeal of a balanced budget.

These comments are a moderation of a position that I took as recently as 1989 in *Governing the $5 Trillion Economy*. I thought then that it was neither possible nor desirable to resuscitate the budget-balancing ethic and that it was necessary and possible to move to a more results-oriented calculus of the desirable size of the budget deficit or surplus, with no presumption that the best answer was zero. In my present opinion, we are still a long way from being able to work out this economic calculus in a way that would command sufficient agreement to discipline the powerful political pressures on the budget. At the same time, the significant residue of attachment to the budget-balancing idea is worth exploiting in the framing of a program. I still hope that we can improve our ability to calculate the effects of budget decisions and to bring them to bear on the political process. We do not have time to wait for that calculation as the sole guidance to policy.

The suggestions I make here may not serve. The disintegration of budget policy that I foresaw in 1967, and that has resisted numerous efforts at correction, might successfully resist the presidential initiative I propose. In that case, real reform will probably have to await a crisis of some kind. But the attempt to forestall such a moment may still be worthwhile. *(January 1993)*

22

Twelve Years of the AEI Economist

This is the last issue of the *AEI Economist*. Beginning in January 1990, my writings on economics will be included in AEI's new magazine, *The American Enterprise*. It seems fitting to conclude the publication of the *AEI Economist* with some reflections on the economic developments, policies, and talk covered in the past twelve years.

The developments, the policies, and the talk must be distinguished from each other. The developments can be more or less objectively described. It is harder to evaluate the performance, to judge whether the performance was good or bad. We can also describe policies, but with less confidence than we can describe developments. To what extent was the budget deficit a policy, for example, and to what extent was it the result of developments? A much more difficult question is the effect of the policies on the developments. Did the economy grow as it did because of the budget deficits or in spite of them? Did inflation come down because of a shift in monetary policy? Such questions cannot be answered by looking at these twelve years alone but only by reference to some general theories of the relation between policies and developments validated by observing policies and developments in a variety of past circumstances. Such general theories as we have, however, are weak.

We can also describe the talk about economic policy and the changing fashions in that talk. But the relation between the talk and the policy is uncertain. Did we have the tax cut because we had the Laffer curve, or did we have the Laffer curve because we wanted the tax cut? It is probably true that "ideas have consequences"; it is at least equally true that desired and actual consequences have ideas.

So, we are in a world of loose and tenuous connections between policy and developments and between ideas and policy. With this disclaimer of what economists—or, at least, this economist—know for sure, I offer some reflections on what has happened and what the *AEI Economist* has been writing about in the past twelve years. I consider five recurrent themes—inflation, supply-side economics, the budget deficit, the trade deficit, and the problems of being a rich country.

Inflation

Inflation was the main subject with which we started twelve years ago. Although the rate of inflation had receded from the double-digit figures of 1974 during the severe recession of 1975, it had risen again to around 6 percent in 1976 and 1977. Three interrelated questions about inflation confronted us:

- Should an inflation rate of 6 percent be accepted as the objective of policy?
- How severe would be the costs of getting the inflation rate down, if that were the objective?
- Are there feasible ways to reduce the costs of getting the inflation rate down?

The first of these questions was largely a matter of psychology and politics. In strictly economic terms, once everyone has adapted as well as possible to the fact and expectation of 6 percent inflation, the system could work about as efficiently as if the fact and expectation were zero inflation. The standard argument for the costs of a fully anticipated inflation is that "money" pays no interest, so that the anticipation of inflation causes people to resort to less efficient ways of managing transactions. But now, all forms of money except currency bear interest, which is accommodated to the rate of inflation. Moreover, plastic cards and computers have much reduced the use of currency, except for illegal transactions. The efficiency cost of a 6 percent inflation rate, then, may be small.

The chief argument against accepting permanent and fully anticipated inflation at 6 percent per annum was that the condition could not really be achieved. Continuation at that rate, and not more, could be fully anticipated only if that were the announced policy of the government and if everyone believed that the government could and would achieve it. But people, it was argued, would not believe in such a policy even if a government announced it. The reason for such a policy would be the government's unwillingness to face the likelihood of unemployment resulting from an attempt to bring inflation down below 6 percent. But if that were the government's priority, why should anyone believe that it would pay the price of unemployment needed to stay at 6 percent inflation or to get back down to 6 percent if mistakes or external events raised the rate above that figure? So while the inflation rate might stay at 6 percent, people would live with the anxiety that it would not remain there. And if it ever did rise above that level, people would expect it to remain at the higher level. That would make getting back down to 6 percent costly, and the government that had previously decided not to get down from 6 percent would then decide not to get back down from 8 percent, or wherever it happened to be.

That picture of how the public would react if the policy were to accept the 6 percent inflation was plausible but not the only plausible picture. One can imagine a government deciding not to try to reduce the inflation rate below what had already been in force for some time and to which the economy had been adapted. But it would be committed to keeping the rate from rising and especially to getting it back down to 6 percent, if it rose above that, before the economy had become adapted to the higher rate. This intention might not be believed by the public at first, but if the government honored its commitment and accepted the costs, including unemployment, of sticking to the 6 percent rate when it tended to go higher, credibility would be achieved, and the 6 percent rate would be stable.

Our theory or historical evidence was inadequate to tell which of these pictures was more realistic. The problem of stabilizing the inflation rate at zero did not seem different from the problem of stabilizing it at 6 percent. Either case required convincing the public that the government was serious.

Perceptions of the amount of unemployment entailed influenced the willingness to adopt such anti-inflation policies. While opinions varied greatly, two schools of thought could be distinguished. One school extrapolated from previous periods of declining demand to calculate how much increase of unemployment would accompany a given decline in the inflation rate. The second school said that this method seriously overestimated the costs of reducing inflation because it used observations from episodes in which firm government commitment to bringing inflation down was absent. Members of this school thought that with a strong government commitment the private sector would adapt its wage and price setting and the unemployment costs of disinflation would be reduced.

Those who thought that the costs of reducing inflation would be severe, even with as credible a commitment as the government could make, believed the costs could be significantly reduced if the government followed an "incomes policy." This policy implied an effort to influence the price-and-wage-setting behavior of businesses and unions directly, by means other than weakening the demand for product and labor, but without mandatory controls. The idea that there was such a remedy for the hard choice between stabilizing the price level and maintaining full employment—what I called the nonfattening hot fudge sundae—had been a theme of economic discussion at least since the mid-1950s. It persisted despite numerous apparent failures, and new variants were devised to correct the revealed defects of the variants already tried.

As it turned out, events overtook this discussion. Before we could decide whether to accept a continuation of 6 percent inflation or try to get down to a lower number or zero, we found ourselves facing double digits. Whether this degree of inflation would have been avoided, or less painfully corrected, with a firmer commitment even to the 6 percent rate, we will never know. No one thought that 10 or 12 percent inflation should be accepted. The initial reaction was that the inflation rate should be gotten "down," although without any more specific goal than that and without indicating any subordination of other objectives in possible conflict with reducing inflation. The government also tried to achieve voluntary cooperation from business and labor, under the aegis of a succession of inflation "czars" (although the word *czar* does not suggest voluntariness).

By the middle of 1979, the situation was obviously becoming too serious for such dilatory responses, and a turn was made in October 1979 with the announcement of a new monetary policy that meant at least a much more determined effort to reduce inflation. A new strategy of monetary policy to achieve that objective was also implied. That is, it seemed to mean more attention to the quantity of money, as distinguished from interest rates, as the lever by which policy would control inflation, and to the gradual reduction of the growth of the money supply.

This shift in policy was followed, after some lag, with a substantial reduction in the inflation rate, from 13.5 percent during 1980 to 6.2 percent during 1982 and 3.2 percent during 1983. While the change in monetary policy alone probably did not cause this decline in inflation, everything that economists know, or believe, would lead them to expect inflation to decline with a decline in the rate of growth of the money supply. But the decline in the inflation rate was larger than would have been expected from the size of the slowdown of the money supply. Possibly so large a decline in inflation should have been expected, because the slowdown of money growth itself so affected expectations of inflation that it caused an increase in the demand for money and thereby a reduction in the velocity of money—thus the observed decline in inflation. But we do not know that. Something other than the slowdown of money growth may have been at work to cause so large a drop in inflation.

The decline in inflation was accompanied by a substantial recession—by some measures the worst of the postwar period. Whether this recession was larger or smaller than should have been expected to accompany the disinflation we actually had was the subject of dispute among economists and never resolved. Some people thought that we may have actually experienced less recession than expected with that much disinflation because the decline in oil prices and the rise of the dollar fortuitously reduced U.S. inflation by means other than restriction of demand. Others thought that we would have had less recession accompanying the disinflation if the commitment to disinflation had been more credible.

The experience of 1981 and 1982 cast a great deal of doubt on the idea that monetary policy could be run by keeping the rate of growth of the money supply constant. The decline in inflation and of total gross national product had been much bigger than monetarist theory would have predicted as the average result of the slowdown of monetary growth. Of course, the word *average* is important to the theory. The theory does not deny the possibility of large occasional variations in the relation between money growth and the inflation rate, and the theory was not disproved by the sharp variations in the early 1980s. But it would have taken an extremely solid devotion to the theory not to be shaken by the experience of the 1980s, and the Federal Reserve clearly did not have such devotion.

By the fall of 1982, the Federal Reserve had given up the idea of stabilizing the rate of growth of the money supply, except possibly as a distant objective, and had returned to the earlier policy of flexible adjustment to conditions as they emerged, sometimes less sympathetically described as flying by the seat of the pants. From 1982 to 1988, the inflation rate averaged about 3½ percent, fluctuating moderately around that level. Inflation was no longer a burning issue, and the question of the ultimate goal for the inflation rate was inactive.

In 1989, the inflation question reappeared. It would probably be more accurate to say that the problem has hovered on the edge of visibility, reappearing in months when the annual rate exceeds about 4 percent and disappearing when it falls below that figure. Moreover, the issue of the ultimate goal has also reappeared. While no one seems to be prepared to say that his ultimate goal is an inflation rate significantly different from zero, the ultimate goal is apparently much more ultimate for some people than for others. At least, the Federal Reserve seems to pay more attention to reducing inflation as a near-term objective than the White House, whose near-term goal typically seems to be that the rate should not rise. But no one in authority is taking a firm position for any inflation goal as against possibly competing objectives.

The lessons of experience with inflation and monetary policy in the past twelve years are mainly negative:

• Hardly anyone talks about incomes policy any more. The unsatisfactory results of efforts in that direction in the latter days of the Carter administration probably had something to do with this. But it would be too optimistic to say that there has been permanent education from such experience. The main factor is that we have not had a sharp conflict between price-level stabilization and unemployment in recent years, since progress was being made on both fronts. If what used to be called "the inflationary dilemma" returns, proposals for incomes policy will probably surface again.

• The idea that fiscal policy could do anything about inflation has faded. For one thing, the simultaneous appearance of large budget deficits and declining inflation went far to dispel the notion that budget deficits were per se inflationary. In any case, fiscal policy

seemed so mired in other problems that it had no maneuverability
left for dealing with inflation.

• As a consequence of that, and of the kernel of truth that seemed
to remain from the monetarist revolution, monetary policy became
the instrument for controlling inflation.

• The idea that high inflation could be reduced without an inter-
vening episode of recession did not stand up very well. The possibility remained that commitment and credibility in the anti-inflation
effort would bring expectations into line without a recession, because
one could say that it had not been tested. But it did not seem a
good bet.

• The argument of twelve years ago about whether to accept and
maintain an inflation rate of, say, 6 percent, if that is where one
starts, or to strive toward a goal of zero inflation seems now to have
been about an unreal issue. In fact, we did not pursue either of these
policies. We not only did not have a determined policy to get down
to zero but also did not have a determined policy to keep from
exceeding 6 percent. The real issue turns out to be whether to have
any determined policy, any commitment to a specified inflation rate,
at all. Ironically, the actual inflation rate in the past twelve years has
been almost exactly 6 percent per annum. Perhaps it would have
been better to have worked our way down to zero beginning in 1977.
But it would surely have been better to stay constantly at 6 percent
than to follow the path we did, rising to 13 percent, declining to 2
and then rising again to 5 or so.

Our present danger is not that the inflation rate will stay around
5 or 6 percent rather than getting down to zero but that there is no
commitment, shared by the president and the Congress, as well as
by the Federal Reserve, and understood by the public, to any specific
inflation target.

Supply-Side Economics

When I coined the term *supply side* in 1976, I did not think that I was
providing the slogan for a new ideology and for a winning presidential
campaign. I was only identifying one of what I thought were the
seven schools of thought among economists at that time about fiscal
policy. It may be (slightly) amusing to see what the other six were:
(1) the pure, old-fashioned Keynesian functional financers; (2) the
fiscal-monetarists; (3) the monetarist-Parkinsonians; (4) the moneta-

rist neutrals; (5) the conventional eclectics; and (6) the growth-oriented eclectics. What I said about the "supply-side fiscalists" was:

> They also (like the monetarists) believe that aggregate demand is determined by money. However, aggregate supply is determined by taxation, including negative taxation, or transfer payments. Both inflation and unemployment can be reduced by reducing taxes and transfer payments, and that should be the objective of policy.

I was not at that time taking any position on the validity of the notion. My interest was "taxonomic." In a later article, I pointed out that the supply-side of the economy had been an interest of economists from the beginning of the science and that the influence of public policy, especially of taxation, on the supply of resources and the growth of output had long been recognized and had been the subject of economists' concern. This side of things had also been overshadowed for a time, naturally, by the experience of the depression, and it was a service to bring the supply side back to attention.

What made the supply-side argument politically effective and economically controversial, however, was not the simple and orthodox idea of paying attention to the effects of policy on the supply of output. What made the difference was the implicit notion of the magnitudes involved, although this issue was rarely faced explicitly. As a political slogan, *supply side* meant two things. It meant, first, that small changes of policy—specifically small changes in tax rates—could make a very big difference in the rate of economic growth. It meant, second, that increases in the rate of economic growth achievable by the recommended tax changes would make a very big difference in the quality of life in America. Taken together, it meant that the supply-side policy would make the difference between the "malaise" under which we suffered in the Carter years and the "sunrise in America" that was promised for the Reagan years.

In its extreme form, supply-side economics meant that a reduction of tax rates would raise the revenue. What made the proposition so appealing politically was that it permitted us to have a tax reduction, which everyone likes, without having to increase the budget deficit or cut government expenditures. The idea that a tax cut would raise the revenue was a natural but erroneous deduction from the sensible notion that if the tax on something is reduced, there will be more of it. If the tax on labor income is reduced, people will work more and earn more and have more taxable income (although there are reservations about this, that I will not go into). But the next step—that they will pay more taxes—does not follow; how much more people would pay in taxes depends on how much more income they earn in relation to how much taxes are cut (what economists call the "elasticity").

During all the talk about supply-side economics, no one ever demonstrated that the quantitative relations would make this extreme version of the theory believable. Some associates of Mr. Reagan have denied that he or they ever believed in the extreme version. But certainly the idea that we could have a tax cut without reducing the revenue helped to make the tax cut irresistible and the proponents of the big 1981 tax cut did nothing to disabuse the public of that idea. Looking back now, probably no one would say that the 1981 tax cut actually increased the revenue, although some would say that it would have done so if it had not been for the 1982 recession—an untestable proposition. Of course, the revenue has increased since 1981, but in a growing economy revenue tends to rise anyway. The question is whether the revenue rose more with the tax cut than it would have risen without it, and the evidence is against that. There are no live proposals to increase the revenue by cutting taxes, with the special, limited, and improbable exception of the proposal to cut the rate of tax on capital gains. And despite the cliché that raising taxes is economically and politically unacceptable, since 1981 we have had tax increases that, according to the 1990 budget, raised the fiscal 1988 revenue by $140 billion.

A less extreme version of supply-side economics held that although the tax cut would not raise the revenue, it would raise the sum of revenue and private saving by increasing the incentive to save. The sum of revenue plus private saving is important because that total limits the sum of government spending plus investment by Americans. So if revenue plus saving would increase, the tax cut would not necessitate a cut in government spending plus American investment. But that result has not been visible either. The rate of saving has declined since the tax cut, not increased.

None of this argument denies that the tax cuts, and tax reforms, have had a positive effect on the supply of labor, capital, and enterprise and on the rate of economic growth. But it is extremely doubtful that these effects have been on the scale predicted or hoped for. If they had been on such a scale, they should have been more clearly visible than they have been.

Experience in the 1980s raises another question about supply-side economics. It was implicit that success on the supply side was what the country needed—that it would solve our major problems. That proposition no longer seems so clear. We have had a considerable increase in output since 1980, whether due to supply-side measures or not. But our problems of crime, drugs, poverty, deficient education, and uncertain economic relations with less-developed countries and our allies undercut our hope that their solution depends very much on whether total output in the United States rises in the next decade by 2 percent or 3 percent or 4 percent per annum.

The 1980s leave supply-side economics in a moderate and defensible position. It is a needed corrective to the demand-side obsession that occupied economics for a generation or more after the depression. It reminds us that we should be concerned with the effects of policy, including tax policy, on incentives to produce and that these effects should be given weight in evaluating policy. But it also tells us to be realistic in estimating the size of these effects and their importance relative to other objectives.

The Budget Deficit

Shortly after the 1981 tax cut was enacted, the country awoke to face a large budget deficit. By December 1981, deficit numbers as large as $100 billion surfaced, to the general amazement. Since then, or at least since the country showed that it was coming out of the 1982 recession, the budget deficit has been economic problem number one in popular opinion.

Sensible discussion of the deficit is difficult for several reasons. First, many people see the deficit as a moral, ideological, and symbolic issue. Without being able to say two consecutive sentences about the effects of a deficit, they are very suspicious of anyone who is not exercised about it. Second, others are inclined to deny any significance to deficits at all, either because they do not want to be blamed or because they do not want to belong to the "booboisie" that cares. And because no one knows what it is about the deficit that does or should concern us, we have no fixed definition or measurement of the deficit. The real content of the deficit is different at different times and to different people, and it is hard to make any valid general statement about "the" deficit. Also, since so much attention is paid to the symbol and so little to the substance, the government is greatly tempted to concentrate on manipulating the symbol without affecting the reality, a temptation that it has not resisted. Nevertheless, some things have been learned:

• The public reaction to large deficits has become less emotional as there has been more experience with them. That this should have happened during the Reagan administration is ironic. For years, conservatives complained that Keynesian economics had undermined the public resistance to deficits. But our greatest exposure to large deficits in peacetime came during the most pre-Keynesian administration of the past sixty years and served to accustom the country to them.

• We no longer think that large deficits necessarily cause inflation.

• The idea that a large budget deficit can keep the economy from expanding, an idea that had some currency during the 1982 recession, has been shown to be incorrect.

• The idea that an increase in the budget deficit tends to be matched by an increase in private saving, so that the increase in the deficit does not crowd out private investment, has been tested. This idea has not stood up very well in the recent past, when the increase in the budget deficit was accompanied by a decline in private saving, at least as usually defined. This is not sufficient to disprove the idea. Like all *ceteris paribus* propositions, which say what would happen if everything else were constant, this idea is difficult to disprove. But the experience of the 1980s did not add to its plausibility.

• The experience was also not kind to Parkinson's law, which says that government expenditures rise to meet any increase in the revenues. Expenditures rose by much more than the revenues from 1980 to 1986, when the deficit was rising, and since then expenditures have risen much less than revenues, when the deficit declined. The feeling of a shortage of revenues probably tended to restrain the expenditures, but there was obviously not a one-for-one relation between expenditures and the availability of revenues.

• We have seen for the first time the significance of the greatly increased international mobility of capital. Because capital can flow here from abroad, a budget deficit here does not necessarily crowd out private investment in the United States. By attracting an inflow of capital, a deficit here can crowd out investment in the rest of the world. The budget deficit does, however, crowd out investment owned by Americans.

• We are coming increasingly to realize that the true significance of budget deficits is their effect on total investment, on the size of the U.S. capital stock, and, through that, on future incomes. This realization is reflected in the growing attention to the question of "intergenerational equity." But how to factor this consideration into budget policy is a subject still in its infancy.

The Trade and Payments Deficits

The biggest economic surprise of the past twelve years was the appearance of deficits in the U.S. balance of international trade, running between $100 billion and $150 billion a year. When the idea of such large trade deficits came to my attention, I was at a meeting shortly after we realized that we would have budget deficits of more than $100 billion. One economist, William Niskanen, suggested that this deficit would cause an inflow of foreign capital and a trade deficit of about the same size. Other economists, including me, were incredulous. Our largest previous deficit in trade in goods and services had been less than $10 billion. Some suggested that if the trade deficit even threatened to get into the neighborhood of $100 billion, protectionist sentiment would rise up to restrain it.

We were wrong on both counts. The trade deficit rose to $150 billion. And although there was a rise of protectionist sentiment, and protectionist policy, that did not limit the size of the deficit because it could not.

Nothing that I have written in the past twelve years has met such resistance and rejection from readers, including some economists, as the proposition that the United States has not been injured by its international trade and payments deficits. The belief that something is terribly wrong persists despite many years of experience to the contrary.

Two views of the international economic problem may be distinguished: the macro is concerned with the effects on the economy as a whole; the micro is concerned with the effects on particular sectors, although it may, of course, be maintained that those sectors were of national concern.

The original complaint about the trade deficit was that it was costing American jobs; a standard figure for the amount of this alleged job loss was 3 million. No basis for such a claim ever existed, as the statistics of employment growth in the past decade demonstrate. Similarly, claims that the trade deficit would prevent the recovery of total output have been denied by the facts. The performance of productivity in the economy as a whole has been no worse during the period of the rising trade deficit than during the previous period from 1973 to about 1982 when the trade deficit was small and of no great concern.

As the strength of the recovery in employment and output in spite of the trade deficit became clear, concern increasingly focused on what would happen when the trade deficit ended. The argument was that the trade deficit could go on only as long as the rest of the world was willing to invest in the United States. That presumably would not go on forever. Foreigners would not only not continue to invest here but also at some point might want to take back some of the funds they have already invested here. If this change comes suddenly, there will be a shock to the American economy. Even if it comes only gradually, American output will be drained to pay at least the interest on dividends on the foreign investment here and possibly also some repatriation of capital.

In my opinion, these worries are groundless. A sudden reversal of the capital flows would be a shock to the American economy, but this seems to me no more likely to occur, or more difficult to adapt to, than other shocks that can be imagined. It would be a shock to cut defense spending from 6 percent to 4 percent of GNP, to discover that the American people had enough automobiles for a while, or to find that businesses had misjudged their inventory requirements. The stability of the system does not depend finally on the avoidance of such localized shocks but on the existence of general stabilizing forces, such as monetary policy. As for the future gradual repatriation of interest, dividends, and, possibly, capital, that would involve only the payment of the earnings on capital that would not otherwise have been in the United States or the return of some of that capital itself. It would not make the United States poorer than if the capital had not come here in the first place.

Despite my arguments to this effect, the concern about the continuing capital inflow and its possible future reversal persists. Fortunately, this concern has little real consequence for policy. Many people would say that the way to reduce the capital inflow, and the trade deficit, is to reduce the U.S. budget deficit. But we already have plenty of reasons for wanting to do that, and concern about the international position does not seem to affect the forces at work on that problem. Beyond that, some suggest that the private savings rate should be raised in the United States and reduced elsewhere, suggestions that are unlikely to have any practical issue. Unfortunately, worry about the trade deficit and the capital inflow provides unjustified argument for protectionist measures, even though most economists would agree that such measures would not affect the trade deficit.

Economists have learned at their mother's knee to be wary of claims for protection for particular industries; their concern, therefore, has been mainly with "macro" effects. The popular concern and the political force have been more strongly focused on what happens to particular industries. First, people were concerned about the manufacturing industry, as if that industry had an exceptional right to national attention. But the share of manufacturing in total output remains where it has been for several decades, around 21 percent. Manufacturing employment has declined from its peak, because productivity in manufacturing industries has risen strongly, but the decline in employment has been small, about 8 percent.

Some American industries, and their owners and employees, have undoubtedly been hurt by foreign competition. That some of these were particularly high-wage industries creates the fear that American incomes are being depressed by this process. But Americans were the main customers of these high-wage industries, and these customers benefit from the availability of cheaper foreign products. A redistribution has occurred within the American economy, but not a net loss. In any case, this kind of effect is not connected with the trade deficit. If we import $10 billion of automobiles from Japan, it makes no difference to the automobile industry whether the Japanese use the $10 billion to buy oranges, in which case there is no trade deficit, or Los Angeles real estate, in which case there is a trade deficit.

Recently, the argument about trade, which is really an argument against trade, has become even more specialized. It now focuses on "high-tech" industries, which are said to have an exceptionally high potential for growth and for contributing to the growth of the national economy. Some claim that these industries will not develop here unless they are assured of a protected market and are possibly subsidized or favored in other ways.

That such cases may exist is hard to deny in the abstract, although the argument does not usually specify many particular cases. The real question is whether the American economy is suffering from failure to find and nurture such industries as we could have done. The evidence commonly given is that someone else—almost always the Japanese—is producing something that we are not. But that says only that international trade is going on, not that something is wrong. The issue can be put this way: suppose that in the past ten years an agency of the U.S. government had been charged with selecting industries to protect, to negotiate market-sharing agreements on their behalf with other governments, and to subsidize those industries in other ways. Suppose that this agency had been like other government agencies we know of—like HUD, for example, or the Federal Home Loan Bank Board—and had the kind of relations with congressmen that other agencies have. Suppose that it had an advisory board of leaders of business and labor with the same degree of responsibility for consumers and taxpayers that we are accustomed to. Would the country have been better off? Perhaps the answer is not obvious, but that is the kind of question the new protectionism has to answer and has not.

This high-tech argument, however, has nothing to do with the balance of trade. Whether the United States should sponsor the high-density TV industry does not depend on how many oranges or pounds of beef we sell to Japan. Moreover, this argument does not explain our protection of steel, automobiles, textiles, rice, sugar, cheese, or a long list of other things.

The present stance of American policy with respect to international trade is hard to evaluate. Surely, an unfortunate increase in protectionism occurred in the 1980s. But one has to understand that Americans considered many developments as "provocations" to protectionism, even though erroneously. These included the trade deficit, the general recession of 1981–1982 and the localized recessions that continued for a while thereafter, the conspicuous appearance of large numbers of foreign products of kinds that we always thought we were very good at, and the special relation with the Japanese, whom many Americans were prepared to suspect of sinister behavior. When all this is considered, the administration may deserve some credit for not having gone further in a protectionist direction. But the jury is still out.

The issue is not really whether we will slide slowly or rapidly into more protectionism but whether the United States will take the lead in trying to steer the world economy toward free and nondiscriminatory trade, as it has done in the past, or leave that leadership role vacant. The significance of the outcome will not be primarily economic but political. Will economic relations help hold the Western Alliance together or be a source of conflict? Will the less-developed countries find their best opportunity for progress by participating in our system? Will the countries of the former Communist bloc be encouraged to join the free world economy? The answer to such questions will depend on the farsightedness and magnanimity of U.S. policy. Whether we will be adequate to this task is uncertain.

The Problems of a Rich Country

A persistent argument during much of the past twelve years was that the United States could not afford the defense program on which President Reagan was embarked. The main intellectual support for this argument was presented by Professor Paul Kennedy in his book, *The Rise and Fall of the Great Powers*. The book maintained, with reliance on historical precedents, that the planned rate of defense spending would so weaken the American economy that our national security would be impaired rather than strengthened by the expenditures. In a number of articles, I held that this claim was absurd when we were spending 6 or 7 percent of the GNP on defense and when the American people were enjoying the highest per capita consumption of any time in the history of any country. I maintained that America was rich enough to be strong.

There were two ways to look at the affordability of the defense program. On the one hand, we have a GNP of $5 trillion, of which we now spend $300 billion for defense and $4,700 billion for other things. The question is whether another, say, $10 billion for defense is more valuable than the least valuable $10 billion of the uses for which the other $4,700 billion now goes. On the other hand, we have a federal expenditure budget of $1,100 billion, which cannot be increased without either raising taxes or increasing the deficit, both of which are ruled out. We also have $500 billion of entitlement expenditures and other "mandatory" expenditures and $150 billion of interest expenditures, both of which are untouchable. So we are left with $300 billion of defense expenditures and $150 billion of "discretionary" expenditures. The question is whether another $10 billion of defense expenditures is worth more than the least valuable $10 billion of the other $150 billion. Conceivably, the two approaches could lead to the same answer, although that is unlikely. The first is the realistic approach, because in the second the choices are constrained by limits that do not exist in the real economy or in any deliberate decision about national priorities. The choices are constrained by artificial rules adopted for political convenience. This argument with respect to the defense program has faded. The apparent change in the Soviet posture has made the argument about what we can afford for defense seem less necessary.

The question of what America can afford now appears with respect to other possible objects of expenditure. There are serious proposals, some coming from the White House, to spend more for drug control, for child care, for education, for economic aid to countries of Eastern Europe, or for space exploration. And in every case, the question is raised of whether we can afford it. In some cases the questions are ludicrous. When President Bush proposed a new program for space exploration, for example, commentators said that of course we could afford President Kennedy's program in the 1960s but cannot afford President Bush's now, even though real per capita consumption in the United States is almost twice as high as it was when Kennedy was president. Many people have said that our economic constraints severely limit the amount of assistance we can give to Eastern Europe but that Japan could do enormously more. In fact, Japan's real per capita income is about three-fourths of ours, and its total real income is about one-third of ours.

Perhaps none of these proposed expenditures would be worth its cost; that is surely a legitimate question for discussion. But the point is that the present way of looking at the budget keeps us from counting the costs realistically. The cost of any of these proposed expenditures is in reality the least valuable use of the national output that would have to be sacrificed to make it. But as the decisions are now made, the cost of any expenditure seems to be the sacrifice of another expenditure within a very small sector of the federal budget, because the apparent range of choice has been artificially limited by arbitrary rules about taxes, deficits, and entitlements.

As I look back at the twelve years about which I have been

writing in the *AEI Economist,* I am struck by the fact that for all our problems of instability and lagging productivity, this is still a very rich country—the richest there has ever been. The American economy is amazingly effective in producing, and in producing what the American people want. Although the American society has many problems, most of them have major noneconomic dimensions. Insofar as they have economic dimensions, they do not result from inadequacy of total national output: they result from failure to allocate the national output in ways that satisfy our most important needs. In part, that is a matter of private decisions, but it is also, and increasingly, a matter of collective decisions made through the government. Our way of thinking about these decisions has not caught up with their seriousness and complexity. *(August 1989)*

23

The $50 Billion Option

E ver since the 1992 Los Angeles riot, the papers have been filled with suggestions for improving conditions in the inner cities. Although I am not an expert on this subject, many of these suggestions seem constructive to me. They do not fall into the category that President Bush, in his Marie Antoinette style, called "dumping largesse" on the problem. Everyone now recognizes the need to improve the competence and behavior of the people in the ghettos by investing in their skills and strengthening their incentives for good behavior.

Suggestions for Improving Conditions

Some of the suggestions that seem to deserve serious consideration are, in no particular order:

- community centers for prenatal care and physical and psychological nurturing of children in the early months of life
- full funding of Head Start and major upgrading of its quality
- residential schooling for children from the worst environments
- a voucher system to provide incentives for the improvement of schools
- full funding of the terms of the Welfare Reform Act of 1988 to provide counseling, training, work experience, and child care for welfare recipients
- revision of welfare programs to reduce the loss of benefits, including Medicaid, that a beneficiary receives if she takes paid employment

- revision of welfare programs to reduce the incentive to bear children who will require public support
- finding absent fathers and requiring them to contribute to the support of their children
- "enterprise zones," that is, subsidy for economic development in selected backward areas
- using military facilities and personnel to train and acculturate ghetto youth
- strengthening of community police forces

We can be certain that no combination of measures on this or any other list will be implemented, or even seriously considered, on a scale commensurate with the problem. This fate was sealed by President Bush's 1992 commencement address at Notre Dame, when he said that the federal government could not solve the problem "alone." Of course, no one ever expected the federal government to solve it alone. That expression is code language for "Don't count on me, Jack!"

The president has endorsed many of the proposals on this list, but only in homeopathic doses. He is for increased spending on Head Start, but not enough to make it available to all poor children or to improve its quality. He is for enterprise zones, as long as their cost does not appear on the expenditure side of the budget. He is for school vouchers, but not for federal money to contribute to the value of the vouchers.

Of course, the Democratic leadership is no better. They are still back in the era of nationwide pump priming, to raise the condition of ghetto youth by public works programs to employ members of the construction workers' unions.

A Large Urban Program

Why won't we even consider a large, comprehensive program? I think that there are two reasons. The first, probably less important, is that many influential people have convinced themselves that the federal government can do nothing. The key is behavior, they say, and the federal government cannot influence behavior. Of course, that is wrong. The federal government has been influencing behavior for a long, long time. The Homestead Act of 1862, offering 160 acres of public land to anyone who would settle on it and farm it, influenced millions of people to go west and fill up the country. The Interstate Highway System has influenced the behavior of tens of millions of people in choosing a place to live. The whole conservative complaint against the Great Society programs is that they did indeed influence behavior, but in the wrong direction.

The second, more important obstacle to a large, comprehensive program is a familiar one, *money*. Except for the demonstrators in the streets, who have no program at all, everyone starts and ends with the proposition that there is no money, or very little. Proposals for dealing with the urban problem must be fit within the nooks and crannies of the $1½ trillion budget, so as not to disturb its contours. With such a constraint, programs under consideration look pitifully inadequate. Someone said, "Make no little plans; they do not stir the blood." The plans in sight will not inspire hope in the ghetto or voluntary cooperation outside it. A critical mass may need to be reached before programs can be successful. Responsible behavior may need to be not a little more common but much more prevalent before it becomes the standard to which almost everyone will adhere. The streets may need to become not a little safer but much safer before investment is attracted. A big program may be much more effective per dollar and per unit of effort and attention than a little one.

Perhaps we do not want a big urban program. Perhaps, as some say, we do not know enough to devise an effective one. But the idea of a big program should not be rejected, as now seems likely, without anyone's having seen what a big program would look like. The president is not well served if no one has put before him the option of an urban program that would cost, say, $50 billion a year, so that he can accept it, accept it in part, or reject it. The Congress and the American public should also have such an option to consider.

The president ought to ask his staff to prepare for him the best program they can with no other budget constraint except that it should not cost more than $50 billion a year. He should also invite other institutions and individuals, private and public, to submit proposals subject to the same limitation. I can imagine programs forthcoming from people at the Urban Institute, the American Enterprise Institute, the Heritage Foundation, the Conference of Mayors, the Urban League, and many other organizations. Some of these programs would not cost $50 billion a year. Some might even call for a reduction in the present level of spending for cities. The point is to get these options into the arena of public discussion and decision making.

The question will still be asked, Where will we find the money if we decide that a big program is worthwhile? The question answers itself. To say it is worthwhile means that its benefits are more valuable than some existing use of an equal amount of money. So the source of the money for the new program is the uses of money that are less valuable. For a more specific answer, I refer readers to a useful series of annual reports by the Congressional Budget Office, entitled "Reducing the Budget Deficit: Spending and Revenue Options." There one will find tens of billions of dollars of "largesse" for the middle and upper classes, including subsidized Medicare, subsidies to agriculture, partial exclusion of social security benefits from income tax, and exclusion of employer-provided fringe benefits from income tax. Options exist for finding the money. The only question is whether the American people think the gains from a large urban program are worth what would have to be given up.

I am sure that most readers of this essay will believe that I am recommending an urban program costing $50 billion a year. That is not the case, because I don't know whether that would be a good idea or not. But I think it important that the people and the government should have the clearest possible view of their options, unlimited by false and conventional ideas about what the economy can afford. *(June 1992)*

PART FIVE
The State of Economic Talk

24

Fugue for Talking Heads

H ave you ever considered how wasteful the standard panel discussion on TV is? Typically the scenario goes something like this:

There are a moderator and four panelists—a Democratic congressman, a Republican congressman, a conservative pundit, and a liberal pundit. The moderator announces the subject and introduces the panelists by name and position in the spectrum. Then he asks one of the panelists a question. After the answer, the moderator refers either the question or the previous answer to another panelist. And so it goes—moderator, panelist, moderator, panelist—until fifteen minutes have passed, the moderator thanks everyone, and the performance is over. Nothing much has been said.

Contrast that with a performance of a string quartet. There is no moderator or conductor. The performers are not introduced. Everyone in the audience knows who they are by where they sit and by the instruments they hold in their hands. They start without any outside intervention and end in the same way. But the key thing is that almost all the time *they are all playing at once.* They get a lot done in fifteen minutes, many times more than if they had all played seriatim as in a panel discussion.

I can imagine a much more efficient panel discussion that would go like this:

The four panelists are seated in a semicircle ranged from left to right—Democratic congressman (DC), liberal pundit (LP), conservative pundit (CP), Republican congressman (RC). At a nod of the head from the Democratic congressman, the recitation begins.

All together: "It will soon be January 20. Yes, it will soon be noon of January 20. Now comes the witching hour for talking heads. It has been a year of ups and downs for Clinton."

DC, LP: ⎫ "More ups than downs."
RC, CP: ⎭ "More downs than ups."
All together: "Nafta."
DC, LP: ⎫ "Nafta was a great triumph for Clinton."
RC, CP: ⎭ "Nafta was a great triumph for Gingrich."
All together: "The main thing is the economy, which is rising—
DC, LP: ⎫ "—Healthily."
RC, CP: ⎭ "—Weakly."
DC, solo: "It's too bad the Republicans defeated the president's stimulus package."
RC, solo: "It's a good thing we stopped the president's stimulus package."
CP, LP: "Consider the budget package. That was the big economic news. It was a . . ."
DC, LP: ⎫ "Triumph! Investment to spur growth."
RC, CP: ⎭ "Disaster! Taxes will stunt growth."
All together: "Look at the shape of the world and what Clinton has done."
RC, CP: ⎫ "Bosnia, Somalia, Haiti!"
DC, LP: ⎭ "Middle East, Russia, Japan!"
All together: "Next year. Critical year. Defining moment. Turning point. Congressional elections."
DC, RC: "Health care will be the key issue."
RC, CP: ⎫ "Socialism! Rationing!"
DC, LP: ⎭ "Security! Economy!"
All together: "But fundamentally, it will be values that count."
DC, LP: ⎫ "Memphis speech! Biting the Bullet!"
RC, CP: ⎭ "Sex, sex, sex."

In this way, TV could cover in five minutes what now takes at least fifteen. The time saved could be accumulated and used for a day of silence at the end of each year.

Now, you may say that a drawback of this proposal is that although it economizes on the time of the performers, it does require a script writer. There have been some musicians, especially jazz performers, who have been able to play together extemporaneously without a written script. But that is a rare ability, and we will have to count on providing a script for the panelists. That is not a serious problem, however. One script could serve for many panelists and with only slight modifications could remain relevant for long periods of time. In fact, even with supposedly spontaneous and independent contributions by panelists today, the performances do not change much from year to year.

Now that I have thought this all out, I think I will apply to the National Endowment for the Humanities for a grant. This could be a small but real service to humanity. *(December 1993)*

25

The Age of Ignorance

I suppose I am as tuned in to the information age as the next fellow. I get three daily newspapers and several magazines. I watch all the talk shows, the news shows, the televised hearings of congressional committees, and even, on occasion, televised performances of the Senate or the House. I have a modem and instant access to millions of bytes of information. I am on the free mailing lists of innumerable organizations kindly seeking to enlighten me. I work and talk almost every day with well-informed people.

And yet, I am more and more impressed by my ignorance. I have the impression that the body of knowledge is the area within a circle whose radius is constantly rising. But I am on the circumference of the circle, where knowledge fades off into ignorance, and the size of the circumference is rising as the length of the radius rises. The more I learn, the more I become aware of how much I ought to know but do not. So I am not denying that we know more than we did a hundred years ago. But I doubt that we know more relative to what we expect, and are expected, to know.

After months of watching the MacNeil/Lehrer NewsHour, I finally learned approximately where Bosnia-Herzegovina is, that like Gaul it is divided into three parts, and that there is no *i* before the *a* in Herzegovina. But, knowing that, I realized that I would have to know enormously more even to begin to think about what U.S. policy should be, which presumably it is my duty as a citizen to think about. I did not know how to find out what I would have needed to know. And I had barely scratched the surface on Bosnia-Herzegovina before

I discovered that there was another place, Kosovo, that I had never even heard about, that was critical to the whole story.

Now I think that President Clinton is telling us that we can stop thinking about Bosnia-Herzegovina, because the question of doing something about it is dead. But I do not know whether that is what he means to tell us, or whether he would be right to tell us that.

Even if I forget about the Balkans, I have a full slate of things that as a responsible citizen I ought to know about but do not. I will not even mention Cambodia. Which group the Khmer Rouge are will always be a mystery to me, and now that I mention it, I am not sure whether they go with Cambodia or Laos.

But there are many things closer to home that I don't know. I don't know whether the issue of gays in the military is like or unlike the issue of blacks in the military. I don't know whether Professor Jeffries has a constitutional right to be the head of a department at City College, or whether a woman has a constitutional right to have an abortion. I don't know whether, if we stop giving aid to unmarried women who have children, there will be more or fewer children living in poverty.

Even in my own field, there are important things I don't know. I don't know whether increasing the budget deficit stimulates or depresses the national income. I don't know whether it is M2 or M1 that controls the level of total spending. I don't know by how much a 10 percent increase in the top rate of individual income tax will raise the revenue.

I do not say these things to brag about my ignorance. I believe that most people are as ignorant as I am, although they may not know it. I am always amazed at the results of public opinion polls. The proportion of people who answer "Don't know" is usually something like 8 percent, whereas it really should be something like 100 percent. I believe that if you ask a sample of Americans what the temperature is on Mars, about 8 percent would say that they don't know.

The experts on talk shows are even worse. I have watched thousands of hours of talk shows and I cannot remember one of the guests ever saying, "I don't know." I understand how that works. The producer calls up potential guests and asks them how they would answer sample questions. Any guests who say "I don't know" are not invited to appear on the show.

So what are we to do about this ignorance? The first answer to that, of course, is that I don't know. But the second answer is that we will live with it, as we do with other human frailties.

When I had the honor of being a professor at the University of Virginia, I was pleased to go around quoting Thomas Jefferson's saying: "Whoever expects to be ignorant and free in a state of civilization expects what never was and never will be." But I now suspect that our patron saint was stretching it a bit there. We have been living for some time in ignorance and freedom—indeed, with increasing freedom since Jefferson's time. Perhaps he would say that we have not been in a state of civilization.

But there may be some precepts for how to live with our ignorance. One is diversification. I have learned that I do not know how to pick winning stocks. So I have concluded that I am best off buying the Standard & Poor's 500. We need to seek the equivalent in public affairs. We are not able to buy a presidential package consisting of 43 percent Clinton, 38 percent Bush, and 19 percent Perot. But we do achieve a certain kind of diversification by the change of presidents and parties from time to time. Although all presidents make mistakes, they do not all make the same mistakes, and by changing presidents we reduce the risk of mistakes cumulating to catastrophe. *(June 1993)*

26

The Mythology of Tax Reduction

"Cut taxes!" is the "Open Sesame!" of the Republican party. It is expected to open the door to innumerable good things for the economy and, probably more important, to open the door to another four years in the White House.

Cutting taxes may or may not be a good thing. But the current Republican infatuation with it reflects belief in a number of ideas that are purely mythological. I would like to call the roll of some of these ideas:

1. *The myth that cutting taxes is a sure prescription for electoral victory.* Since there is so much interest in Harry Truman these days, partly because he is an example of a come-from-behind victor in a presidential election, we can start with him. In 1947 and 1948, a Republican Congress passed tax-cutting bills three times, and each time Truman vetoed them. The third time Congress overrode the veto, and the tax cut became law. The "rich man's tax bill" became a major theme of Truman's whistle-stop campaign in the fall of 1948. He won an election no one expected him to win, and the Republican Congress went down in defeat.

In 1954, the Republicans were again in control of Congress and, with the reluctant agreement of President Eisenhower, passed another tax-cut bill. In the November elections, they lost the Senate, not to regain it for twenty-six years. They lost the House and have still not regained it, some fifty years later.

Lyndon Johnson won a smashing victory in 1964, after the Kennedy-Johnson tax cut, but he had a lot of other things going for him against Barry Goldwater. Similarly, Ronald Reagan had a lot of other things going for him in 1980 in addition to his promise of a tax cut.

When Ronald Reagan ran for reelection, he had on the record his support for big tax increases in 1982, 1983, and 1984. If the perception of him as being antitax contributed to his reelection, that was as much a tribute to the image as to the reality. In 1986, the Republicans, the antitax party, lost the Senate. George Bush's promise not to raise taxes probably helped him in 1988.

The record is mixed. One would expect giving or promising tax reduction to be helpful in an election, just as the city bosses' gifts of free turkeys and free beer were helpful. But tax reduction does not seem to be decisive, or to overcome other handicaps. And being seen as in favor of a "rich man's tax cut" is probably a negative, which may be a problem for those who make cutting the capital-gains tax the crown jewel of their domestic agenda.

2. *The myth that cutting taxes will raise the revenue.* One has to be a little apologetic about raising this subject. We have recently been assured by responsible authority that, contrary to common impressions, neither Ronald Reagan nor members of his team believed that cutting taxes would raise the revenue. But this idea still seems to lurk in the underbrush of tax-cut thinking, and it is worthwhile to point out that it is invalid, except possibly for a few particular taxes.

3. *The myth that cutting taxes will force a reduction of expenditures.* After the experience of the 1980s, this no longer looks like a reliable proposition, if it ever did. If it were true, explaining the large deficits would be very difficult.

4. *The myth that cutting taxes caused the Reagan economic miracle.* In fact, there was no economic miracle. The rate of increase of total output from 1981 to 1988 was a little less than in the postwar period up to 1981—much less than from 1948 to 1973, but more than from 1973 to 1981. Cutting taxes was supposed to increase private saving, but that did not happen. Private saving as a percentage of gross national product was a little less in the 1980s than it had been in the 1970s. Neither was any effect of the tax cut on the labor supply visible to the naked eye. Sophisticated studies of the subject suggest that the tax changes of the 1980s may have increased the supply of labor by an amount ranging from zero to 2 percent.

It is probably true that the tax changes of the 1980s had some, although small, favorable effect on the national output, if the tax changes are taken by themselves. But the tax changes cannot be taken by themselves. They contributed to the deficits that had a negative effect on the national output by reducing the savings available for productive investment. A recent study published by the Federal Reserve Bank of New York concludes as follows: "Our reading of the available impressionistic and econometric evidence suggests that the favorable effects of reductions in marginal tax rates on potential output appear to have been smaller than the adverse consequences of large and persistent budget deficits."

This observation about the 1980s is relevant for the current discussion about tax cuts for growth versus what is sometimes described as a "Victorian" obsession with the budget deficit. It suggests that a tax cut that increases the budget deficit will not, on balance, promote growth.

The enactment of the big Reagan tax cut in 1981 was followed by the recession of 1981–1982. This was the second deepest recession of the postwar period as measured by output, and the worst as measured by unemployment. What is sometimes described as the Reagan miracle was the recovery from that recession, a recovery that was not extraordinary. This recovery came while taxes were being raised in the legislation of 1982, 1983, and 1984.

5. *The myth that taxes in America are very high by American historical standards.* As a fraction of gross domestic product, federal taxes in 1993 are just as high as in fiscal year 1960, the last year of the Eisenhower administration (18.3 percent). The tax percentage of 1993 was a little higher than in the average of the years 1960 to 1980, if we exclude the years when the Vietnam War surcharge was in effect (17.3 percent). But there has been a major change in the composition of the receipts. In fiscal year 1960, payroll taxes for social security were 2.9 percent of GDP. In 1993, they were 6.8 percent. All other taxes have fallen from 15.4 percent of GDP to 11.5 percent. Individual income tax receipts are the same percentage of GDP as they were in 1960 (8.1 percent). The big decline has been in the yield of the corporate profits tax.

The rise in the payroll tax raises a question of interpretation. In one view, the "tax" is not a tax at all but is a price that individuals and their employers pay for retirement and health benefits they are receiving or will receive in the future. If that is the case, then taxes have declined substantially relative to GDP since 1960. But if the payroll tax really *is* a tax, there has been a substantial shift in the tax burden in the past thirty years or so, and reduction of the individual income tax would accentuate that shift. An across-the-board cut in the individual income tax is thus *not* an equal cut if payroll taxes are excluded. It is a bigger cut for upper-income people, because the payroll tax is a smaller part of their total tax bill. In the move to reduce taxes, the payroll tax would seem to have a strong case for inclusion. But only Senator Daniel Patrick Moynihan shows much interest in that.

6. *The myth that taxes in America are high by international standards.* According to the latest comparable figures available (1989 for the United States and Western Europe and 1988 for Japan), total government receipts as a percentage of GDP were 31.8 percent in the United States, 34.3 percent in Japan, and 44.2 percent in Western Europe.

Cutting some taxes is undoubtedly a good idea in some economic and budgetary conditions. But the case for it now, either as political battle cry or as serious economic policy, requires more evidence than can be gotten out of these common myths. *(August 1992)*

27

Term Limits for Pundits

I have never been much impressed by the argument for term
limits for congressmen. It reminds me of a story I first heard
from my former colleague, Earl Butz. A farmer goes to the
lawyer in his village and asks him how much it would cost to get a
divorce. The lawyer says it would be $500 but asks why he wants a
divorce. The farmer says he wants to divorce his wife so he can
marry her sister. And the lawyer responds by opining that there isn't
$500 worth of difference between them.

I have seen lots of congressmen, old and new, and I cannot see
that there is much difference between them. I am especially surprised that people who call themselves conservatives are so eager
for term limits. I should think they would prefer to be governed by
old congressmen who have given up hope that the government will
do anything except provide a reasonable amount of pork to get them
reelected, rather than by new congressmen who come trailing clouds
of goals and programs. Also, aren't conservatives worried that
denying the claims of congressmen to retain their comfortable seats
may lead to denying the claims of other people to retain their
comfortable fortunes?

But I suppose there must be something to the term limit idea.
After all, God does set term limits on us all, although He is
more generous about the length of the term than some of the
current reformers.

It does seem to me, however, that the idea is at least as
applicable to some other institutions as it is to Congress. I think
specifically of pundits—the people who write newspaper columns of

opinion about public policy. Surely many of them occupy their space long after they have a contribution to make.

The typical pundit career runs like this: he (the typical pundit is male) goes to a good college where he studies history, political science, philosophy, and perhaps a little economics, and he is editor of the student newspaper. He then gets a job as a sports reporter, where he learns to write to deadline and acquires familiarity with many sports expressions, like "touching all the bases," that he will use for the rest of his life. Having demonstrated imagination and literary skill, he is then promoted to apprentice pundit. He surveys the policy scene with fresh eyes and measures what he sees against the great ideas he learned in college. The resulting columns are widely praised, and he acquires the position of tenured pundit.

From then on it is downhill. That is not surprising. If he is going to write two columns a week, each of 750 words, and do that for fifty weeks a year, and do it for forty years, from age thirty to age seventy, he is going to write 3 million words. That is a lot of words to write incisively. It is about seven times as many words as are in *The Wealth of Nations*. Anthony Trollope is said to have written 3,000 words a day, day in and day out. But he was unusually lavish with words. He took almost 250,000 words to get Phineas Finn married—the first time. Our pundit has to eke out his 3 million words in 750 word bites, each a rounded essay on a different subject.

That is hard. I was once an apprentice pundit. I had to write only one column a week, and I did it for only six years. But I found that I was spending all my available time trying to think of a subject that I could write 750 words about without having to do more research than I had time for. The product becomes quite thin.

Then the pundit falls into various bad habits to keep the words coming. He begins to write little junior-high-school essays, like "what I did on my vacation," "what the taxi driver said," "what new books I have read." Or he forms a relationship with one or more government "sources," who provide him with information and in the process use him to promote their own ambitions. Or he becomes a spokesman for some "cause" that gives him an endless series of controversies to engage in.

Now, you will say, the market will take care of that and retire the pundit when he becomes unreliable or boring. But the market in this case is imperfect. Buying a newspaper is a package deal. You get the pundits along with a lot of other things; you can't get the paper without the pundits. I have been subscribing to the same newspaper for more than fifty years, and no one has ever asked me whether I like the pundits. For all the publisher knows, I may be buying the paper for the crossword puzzle or to wrap herring.

Anyway, there is not a level playing field (to coin a phrase). The incumbent pundit does not have to compete with would-be pundits. Frequently after I write a newspaper column, I get letters from people who first compliment me and then enclose an unpublished manuscript that made my point earlier and better. Surely there are village Lippmanns and Menckens out there, doomed to lie unpublished because the space on the Op-Ed page is already occupied.

Of course, there are exceptions to my thesis—pundits who are evergreen and get even better as they get older. But I suppose that is also true of some congressmen and senators, and if I had time for a little research I would come up with some names. But policy has to deal with the general state of affairs, and I am suggesting that term limits would improve punditry in general, even though it would unfortunately crop some wise heads along the way.

Perhaps legislation limiting the term of pundits to, say, twelve years would be unconstitutional. I don't know whether the First Amendment protects anyone's right to tenure as a newspaper columnist. If it does, we might appeal to the consciences of pundits to turn off their word processors after a certain number of years.

What would become of the used-up pundits? A fitting answer, in my opinion, would be for them to run for Congress.

I hasten to add that none of this applies to me. I do not write to a fixed schedule. I write only when I have something to say—as you can see. *(January 1993)*

PART SIX

The State of Economics

28

Economics—Dismal Science or Dentistry?

M any literate people who know little else about economics know that it is the "dismal science." But what this means—in what sense it is dismal—is unclear.

Origin of *The Dismal Science*

The Oxford English Dictionary gives several possible meanings of the word *dismal*. The one relevant to our subject is "of a character or aspect that causes gloom and depression; depressingly dark, gloomy, dreary, or cheerless." We know that is the definition relevant to our subject because one of the two quotations given by the OED to illustrate the use of the word *dismal* is about economics. In an 1849 essay, "The Nigger Question," Thomas Carlyle writes,

> The Social Science—not a "gay science" but a rueful—
> which finds the secret of this Universe in "supply and
> demand," [and reduces the duty of human governors to
> that of letting men alone, is also wonderful. Not a "gay
> science," I should say, like some we have heard of; no, a
> dreary desolate, and indeed quite abject and distressing
> one;] what we might call, by way of eminence, the *dismal
> science* [Material in brackets omitted from original in OED
> quotation.].[1]

---

1. *The Works of Thomas Carlyle: Critical and Miscellaneous Essays,* vol. IV (New York: Scribner's, 1904), pp. 353–54.

The other citation in the OED is of the Dismal Swamp. The conjunction of the dismal swamp and the dismal science as illustrations expected to help the reader understand what the word *dismal* means is puzzling. The user of the OED probably has in his mind some picture of a swamp, so that when he is told that a swamp may be called dismal, he gets an idea of what the word *dismal* means. But what does the user of the OED know about "the Social Science . . . which finds the secret of the Universe in 'supply and demand'" (Carlyle at this point has not mentioned economics) that helps him to understand the word *dismal*? Probably very little.

But to return to Carlyle, who coined the term *dismal science*, as applied to what was then called "political economy," the term *economics* not then being in use. Carlyle first reacted against the economics of Thomas Malthus, to which he applied the adjective *dismal* but not yet with the noun *science*. Malthus held that wages would be forced down to a subsistence level because the supply of food could not keep up with the growth of the population unless the increase of population was restrained by poverty (or war or pestilence). In later editions of his work, he allowed for the possibility that this fate could be avoided if people practiced abstinence.

Today, we would say that the Malthusian theory was wrong— that it was bad science. It did not take into account the potential of technological advance to accelerate the production of food and to hold down the rate of population growth by means other than abstinence. But that was not the essence of Carlyle's disagreement with Malthus. It was not so much that he denied the truth of Malthus's message as that he disliked it; he did not like the picture it gave of man's motivation and behavior. He thought Malthus's picture was dark and cheerless, which is why it was dismal, but that did not necessarily mean that the picture was inaccurate.

Carlyle's main fury was not against Malthus, however, but against the classical economists of his time—David Ricardo, James Mill, McCulloch, and, in his early stages, John Stuart Mill. Exactly what the classical economists meant is even now a subject of study and disagreement among experts. But as popularly understood in Carlyle's time, their description of society ran essentially like this:

> All individuals are motivated by the desire to maximize their private incomes, and all relations among persons are governed by the effort to achieve that. Individuals know

better than anyone else how to use the resources they have, and if they could freely exchange with others, they would all reach the best possible results for the volume of production, the composition of production, the methods of production, and relative prices. Accordingly, the proper policy is "laissez faire"; the government should not intervene in economic affairs.

Carlyle disliked all these propositions. I use the word *disliked* here purposefully. He did not try to disprove the propositions of the political economists, either by logic or by empirical evidence. He often pointed to the misery in which people lived in England and, even worse, in Ireland. But a modern economist would dismiss that as "casual empiricism." He adduced no statistics; in fact, he was contemptuous of statistics. Carlyle described the economists' propositions in his own terms to show how much he disliked them and to cause his readers to dislike them as well. He was saying that if all personal relations are governed by the "cash nexus," if all people are "nomads," wandering from place to place in search of money-making opportunities, without attachment to any other person, that is a very dreary picture of life.

Carlyle's style of talking about political economy clearly reveals that he is making an aesthetic or moral judgment, not a scientific one. A good example is in his 1850 essay, "The Present Time." In the guise of a fictional speech by a fictional prime minister about what we would now call "welfare reform," he addresses economists as follows:

Respectable professors of the Dismal Science, soft you a while. Alas, I know what you would say. For my sins, I have read much in those inimitable volumes of yours,—really, I should think, some barrowfuls of them in my time,—and, in these last forty years of theory and practice, have pretty well seized what of Divine Message you were sent with to me. Perhaps as small a message, give me leave to say, as ever there was such a noise made about before. Trust me, I have not forgotten it, shall never forget it. Those Laws of the Shop-till are indisputable to me; and practically useful in certain departments of the Universe, as the multiplication table itself. Once I even tried to sail through the Immensities with them and to front the big coming Eternities with them; but I found it would

not do. As the Supreme Rule of Statesmanship, or Government of Men,—since this Universe is not wholly a
Shop—no. . . . By the side of the shop-till,—see your
small "Law of God" is hung up, along with the multiplication
table itself. But beyond and above the shop-till, allow me
to say, you shall as good as hold your peace.

This is not the language in which one discusses a science and
tries to test it by reference to objective facts. Indeed, reading
Carlyle, one is more puzzled by his calling political economy a science
than by calling it dismal. He treats political economy as a work of
art, of literature, about which the point is not whether it is true or
not but whether it is beautiful or not, inspiring or not, moral or not.
He does not deny that economics has validity and utility in a limited
range of human affairs. But in his view, if economics were all there
is, it would be too ugly a world to contemplate.

Perhaps Carlyle was justified in treating the economics of his
time (I say nothing about ours) as a "story" made up in the
imagination of a few people. The authors of the story presented it
as the logical deduction from a few assumptions, but neither the
assumptions nor the deduction had been tested for conformity to the
facts. As Nassau Senior, one of them, said, "Political economy is not
greedy of facts; it is independent of facts." So Carlyle could look at
the story and declare that it was ugly, or "dismal," without having to
adduce any facts.

Carlyle's attitude to economics was like the attitude of many
Victorians, and even of some of our contemporaries, to Darwin's
theory of evolution. They rejected the theory, not on the basis of
any contradictory facts, but because they did not like to think of
themselves as descended from monkeys or "worse." Just so, Carlyle
rejected economics because he did not like to think of himself as
having the motivation and morality of a shopkeeper. Of course,
Darwin had more evidence than the classical economists, but that is
not the point.

The later reaction to Freudian psychology was similar. People
rejected it because they did not like the story it told about human
behavior, presumably including their own. It is interesting that after
Freud failed to win a Nobel Prize for medicine, many of his supporters thought that he should be awarded a Nobel Prize in literature. In
that case, his writings would have been judged not on the basis of
their truth but on some aesthetic or stylistic standard.

Carlyle may have misunderstood the story that the classical economists were telling. He interpreted them as claiming that "profit maximizing" or "utility maximizing" was the general and universal law of human behavior, whereas they might have been saying that these motivations ruled only in a limited sphere, a proposition that he would have accepted. Alfred Marshall, one of the giants of economics, made this point in his *Principles of Economics* in 1890:

> Thus though it is true that "money" or "general purchasing power," or "command over material wealth," is the centre around which economic science clusters; this is so, not because money or material wealth is regarded as the main aim of human effort, nor even as affording the main subject-matter for the study of the economist, but because in this world of ours it is the one convenient means of measuring human motive on a large scale. If the older economists had made this clear, they would have escaped many grievous misrepresentations; and the splendid teachings of Carlyle and Ruskin as to the right aims of human endeavor and the right uses of wealth, would not then have been marred by bitter attacks on economics, based on the mistaken belief that science had no concern for any motive except the selfish desire for wealth, or even that it inculcated a policy of sordid selfishness (p. 22, 5th ed.).

So we may leave Thomas Carlyle as having made an unscientific judgment about an unscientific story that he misunderstood and that its authors may have misunderstood also.

Today's Meaning of the "Dismal Science"

What do people mean today when they call economics the "dismal science"? One obvious answer, although an incorrect one, is that they find economics "dull." This is reflected in the old chestnut about an economist being a person who is good with figures but lacks the charisma to be an accountant. We have to distinguish again between economics in the sense of the economy or economic conditions as a subject, on the one hand, and economics as the study of that subject and writing and talking about it on the other hand. People do not find the subject itself dull. When they say that economics is dull, they are referring to the writing and talking about it.

"Dull" is not the same as "dismal." One might receive a report from his doctor that would be quite dismal but that would not be dull at all. When President Nixon swore in Paul McCracken, Hendrick Houthakker, and me as members of his Council of Economic Advisers, on February 4, 1969, he said:

> I have been reminded over and over again that as economists they are part of the dismal science. I can say it may be a dismal science, but from the reports I have been receiving [from them], it is not a dull science by any manner of means.

Still, if dull is not the same as dismal, there is a certain connection between the two ideas, and sometimes economics may be called dismal when what is meant is that it is dull. So it is worth speculating on why economics is considered dull.

Is Economics Dull?

Probably, most people consider the talk and writing of economists dull most of the time, just as most laymen consider most of the talk and writing of other scientists dull. And it is not just sciences of which that is true. I find cricket dull, for example, whether seen on television or written about in the newspapers. I do not know the rules or the language or the history. Economics has a language, a set of theories, and a history of its own, and listening to or reading a discussion of economics if these ingredients are unknown must make it very dull. (I can testify to that, because I find most economic writing in journals taxing beyond hope of profit, and therefore dull.)

Not all writing or talking about economics is equally dull. But as it happens, the discussion of economics that laymen find least dull also has the least economics in it and the most of something else—politics or soothsaying.

But why do people consider economics "the" dull, or dismal, science when they do not apply the same adjective to physics or chemistry or astronomy? It is probably not that they understand these other sciences better but that they concede to them the right to their own language and system of discourse, which they do not expect to understand, but do not make the same concession to economics. They believe that economics deals with subjects that lay people, noneconomists, are quite familiar with, and that they are entitled to have the economist speak to them in a way that they find not only understandable but also interesting. They have a similar attitude toward sociology, political science, psychology, and literary criticism. A person who had read a Shakespeare play in high school and thought that he understood it and loved it would find a modern academic analysis of that play dull, impertinent, and irritating. An economist might say that the dullness of which he is accused is in the eye of the beholder. As Henry Kissinger said, after he reached a high level of self-confidence, if his dinner partner found him boring, it must have been the fault of the dinner partner.

But to say that economics is the dismal science is to say something more than that it is dull or boring. One might think that people would have changed their opinion about economics after 150 years of great economic progress since the time Carlyle was writing. But people do not give economists credit for that progress. If asked what men deserve credit for the great increase in output per capita, some people would mention James Watt or John Deere or Henry Ford. Hardly any would mention Adam Smith or Alfred Marshall or Friedrich von Hayek. And economists are not in a good position to claim credit. In the economists' view of the world, everyone, including economists, acts to maximize his own interest, in which case no one deserves credit.

The Reputation of Economics

The basic problem that people have with economics, I think, is that it deals with scarcity, a condition in which wants are unlimited and the resources to satisfy those wants are limited. That is not by itself sufficient to make economics dismal. Medicine, after all, deals with morbidity and mortality, but that does not make medicine a dismal science. Medicine is seen as a science that seeks to improve adaptation to the facts of morbidity and mortality by curing illnesses and prolonging life. If economics is a science that seeks to improve adaptation to scarcity by achieving the most and best use of the limited resources, no one would call it dismal. But that is not the picture of economics that people have.

Economics has a reputation, with some reason, for saying that nothing can be done or should be done. Whether that should be considered a dismal state of affairs is probably a matter of taste. One of economists' favorite stories about themselves is of two men, one an economist and one not, walking along a street together. The noneconomist says, "Look, there's a twenty dollar bill lying on the sidewalk!" The economist replies, "No, there can't be. If there had been, it would already have been picked up." The economist's model of the world is that all beneficial adjustments have already been made, because people are motivated to take all actions that are beneficial to themselves. This can be considered an optimistic view because it means that no one has lost twenty dollars, or if someone has, it has not remained lost; it can be regarded as a dismal view because it means that no one has a chance of finding twenty dollars. More generally, it can be considered an optimistic view because things are as good as they can be; it can be considered a dismal view because things cannot be any better.

A related proposition about economics is that "there is no free lunch." (As applied to economics, this law is attributed to Milton Friedman, although as applied to saloons it obviously has an earlier source.) While this is sometimes taken as a dismal statement, it may be considered optimistic in the sense that no free lunch has gone uneaten: that is, no opportunities have been wasted. Moreover, it does not deny the possibility that some lunches, though not free, are worth paying for.

"Dismal" Views of the World

Different economists at different times have espoused four different views of the world that may be rated on the "dismalness" scale:

• *The textbook version of classical economics.* The real world conforms to the ideal picture of an economic system in which there are perfect competition and perfect information and in which natural private forces lead to the best possible volume and composition of output, produced by the most efficient methods, and to the best possible distribution of the resulting income among the population. Since everything is already as good as it can be, there is nothing to be done.

• *The positive program for laissez faire.* The real world does not match this ideal picture. Competition is not perfect, information is not complete, the system is subject to fluctuations in total output and to involuntary unemployment, private decisions may not be optimum because individuals do not have incentives to take account of all the consequences of their actions, and the distribution of income may be "unjust" or "unlovely." These conditions could be corrected in part by government policy.

• *The negative program for laissez faire.* The real world would conform to the ideal picture to a satisfactory degree if the government did not intervene but departs substantially from the ideal picture because of unwise government policies. Although competition would not be perfect, effective competition would emerge if government did not create or protect monopolies. Private forces would generate all the information that is worth its cost to produce. Contracting among private parties would lead to all relevant consequences of actions being considered. The market would develop a stable monetary standard that would lead to reasonable economic stability. The distribution of income would be fair in the sense that people got the income they earned and that no different meaning of fairness can be objectively determined.

This view leaves a great deal of room for improving conditions by government action, but all the required action is negative. The government can improve conditions by ceasing to protect monopoly, to regulate the market, to manipulate the currency, and to interfere with the distribution of income.

• *The hopeless government.* Although in theory the government could improve conditions by positive or negative action, in practice that is not possible. The government is not a *deus ex machina* that can be called on to correct deficiencies in the real world. The government is part of the real world, and the people in the government who make decisions are motivated by the same desire to maximize their private welfare. Presumably, their policies already reflect this motivation, and they cannot be expected to behave differently just because they are told that different behavior would improve conditions in the society at large. In this view, as in the first, there is nothing to be done.

The first view seems to be highly optimistic. Many people would say, of course, that it is also highly unrealistic. But even if it were a picture of the real world, some people would find that real world a rather dismal one. The economists' optimum depicted there is the optimum output possible given the initial distribution of resources (ability to earn income) and the wants that human beings have. But nothing can be said in favor of the initial distribution of resources except that it is what it is. And it has been pointed out, for example, by Frank H. Knight, that what people want is not just the satisfaction of their wants but better wants; and the economists' optimum says nothing about the quality of wants or about their development.

The fourth view is a picture of a world that is unrelievedly dismal: it is a world in which things are as they are, and nothing can be done about it. And however satisfactory that world might be in many respects, it would be a dismal world in which there was no point in striving, in trying to make it better.

But the second and third views are optimistic. They picture a world in which, speaking of the American case at least, conditions are good but in which there is a possibility of making them better by public policy. People will differ about whether the required public policy would be positive—increasing the role of government—or negative. Perhaps a reasonable answer is that the proper policy would be some of both, positive with respect to some aspects of the economy and negative with respect to others. But either view offers something to think about, argue about, and do.

Perhaps the last word on this subject belongs to Marshall's comment on Carlyle. The world depicted by economics would be dismal if indeed that was all there were to life, but it isn't. A comment of Keynes is relevant here:

> But, chiefly, do not let us overestimate the importance of the economic problem, or sacrifice to its supposed necessities other matters of greater and more permanent significance. It should be a matter for specialists—like dentistry. If economists could manage to get themselves thought of as humble, competent people, on a level with dentists, that would be splendid![2]

That estimation of their science would be disappointing to economists. I doubt that Keynes would have been happy if he thought that he would be considered on a par with a dentist. But with so modest a claim, the science could not fairly be called dismal. *(November 1992)*

---

2. John Maynard Keynes, "Economic Possibilities for Our Grandchildren," *Essays in Persuasion*, vol. 9 of *The Collected Works of J. M. Keynes* (New York: Macmillan, 1972), p. 332.

29

Economics in Washington—Fifty-five Years Ago

In 1938, if you were a young economist who had passed his written examinations but not yet written his doctoral thesis, you came to Washington. You did not have the money to stay at the university while you wrote the thesis, and you would have had difficulty finding a job anywhere else, especially without your Ph.D. Of course, you did not expect to spend the rest of your life in Washington. You would work at a job there and write your thesis in the evenings and on weekends. Then, having obtained your degree, you would become an economist like the only economists you actually knew, your professors.

So I came to Washington in 1938, and fifty-five years later I am still here. I would say that I had spent fifty-five years inside the Beltway, but there was no Beltway when I came. But I did spend almost all my professional life inside Washington's first taxi zone.

Washington in 1938

Washington in 1938 was in an early stage of development as far as economics was concerned. It was not that the number of economists in the federal government was small: there had already been a considerable influx since the arrival of Franklin Roosevelt five years earlier. I estimated later that there were about 4,000 federal economists in Washington when I arrived. Today, while the number is probably four times as large, it has not increased much more than the size of the total labor force, proportionately, and has increased much less than the size of the federal government, as measured by expenditures adjusted for inflation.

Although their numbers were already large, federal government economists had not achieved the prominence, either in policy making or in public perception, that they were later to achieve. Moreover, the large crust of nonfederal economics that was to develop later around the federal establishment had not yet emerged.

In 1938, no economist had yet been in the Cabinet or served as chairman of the Federal Reserve: that would not come for thirty-one years, until the Nixon administration. No economist had yet been director of the Bureau of the Budget: that would come in 1961, in the Kennedy administration. There was no Council of Economic Advisers to the president: that was not so far away—in 1946.

The most important economist in Washington was Lauchlin Currie, at the Federal Reserve. At that point, in 1938, he was advising the chairman of the Federal Reserve, Marriner Eccles, a banker open to economics and with access to Roosevelt. Another big name at the time was Harry D. White, director of the Division of Monetary Research at the Treasury, but he and his office concentrated on international monetary affairs and did not get involved in the central issues of domestic economic policy. (Notably, after World War II both White and Currie were accused of Communist connections. White died of a heart attack while being investigated, and Currie emigrated to Colombia. Whatever the validity of these charges, no one ever accused them of trying to subvert U.S. economic policy in a Communist or "leftish" direction, and that was also true of other, less prominent economists similarly accused of Communist associations.)

The Bureau of the Budget, which would later be a center of macroeconomic thinking, was still a part of the Treasury and still populated by accountants.

Able economists worked in some of the agencies—Isadore Lubin at the Bureau of Labor Statistics, Robert Nathan at the Department of Commerce, Mordecai Ezekiel at the Bureau of Agricultural Economics, and Raymond Goldsmith at the Securities and Exchange Commission, for example. Some of them later became important in policy making, but at the time of my arrival, 1938, their role was indirect and limited. Congress did not employ any economists; staff positions that might later be filled by economists were filled by lawyers.

In 1938, there were no economist media stars in Washington. For one thing, no economists were prominent enough on the Washington scene to make them prominent on the national scene. But also there were no media to make stars of them. Of course, there were no TV talk shows, but the only radio talk show I remember from the time was the "University of Chicago Round Table," which sometimes included economists but mainly ones from the University of Chicago faculty. No economists regularly wrote for Op-Ed pages. In fact, I don't think there were any Op-Ed pages. More important, there were no economic journalists. Washington affairs were covered by political reporters. Business reporters worked mainly in New York and covered the financial markets and company news. No writers for the daily press or magazines were economists, whether academically trained or self-taught. No corps of journalists telephoned their lists of economists every day for quotations and wrote about economic conditions or policy in terms that economists would use.

Only one important trade association—the Chamber of Commerce of the United States—was located in Washington, and it did not have an economist on its staff. Most trade associations were in New York or in the home city of their industry, as the American Iron and Steel Institute was in Pittsburgh. There were no private economic consultants to guide businesses in their dealings with government. The big international agencies, like the International Monetary Fund and the World Bank, which were later to employ many hundreds of economists, did not exist.

The universities of the Washington, D.C., area were of low caliber in economics except to the extent that some of the economists in government supplemented their earnings and experience by giving courses at American University or George Washington University in the evening. Probably the main source of education in economics was the Department of Agriculture, which gave some advanced courses, especially in statistics. Some of that work at the Department of Agriculture would have a big payoff in the development of key statistics, such as the unemployment figures, through scientific sampling statistics. But that was still a little bit over the horizon.

The term *think tank* was still unknown. Whatever we called it then, only one of them was located in Washington: the Brookings Institution, successor to a private, nonprofit research institution established in 1916. In the early days of the depression, Brookings had done useful work in trying to evaluate what had gone wrong. But by the time I arrived, its writing was quite outside the stream of effective discussion and rabidly anti–New Deal, for a reason that is even now not clear to me.

The president of Brookings was Harold Moulton. I had encountered him a few years earlier when he gave a seminar on the causes of the depression at the University of Chicago. His explanation was that people did not spend all their income. But he could not answer the students' questions about what happened to the income that people did not spend. Within a few months, of course, Keynes would answer that question simply and definitively: people in the aggregate would not earn more income than was spent for the purchase of their product, so there could be no excess of income over expenditures. If people in the aggregate *tried* to spend less than their incomes, incomes would fall to a level at which they would spend all their income.

Although Brookings research did not have much standing— except possibly with some Republicans in Congress—the institution did serve as a meeting place for economists. The man for whom I worked, Homer Jones, was a former fellow of Brookings and had lunch privileges there. Frequently, I would walk with him from our offices to the Brookings Building on the west side of Lafayette Square. The chef prided herself on not serving the same lunch twice in 365 days. But if you did not like the lunch of the day, you could have skinless and boneless Portuguese sardines, which became a staple of my diet. A group of younger economists could be found in the dining room there, while Moulton and some of his older cronies ate apart in a private room.

Brookings held economics seminars in the evening, perhaps one a month, which I attended. Jones once prevailed on me to give a seminar on the thesis I was planning to write, on the absurdly ambitious subject of the relation of wage rates to unemployment. I soon found myself attacked and overwhelmed by a visiting economist from Harvard who knew enormously more mathematics and somewhat more economics than I did. The experience left me with an abiding allergy to mathematical economics.

Washington in 1938 was a great place for economics and economists, because of the combination of two conditions. First, the economic problem had become clear: it was to achieve and maintain "full employment," although we did not use that term. Second, we knew the solution to the problem: Keynesianism.

By 1937, the year before I came, the period of the main New Deal structural "reforms," or changes, to use a more neutral term, was over. Social security, unemployment compensation, the minimum wage, the National Labor Relations Act, federal deposit insurance, and farm price support programs were all in place. The United States had gone off the gold standard, and control of the Federal Reserve System had been placed more definitely in Washington. The Reciprocal Trade Agreements program had been adopted. The income tax had been raised and made more progressive. Roosevelt seemed to have nothing more in mind, and Congress seemed in no mood to give him more if he asked for it.

Moreover, in 1937 it had seemed that recovery was complete. At least, total output had apparently regained the 1929 level. There were no gross national product or gross domestic product figures then, in either nominal or real terms. But we did have national income estimates in nominal terms, and although there was no entirely satisfactory way of converting them into real amounts of total output, the available figures on consumer and wholesale prices suggested that real output was as high in 1937 as it had been in 1929. Nothing we have learned since contradicts that judgment.

But while recovery, as many thought of it then, was complete, there was still a lot of unemployment. We did not know how much, because there were no good unemployment statistics, but the number was evidently large. (Later estimates suggest that unemployment in 1937 was about 14 percent of the labor force.) So the situation was puzzling to many people. They felt like a person assembling a watch who has followed all the printed instructions but had some parts left over and a watch that didn't run.

And just as the recovery seemed to have been achieved, the country fell into an exceptionally steep recession, beginning in August 1937. The recession ended quite clearly in June 1938, the month when I began work in Washington, but it was a sharp reminder of the continued vulnerability of the economy to serious contraction. So the dominant problem was how to achieve and maintain full employment.

Keynes's General Theory

For most of the economists working in Washington, the key to the solution of that problem, or at least part of the key, was derived from J. M. Keynes. Keynes's *The General Theory of Employment, Interest and Money* had been published in December 1936, a year and a half before I began work in Washington. In that period, Keynes's theory and prescription had swept through the profession like wildfire. There surely has been nothing else like it in the history of economics.

Aside from the little nest at Brookings, we were all Keynesians in some degree. As a contemporary of mine at Chicago, Albert Hart, had said, one could be pro-Keynesian or anti-Keynesian, but one could no longer be pre-Keynesian. That is, one could not get away from some simple Keynesian arithmetic, such as that income equals expenditure, savings equal investment, and total expenditure consists partly of an exogenous element, determined outside the system, and an endogenous element, determined by income. The exogenous expenditure is investment plus government expenditures, and the endogenous expenditure is consumption. By controlling the exogenous expenditures, which included government expenditures, one could control total expenditure, and that in turn would control total employment.

Paul Samuelson later described the feeling of his fellow graduate students on first encountering *The General Theory* in Wordsworth's gush: "Bliss was it in that dawn to be alive, but to be young was very heaven." Samuelson said that he did not initially share that rapture, but he surely had his epiphany not long after. Those who shared that reaction in the years around 1938 were to ride on a wave of growing self-confidence, esteem, and influence for economists that would go on for almost thirty years.

Although I became accustomed to thinking in the Keynesian terms, my reaction, mirroring that of my professors at Chicago, was less starry-eyed. My professors were inclined to say of *The General Theory* that what was true was not new and what was new was not true. They maintained, with evidence, that the simple prescription of running budget deficits in a time of depression had been known and advocated by them as early as 1931. But they did not accept the notion that continuous high unemployment could be a condition of equilibrium. They did not accept the downgrading of the effectiveness of monetary policy that most readers found in *The General Theory*. And they worried that an all-out application of the Keynesian prescription to produce full employment would cause persistent inflation. As my professor, Jacob Viner, put it, the Keynesian policy could degenerate into "a race between the printing press and the trade unions," as the commitment to full employment would remove any restraint on wage increases. Monetary policy, the "printing press," would have to generate enough inflation to make the labor force employable at the rising wage rates.

All these skeptical views were mother's milk to me. But they were basically academic qualifications that were not, or not yet, of practical importance. And, of course, these reservations that I brought with me from Chicago were of no historical significance, since I was very young, very junior, and employed in an agency remote from the making of macroeconomic policy. In fact, the Division of Research and Statistics of the Federal Deposit Insurance Corporation, where I worked, turned out to be an early seedbed of monetarism. One of my older colleagues, Clark Warburton, produced the first consistent, long-term estimates of the money supply in the United States and later used those estimates to demonstrate the close connection between the money supply and the price level. And my own boss, Homer Jones, would later be the research director of the Federal Reserve Bank of St. Louis and in that capacity do more than anyone other than Milton Friedman to explain and promote monetarism.

Toward Keynesian Policy

But the tide was clearly running in a more purely Keynesian direction. Indeed, although I did not appreciate it at the time, the president had already taken what I later described as the decisive step toward Keynesian policy.

Roosevelt had faced the question of what to do about the recession that began in August 1937. On November 8, Harry Hopkins, who was FDR's confidant and frequent intermediary between the president and economists, brought Currie, Lubin, and Leon Henderson (who was a consultant to Hopkins at the Works Progress Administration) to see the president. They gave him a memo urging an increase in federal spending to reverse the recession. But he was unimpressed by the economists' argument. He preferred to stay with the advice of his Treasury secretary, Henry Morgenthau, to try to balance the budget and restore the confidence of businessmen.

FDR did not seem to have much understanding of economists or interest in them. On a famous occasion in June 1934, Keynes visited President Roosevelt. Keynes is believed to have been an admirer of Roosevelt, but after the visit, he said that he had "supposed the President to be more literate, economically speaking." The president said of Keynes: "He left a whole rigmarole of figures. He must be a mathematician rather than a political economist."

But by the spring of 1938, the president was more ripe for the arguments of his Keynesian economists. His stance of balancing the budget had neither slowed the recession nor won any accolades from the business community. While Roosevelt was vacationing in Warm Springs, Georgia, the stock market took what Morgenthau called "another sickening dip." Hopkins called Aubrey Williams, his deputy at WPA, and Henderson to come down to Georgia to help him in persuading FDR to change course. By serendipity, they were joined there by Beardsley Ruml, who was then the treasurer of Macy's Department Stores.

For today's readers, the entry of the treasurer of Macy's into this story may be a puzzle. But Ruml, whom I did not know in 1938 but with whom I worked for many years after the war at the Committee for Economic Development, was a most remarkable person. He had been trained as a psychologist and then became dean of the social sciences at the University of Chicago. How he got to Macy's, or what he did there, I do not know. He had an extraordinary capacity to see a problem both objectively and subjectively. That is, he understood what the problem really was and also how the problem looked to others and how it could be explained to others so that they would share his view of the solution. He was well known and appreciated in business, political, and intellectual circles. Leon Henderson was probably his main connection to the group meeting in Georgia to work on Roosevelt.

With the help of the others, he wrote a memo to the president that even now is amazing for its insights. He offered estimates of the existing level of national income and of the level that would be required to achieve full employment. This gave the size of what we would now call the gap, and he estimated how much government spending would be required to fill the gap, after allowance for the increase in private investment that might be expected. Then, in an argument that no one but Ruml would have made, he provided a bird's-eye view of American history to show how what he proposed fit into a tradition that Roosevelt would want to be part of. He said that the economic growth of the country had been made possible by the "alienation"—that is, conversion into private purchasing power—of various national assets. First, it had been gold; then it had been land; then it had been franchises—rights to engage in certain kinds of business. Now another national asset, expected future tax revenue, should be converted into present purchasing power by running a deficit.

Whether it was this argument that converted FDR, or whether he simply had no where else to turn, I do not know. But on April 14, 1938, the president announced his new spending program in a fireside chat and used some language reminiscent of Ruml's memo. In a history of fiscal policy that I wrote thirty years later, I described this as a decisive turn—the first spending program explained in terms of its indirect effects on the aggregate economy rather than in terms of the jobs it would create for particular workers on particular projects. In June 1938, Congress created the Temporary National Economic Committee (TNEC) to investigate what was wrong with the economy and how to get it moving. Although that was probably not the intent, the TNEC turned out to be a major platform for the propagation of Keynes's ideas in the next two years, before we were diverted by war economics. The TNEC also proved to be a source of a free, five-foot shelf of books about the economy that constituted the basic library of every impecunious economist in Washington.

What was going on in the White House or in Roosevelt's vacation home in Warm Springs, Georgia, was of course not known to the economists of my generation. But we knew that Washington was alive with the sound of economics, and, supplied with the lessons we brought from Chicago or Harvard or Columbia or Wisconsin, we were confident of our ability to participate in the chorus. Sometimes I think that economists in Washington in 1938 were like the young Americans who went to Paris in the 1920s to bathe in the world of art and literature. It was a wonderful time for us, perhaps mainly because we were young but also because economics as a specialized tool of public policy was also young and self-confident. *(March 1993)*

30

Remembering Adam Smith

F rom the day it was published, March 9, 1776, *The Wealth of Nations* was a big hit. But its author, Adam Smith, is probably more popular now than ever before—known to more people with more approbation. Throughout the world, the wigged head of Adam Smith has replaced the bearded face of Karl Marx as the symbol of the beneficent revolution.

But I have a feeling that few of his fans have read *The Wealth of Nations* and that even fewer have read it recently. I suspect this to be true even of those who wear the Adam Smith necktie as a sign that they are CPC—Conservatively Politically Correct.

I had not read *The Wealth of Nations* since I was a student in 1936 until recently when a book discussion group of which I am a member assigned itself some chapters. I then had occasion to read several hundred pages along with expert commentary by Jacob Viner, Joseph Schumpeter, and Andrew Skinner. The experience was fascinating. I venture to pass on a few observations here to remind some of what they read long ago and to encourage others to dip into it for the first time.

The Everyman edition, which I used as a student, had quite legible type fifty-eight years ago, but although I have the same two little volumes, the size of the type has shrunk terribly. Fortunately, the University of Chicago Press has published a new edition with type large enough for adult eyes.

Why Read Adam Smith?

Why should one recall Smith today? We should do it for the same reason that we should visit Monticello, the home of his younger

contemporary, Thomas Jefferson. One doesn't visit Monticello looking for a place to live: it isn't for rent. Moreover, one wouldn't want
to live at Monticello. There is no air conditioning, the kitchen is too
far from the dining room, and too many servants would be required.
We visit Monticello to marvel at what the human mind can do to
combine beauty with utility. And we visit it to see a model not of a
house but of how to think about building a house.

We don't read Adam Smith today to learn economic theory. One
can learn that better and easier from any sophomore economics
textbook. Neither do we read him today to learn about economic life
in eighteenth-century Britain. One could learn that, but few of us
care very much about it.

I believe that we read Smith today to marvel at the genius with
which *The Wealth of Nations* was produced. And we read him as a
model of how to think about the role of government in a free
exchange economy.

The first thing that impressed me in reading Smith now was
what a good writer he was. He was, among other things, a professor
of rhetoric. That by itself is no guarantee of good writing—perhaps
more the contrary. But Smith had an interest in writing, he wanted
to communicate clearly and attractively, and he succeeded.

Starting the treatise with the simple, homely description of the
pin factory was a brilliant stroke. At first, one wonders what that is
doing there. But then it becomes clear that he is leading us to
understand and appreciate the division of labor. And the division of
labor leads us inexorably to the idea of exchange as the natural and
efficient way to organize an economy. At that point, the battle is half
over; the rest is drawing out the implications of the fact that a
modern economy is an exchange system.

Smith was a well-organized writer; he knew what he was doing
and where he was going. At the end of book 1, chapter 4, after
listing three subjects he would discuss, he wrote:

> I shall endeavor to explain, as fully and distinctly as I can,
> those three subjects in the three following chapters, for
> which I must very earnestly entreat both the patience and
> attention of the reader: his patience in order to examine a
> detail which may in some places appear unnecessarily
> tedious; and his attention in order to understand what may,
> perhaps, after the fullest explication which I am capable of
> giving to it, appear still in some degree obscure. I am

always willing to run some hazard of being tedious in order to be sure that I am perspicuous; and after taking the utmost pains that I can to be perspicuous, some obscurity may still appear to remain upon a subject in its own nature extremely abstracted. [In my student text, I wrote in the margin next to this paragraph, "Wonderful," and I still find it wonderful.]

There are tedious passages, and I wish that the British had gone onto the decimal system of currency 300 years ago, so we would be spared the business of guineas and pounds, shillings and pence. But the reader can usually tell when he is approaching one of those deserts and can skirt around without much loss.

The Wealth of Nations is full of well-crafted sentences. The most famous is probably: "It is not from the benevolence of the butcher, the brewer, or the baker, that we expect our dinner, but from their regard to their own interest." That is an acute perception. But notice also the alliteration of the *b*'s at the beginning, the homely appeal to getting our dinner (rather than maximizing gross domestic product, as we might say), and the sting in the tail of the sentence.

Smith rarely uses the pronoun *I*, but his personality comes through, and it is surprising. We tend to think of him as an absent-minded, Scottish professor who led a secluded existence, living with his mother all his life until she died when he was sixty-one. But what we see in *The Wealth of Nations* is a worldly, skeptical, witty man. The book is full of sarcasm—about businessmen, politicians, professors, and clergymen. He doesn't even glamorize the common man, whom he tends to regard as pretty stupid. All of that is pleasant to a reader who does not consider himself to fall into any of those categories.

The Real Adam Smith

But the people who wear the Adam Smith tie are not doing so to honor literary genius but to make a statement of their devotion to the idea of free markets and limited government. What stands out in *The Wealth of Nations,* however, is that their patron saint was not pure or doctrinaire about this idea. He viewed government intervention in the market with great skepticism. He regarded his exposition of the virtues of the free market as his main contribution to policy and the purpose for which his economic analysis was developed. Yet he was prepared to accept or propose qualifications to that policy in the specific cases where he judged that their net effect would be beneficial and would not undermine the basically free character of the system. He did not wear the Adam Smith necktie.

These cases were numerous, and some of them are unexpected. I give here a list, certainly incomplete, largely derived from Viner's article on Smith written for the sequicentennial of *The Wealth of Nations*. The comments in parentheses are mine. The government could legitimately do the following:

- protect the merchant marine and give bounties to defense-related manufacturing industries
- punish, and take steps to prevent, dishonesty, violence, and fraud. (Does this include the Securities and Exchange Commission, and would prevention of violence justify measures to assist ghetto youth?)
- establish indicators of quality of goods, such as the sterling mark for silver. (Does this justify the Food and Drug Administration, the Federal Trade Commission, and the Consumer Products Safety Commission?)
- require employers to pay wages in cash rather than in kind. (Could the government conversely require employers to pay part of wages in the form of health benefits?)
- regulate banking
- provide public goods, such as highways, harbors, bridges, and canals. (What about railways, airlines?)
- run the post office. (Also telephone, telegraph?)
- grant patents and copyrights
- give a temporary monopoly to a trading company developing commerce in new and risky regions. (Is this industrial policy, managed trade?)
- require children to have a certain level of education
- provide protection against communicable diseases
- require the streets to be kept clean. (Environmentalism?)
- set a ceiling in interest rates
- impose discriminatory taxation to deter improper or luxurious behavior

The point is not that all the items on Smith's list belong on our list today. Neither should we consider ourselves committing a sin if we decide to add some things to our list of qualifications on the free market that were not on his. There is nothing in Smith's list, for example, about government action to deal directly with poverty. The evidence is mixed on whether Smith deliberately meant to exclude such action or only neglected to include it.

Smith was prepared to look at the conditions of his time and make a judgment, reflecting a presumption against government intervention, about whether government action in particular cases was appropriate. His admirers do not have to accept his judgments, but they should accept the idea that such judgments have to be made. *(April 1994)*

31

Jacob Viner—Master of the "No School" School of Economics

Out of the TV endlessly squawking
Little men belittling
Others as little.

E lection campaigns can make one a cynic. It is good for the soul to think of some better people—people one has known or could have known who did something useful or admirable extremely well and were helpful to others. Recalling such people is a reminder that quality in the human race is not confined to a few untouchable stars. I think of one such now, Jacob Viner.[1]

Jacob Viner was a member of the economics faculty of the University of Chicago from 1916 to 1946, with a few interruptions. In 1946, he joined the faculty of Princeton, where he remained until his retirement. He died in 1970.

Viner was the greatest authority there has ever been on the history of economic thought. In his time, he was one of the world's two leading experts on international trade, the other being Gottfried Haberler, my colleague at the American Enterprise Institute. Viner was one of a handful of outstanding economic theorists in America and an exceptionally effective teacher, three of whose students later received the Nobel Prize in economics. I was one of hundreds of students who were terrified of him when young, who lived for years

---

1. For convenient access to Viner's thinking, see two collections of his essays, *The Long View and the Short* (1958) and *Essays on the Intellectual History of Economics* (1991).

229

on what they had learned in his classes, and who later were proud and delighted to have known him.

Viner's Independence

I do not have space here even to note his many achievements. I want to concentrate on one of his outstanding characteristics, which I recall from my own experience and can see vividly as I now review some of his writings: his fierce independence, his dogmatic nondogmatism, his resistance to being classified.

Viner served for almost ten years as adviser to a Democratic secretary of the Treasury, Henry Morgenthau, Jr. But I never knew, and do not now know, whether he was a Democrat or a Republican—something everyone knows about almost every leading economist today. For him, as for many other economists, Adam Smith was the great hero. He was the leading expositor of Smith's thoughts. But I cannot imagine his wearing the Adam Smith necktie. He was an admirer of Alfred Marshall and assigned Marshall's *Principles of Economics* as the text in his course. But when he wrote an appreciation of Marshall in 1940, on the fiftieth anniversary of the *Principles,* he said: "But Marshall is now long dead, and the rule 'De mortuis non nisi bonum' is a required rule of morals or of good manners only of men very recently dead. There would be no point, therefore, in treating Marshall, whether the man or his work, with special tenderness or reserve."

Viner evidently loved to tweak the audiences to which he spoke. Addressing the Chamber of Commerce of the United States he said:

> In my old-fashioned liberalism, there are no inherent rights for trade unions, but there are also no inherent rights for corporations. The trade union and the corporation are aggregates of economic and political power with no true attributes of personality. As such, like the state, they are all suspect of the true liberal.

And in his presidential address to the American Economic Association in 1939, reflecting on his experience as an adviser in government, he took down the professors a little:

> The higher officials in Washington, whether they be political appointees or career men, need make no apologies for their standards even to college professors, elect of the

elect though we be. As far as I have observed, the higher officials in Washington as a group work as hard, as disinterestedly, cooperate in common tasks as loyally, think as straight within their own special fields of competence, as does the ordinary run of college professor. They certainly do not live on the moral heights continuously, but they are called upon more often than academic men to rise to them, and, in my honest judgment, they respond to the call as often and as fully as in all probability we ourselves should under like circumstances.

In Viner's time, the words *liberal* and *conservative* were not used as freely as they are today. I do not know how he would be classified by today's standards. When he felt it necessary to define himself, he called himself an "old-fashioned liberal," meaning one who emphasizes the numerous values of freedom, but he was always alert to warn against doctrinaire and simplistic use of the term. At one point he describes himself as a "moderate liberal," meaning "a man with one foot firmly imbedded in the nineteenth century while the other gropes in the air for Utopia." That was not a club with many members or very fixed rules.

Viner, the Depression, and Keynes

The depression of the 1930s and J. M. Keynes's *The General Theory of Employment, Interest and Money* (1936) were great challenges to everything that economists of Viner's generation believed. Both were outside the range of their previous experience.

The economists of the time had not foreseen the depression, they had not recognized its severity as it was going on, and, at the time *The General Theory* came along in 1936, they had no convincing explanation for the depression and no agreed prescription for getting out of it. Then along came Keynes, blatantly rejecting what had been the common wisdom and proposing a new model with which both to explain and to solve the greatest economic catastrophe of modern times. The immediate result was to polarize the economics profession. To some, mainly the older economists, the whole thing was nonsense, subversive, and anyway they had known it all along. To others, mainly but not exclusively the young, Keynes was a great revelation, explaining everything and offering the way to cure everything.

Viner did not join either camp. His review of *The General Theory,* in the *Quarterly Journal of Economics,* was both highly complimentary and highly critical. He says,

> It [the book] brings much new light, but its display of dialectical skill is so overwhelming that it will probably have more persuasive power than it deserves, and a concentration on the points where I think I can detect defects in the argument, though it would be unfair if presented as an appraisal of the merits of the book as a whole, may be more useful than would a catalogue—which would have to be long to be complete—of its points of outstanding intellectual achievement.

There then follow eighteen closely argued pages of criticism of Keynes's fundamental theses.

From the standpoint of subsequent policy, Viner's most interesting point was the danger that Keynesian policy, followed rigorously, would be endlessly inflationary. In a famous statement, he said:

> In a world organized in accordance with Keynes' specifications there would be a constant race between the printing press and the business agents of the trade unions, with the problem of unemployment largely solved if the printing press could maintain a constant lead and if only volume of employment, irrespective of quality, is considered important.

Despite his criticisms, Viner retained his admiration for Keynes. Characteristically, he was contemptuous of the "Keynesians," the followers who were more Keynesian, more extreme and single-minded, than Keynes himself. In 1950, Viner reviewed a United Nations report by an international group of experts on ways to maintain full employment. The experts unanimously agreed on a simple, mechanical program consisting basically of the perpetual provision of whatever size of budget deficit government experts consider necessary to achieve whatever level of employment they consider "full." Viner said: "This capacity of economists to reach agreed and unqualified conclusions should, I suppose, be the occasion for professional congratulations and rejoicing. Instead, it brings a slight shudder to my spine." And I think the shudder is more for the unanimity than for the conclusions.

Viner and Chicago

Sometime during World War II, either in 1941 or in 1942, I met Jacob Viner by chance in Bassin's Delicatessen on Pennsylvania Avenue near Fourteenth Street in Washington, D.C. He was then giving advice at the Treasury, which was only about a block away. He asked me what I was doing. I replied that I was working at the Office of Price Administration and then added, gratuitously, "They don't have much use for the Chicago School there."

His reply was quick and strong: "Chicago School! Chicago School! What's that? I'm not a member of it."

I was later told by George Stigler, surely an authority, that the term *Chicago School* was not in use until after the end of World War II, and Viner himself later wrote that he did not begin to hear about it until after 1946. But the conversation has remained clear in my mind, and I am sure that I did not invent the term. Perhaps it was part of the underground vocabulary of students after Stigler left the university.

Whether the term was in use then, there was certainly something distinctive about the University of Chicago Department of Economics in the 1930s. The curriculum emphasized price theory and monetary theory more than other universities did. With respect to policy, there was a Chicago consensus. Main reliance was placed on competitive markets for the organization of the economy, but there was a major role for government to maintain competition, to moderate economic fluctuations by the active but limited use of monetary and fiscal policy, and to correct extremes in the distribution of income. Nothing I have ever learned from or about Viner, in the 1930s or since, makes me think that Viner was outside that consensus. His reaction against being considered a member of the "Chicago School" at that time was, I believe, more an expression of general aversion to being classified in any way, to giving up his uniqueness and independence, than to any substantive disagreement.

After the war, there was more substantive disagreement as Chicago changed but Viner did not. A key difference was over "monetarism," the view championed by Milton Friedman that the optimum monetary policy was steady increase of a measurable aggregate called "money." Constitutionally allergic to such rules, Viner believed they implied a degree of knowledge that no one could have. Moreover, he called all measurements of money "promiscuous aggregates."

A more general difference was Viner's unwillingness to follow the postwar Chicagoans in an increasingly sweeping and indiscriminate rejection of government action in the economy, including preserving competition and relieving poverty. Viner's reservations were expressed in the heart of the Chicago School, in 1959, when he delivered the Henry Simons memorial lecture at the university. (Simons, who had died at an early age in 1946, had been a professor at Chicago and a leading articulator of the prewar Chicago consensus described above.) Two quotations reveal both Viner's philosophy and his literary style:

- I would not dispute that even a monopoly-ridden market would be preferable to any economic system trying to operate without any kind of a market. But given the prevalence or the danger of substantial intrusion of monopoly into the market, the logic of the laissez faire defense of the market against state-intervention collapses and there is called for instead, by its very logic, state-suppression or state-regulation of monopoly practices, which one may wish to call, as Henry Simons called it, an instance of "positive laissez faire" or, as I prefer, as an instance of deliberate departure from laissez faire.

- A laissez faire program which confined its efforts to preserving or restoring a free market, even a competitive market, while remaining silent on or opposing any proposals for adopting new or retaining old measures in the field of distributive justice, would seem to me glaringly unrealistic with respect to its chances of political success, and also highly questionable with respect to more exalted criteria of merit.

Insistence on independence and uniqueness, if combined with ignorance, results in mere eccentricity. But when it is combined with good historical perspective, keen analysis, and sound judgment, it can be a stabilizing force against faddish oscillations in the economics profession and, indirectly, in national economic policy. That was Viner's case. *(March 1992)*

32

Memories of a Model Economist

E dward F. Denison died on October 23, 1992. He was, in my opinion, the best economist in Washington and one of the handful of best in the country. And yet, at a time when the names of many economists are almost household words, he was hardly known outside the economics profession. He wrote no Op-Ed page articles, he appeared on no talk shows, and he was not on the phone lists of economic journalists who every day round up the usual suspects to get a pithy quotation. The economists on those lists are almost all past, present, or expectant political officials, and they are quoted because their opinions are supposed to give some clue to political developments. Economic journalism should be faulted for paying so little attention to Ed Denison and a few other economists like him. Their readers would have been better informed if this knowledge had been tapped.

I write these few words about Denison partly because what he learned is important and partly because his life story may help brighten the common skeptical view of what economists do. Denison was devoted to the advancement of economic knowledge. I do not mean that he was a single-minded recluse. He was a man of wide interests, a most congenial friend, and helpful colleague. But in that part of his life that was economics, he did economics. He was not in politics and not in show business. I suppose that he was a registered Democrat, but that affiliation no more affected his economics than did his being a Chicago White Sox fan.

Denison's Contribution

Denison's great contribution to understanding the economy was that he launched, around 1960, the study of growth accounting and remained at the forefront of that study for the remaining thirty-two years of his life. He had done good work before that, at the Department of Commerce in the development of the national income accounts, but in retrospect that can be seen as warm-up and toolmaking for his study of economic growth. Moreover, important work on understanding growth had been done before him—the names of Simon Kuznets, Solomon Fabricant, and Robert Solow come to mind—but Denison's careful, comprehensive, and insightful approach opened up a whole new continent. In Denison's words,

> Growth accounting refers to allocation of growth rates of national output or output per person employed among the determinants of output that changed and caused growth; to allocation of international differences in output levels among the determinants responsible for level differences; to estimation of the size of the effect upon output of a given change in each output determinant; and to related estimates.

To paraphrase, growth accounting is an effort to estimate how much each of the factors that cause economic growth contributes to growth. Now that the rate of economic growth has become accepted as the key measure of economic performance, and accelerating it the main goal of economic policy, this subject is obviously of cardinal importance.

It may help to understand Denison's contribution to recount how he got into the subject. In 1957, Denison was on the research staff of the Committee for Economic Development (CED), an organization of businessmen. In that capacity, he had the assignment of doing the background research and preliminary drafting for a statement on economic growth that would be signed and issued by the members of the CED. The final form of the statement was determined by a subcommittee of which the chairman was Harry Scherman, founder of the Book-of-the-Month Club. Scherman was a man of intelligence, creativity, and concern for literary style, but, as he would have insisted, no economist.

The policy statement that emerged was well written and was illustrated by several attractive charts. It turned out to be one of

CED's most-read statements. But it did not satisfy Denison; in fact, it rather frustrated him. Substantively, the statement consisted of a list of disparate factors said to affect the rate of economic growth: some were on what we would now call the supply side and some on the demand side; some were inputs, like labor and capital; some were institutions, like markets; and some were psychological, like entrepreneurial spirit.

What Denison wanted to know, and explain to others, was *how* and *how much* each of these factors contributed to economic growth. And he wanted to answer these questions as far as possible by reference to the facts, not by a priori assumption, speculation, or determination to rationalize a preferred policy. With the support of CED, he began the research to find the answers.

He brought four things to this research:

• *Firm grasp of the economic theory of his time, which was essentially classical theory.*

• *Detailed knowledge of the sources, meaning, and limitations of all the data he used and extreme meticulousness in the use of data.* (He is, I believe, the only economist who, in the analysis of time series, took account of the fact that some years have more working days than others, to give a trivial example.)

• *Determination to define and measure the inputs into the production process as precisely as possible.* The case of labor, which is the biggest input, was especially important. He was not content to measure the labor input by man-hours. Here, following the lead of T. W. Shultz and others at the time who were pioneering the idea of "human capital," he paid a good deal of attention to estimating the value as production input of the education embodied in the labor force. He also wrestled with and offered a solution to the problem of measuring physical capital to take account of quality changes.

• *Imagination in creating and testing hypotheses to explain that proportion of output change that is not explained by change in the quantity of inputs.* That proportion, sometimes called the "residual," is what is meant by productivity change, that is, the change in output per unit of input.

The initial findings of Denison's CED study were first published in 1960 in an essay, "High Employment and Economic Growth in the American Economy," that he and I wrote as a background paper for the President's Commission on National Goals that had been established at the request of President Eisenhower. (Although we were co-authors and each endorsed every word, all the calculations about sources of past growth and the requirements for future growth were from Denison's study.) Denison's work was published by the CED in January 1962 under the title, "The Sources of Economic Growth in the United States and the Alternatives before Us." Later that year, he moved to the Brookings Institution, where he continued to cultivate and enrich the study of growth accounting and produced a number of notable books and articles. I think particularly of his work on comparative growth rates (*Why Growth Rates Differ: Postwar Experience in Nine Western Countries,* 1967) and the reasons for the slowdown in U.S. growth after 1973 (*Accounting for Slower Economic Growth: The United States in the 1970s,* 1979).

I shall not try to report the results of Denison's research except for a few very general points that have remained with me for a long time:

• The difference between 2 percent and 3 percent is not 1 percent but 50 percent. That, of course, is not the result of research—at least, not Denison's—but it is an often-neglected and important proposition that he emphasized. Its significance is that what seems a small increase in the growth rate—say, from 2 to 3 percent—is really a large increase. As a first approximation, such an increase in the growth rate would require an increase of 50 percent in all the resources, effort, and attention that went into generating the 2 percent growth rate.

• The contribution of education to economic growth turns out to be large, about as large or larger, depending on the period studied, as the contribution of investment in physical capital.

• Increases in the inputs of capital and labor, however broadly defined, account for only a little over half of economic growth over long periods of time. The remainder is described as the increase due to the growth of productivity. Plausible explanations of that residual—mainly the shift of resources from low-productivity uses to higher ones and gains from increasing the scale of economic activity—still leave about one-fourth of growth unaccounted for. This one-fourth is attributed by Denison, and others, to the advance of knowledge and causes "not elsewhere classified," which means that we do not really know what is at work there.

Although Denison was interested in economic policy, he did not use his writings on economic growth to argue for or against particular economic policies. He considered it his function to try to contribute to understanding what effect policy A, B, or C would have on economic growth; but the judgment whether policy A, B, or C was worthwhile was not up to him to make. That was properly the function of a political process in which the benefits of more economic growth and the costs of the policies that might achieve it would be evaluated. He sought only to enlighten that process.

When I ask myself why Denison was so exceptional, I think first of his unusually high intelligence. But there was something more, and more rare, than that. It was a moral quality of responsibility. He accepted his responsibility to do his work as thoroughly, comprehensively, and honestly as possible, with no short cuts, no unnecessary displays of virtuosity, no acceptance of unexamined data, no fear of saying that he did not know, and no contamination by pride, ideology, or politics.

In the future, the research of other economists will alter some of Denison's findings and fill in some blanks that he could not. But the study of economic growth will never be without influence by what Denison pioneered. And his life and work will remain a model for what economists should be and do. *(October 1992)*

33

Henry Calvert Simons

H enry Calvert Simons (1899–1946) was born in Virden, Illinois, and died in Chicago. An economist at the University of Chicago from 1927 to 1946, he was the first professor of economics at the University of Chicago Law School. A leader of the "Chicago School," he had an important influence on American thinking about economic policy.

Simons's central theme was stated in the title of his first writing to attract attention, a 1934 pamphlet, "A Positive Program for Laissez-Faire: Some Proposals for a Liberal Economic Policy."[1] The conjunction of the words *positive* and *laissez faire* set him apart from both the conventional conservatives of his time and the conventional liberals (in the American sense of interventionists). Simons visualized a division of labor between the government and the market. The market would determine what gets produced, how, and for whom. The government would be responsible for maintaining general stability, for keeping the market competitive, and for avoiding extremes in the distribution of income. This system would preserve liberty by preventing concentration of power, and liberty is the primary virtue, followed closely by equality.

Simons's work was the response of a free society liberal—or, as he preferred, "libertarian"—to the rise of totalitarianism in Europe, to the worldwide depression, and to the attempt in the democracies, including the United States, to cope with the depres-

---

1. First published as Public Policy Pamphlet no. 15, ed. H. D. Gideonse (Chicago: University of Chicago Press, 1934).

sion in ways that Simons regarded as threats to freedom. Simons's close friend, Professor Aaron Director, later said that Simons acted as if the end of the world was at hand. During the period of Simons's work, if not the end of the world at least the end of the free society could realistically be considered a serious possibility. Simons undertook to help to prevent that, by showing that the free society had not failed but that the government had failed to discharge its role in the free society.

Simons's Policies

The 1934 pamphlet contained the elements of a policy for a free economy that he was to restate and refine for the next twelve years, with some changes of emphasis. As he put it in 1934:

> The main elements in a sound liberal program may be defined in terms of five proposals or objectives (in a descending scale of relative importance):
> I. Elimination of private monopoly in all its forms. . . .
> II. Establishment of more definite and adequate "rules of the game" with respect to money. . . .
> III. Drastic change in our whole tax system, with regard primarily for the effects of taxation upon the distribution of wealth and income. . . .
> IV. Gradual withdrawal of the enormous differential subsidies implicit in our present tariff system. . . .
> V. Limitation upon the squandering of our resources in advertising and selling activities.[2]

In later years, the fifth of these items fell from the list.

The first proposal, "elimination of private monopoly in all its forms," was substantially altered later. In 1934, Simons had said, "The case for a liberal-conservative policy must stand or fall on the first proposal, abolition of private monopoly; for it is the *sine qua non* of any such policy."[3] His measures for achieving this included limitation on the absolute size of corporations and on their relative size in their industries. He suggested, for example, that "in major industries no ownership unit should produce or control more than 5 per cent of the total output."[4]

---

2. Ibid., p. 57.
3. Ibid.
4. Ibid.

By 1945, he was saying, "Industrial monopolies are not yet a serious evil."[5] Simons's concern about private monopoly had always been about its interaction with the state. He feared that government would support private monopolies and then have to become more powerful to control the warring monopolies it had created. The 1934 pamphlet was written at the time of Roosevelt's National Recovery Administration, which was promoting the universal cartelization of business under government aegis. But in 1945, all that was past, and the political influence of business seemed too small to be a danger.

In 1945, what he had said about business monopoly he now said about labor unions. In 1934, Simons had expressed concern about labor monopolies, but in a rather subdued way. In the decade after the 1934 pamphlet, labor union membership quadrupled, and this growth showed no sign of diminishing. In his final credo (1945), Simons said "the hard monopoly problem is labor organization." For this problem he could offer no "specific," only a rather uncertain question about "the capability of democracy to protect the common interest."[6]

As World War II drew to an end, the preservation of free international trade received more of Simons's attention. Peace was essential for all the goals he cherished. Even the fear of war would require a centralization of power in government that would be incompatible with personal freedom. Simons believed that economic nationalism would be the greatest threat to peace after World War II. Therefore, he devoted much of his work in the mid-1940s to arguing for a liberal international economic order.

Chief Contributions

While the emphasis of some points in Simons's initial policy agenda shifted, two items remained of major importance and constituted Simons's chief contribution aside from the general idea of conjoining "positive program" with "laissez faire." These were the need for monetary certainty and stability and the need to finance government primarily by progressive taxation of "income" defined in a comprehensive way.

---

5. "Introduction: A Political Credo." In *Economic Policy for a Free Society* (Chicago: University of Chicago Press, 1948).

6. Ibid., pp. 35–36.

His analysis of the monetary problem and proposals for its solution, already outlined in the 1934 pamphlet, were elaborated in a 1936 essay whose title defined the issue for years to come, "Rules versus Authorities in Monetary Policy."[7] Simons believed that economic instability was due largely to the instability of the financial system. The system rested excessively on private debt, mainly short-term debt. Variations in the quantity and quality of this debt caused destabilizing variations, in the quantity of money, in the quantity of "near-money," and thereby of velocity, and in the financial requirements of business. The monetary authority, the central bank, was unreliable in discharging its responsibility to counter these devastating tendencies.

Simons's remedy for this condition was a radical reform of the financial structure and the establishment of a rule to govern the conduct of monetary policy. He regarded as an "approximately ideal solution" one in which all property was held in equity form. Failing that, he would have preferred that all debt be in the form of perpetuities, or at least of very long maturities. He did not, however, expect to achieve even that much. But he was specific in recommending the insulation of the banking system and government finance from the malignancy of short-term debt. Banks would be required to hold reserves in currency and Federal Reserve deposits against 100 percent of their deposits. The government would have only two kinds of debt: currency and consols, bonds of infinite life.

This arrangement would give the government effective control of the quantity of money, a control that it would exercise by fiscal means—by altering the size of its own debt or the division of the debt between currency and controls. This control would be exercised "under simple, definite rules laid down in legislation," to provide the private sector with the maximum certainty.

Simons wrestled continuously with the question of what the rules should be. His indecision appeared at the beginning, in 1934, when he referred to controlling "the quantity, (or through quantity, the value) of effective money."[8] He debated with himself on this issue in the "Rules versus Authorities" and elsewhere. He recognized that a rule aimed at the price level (or the value of money) would

---

7. "Rules versus Authorities in Monetary Policy," *Journal of Political Economy*, vol. 54 (February 1936), pp. 1–30.

8. "A Positive Program for Laissez-Faire," p. 57.

necessarily leave the authority with discretion to decide what quantity of money would achieve the goal. But he also feared that with the existing financial situation, the velocity of money would be so variable that a quantity rule would yield great price-level instability. His solution to this dilemma was to opt for the price-level rule until reform of the financial system would reduce the quantity of near-moneys and the instability of the debt structure, after which stabilizing the quantity of money would be the preferred rule.

Simons's only two books were on taxation. The first, *Personal Income Taxation*, was his doctoral dissertation, written in the early 1930s and published in 1938. The second, *Federal Tax Reform*, was commissioned by the Committee for Economic Development, an organization of businessmen, mainly written in 1943 and published posthumously in 1950. A few main elements ran through all his work on taxation. The nearly exclusive source of revenue should be taxation of personal income, meaning what has come to be called the Haig-Simons definition of income as the sum of the value of the taxpayers' consumption plus the addition to his net assets.[9] This definition should be applied as comprehensively as possible, for the sake of equity and economic efficiency. Simons fully explored the implication of that for the treatment of capital gains, gifts, income in kind, and corporate profits. Finally, he emphasized the use of the progressive income tax as a means of reducing inequality both because reducing inequality was important and because the progressive income tax was a way of reducing inequality that was much more compatible with a free economy than other measures commonly proposed for that purpose.

The Chicago School

Simons was a leading member of the "Chicago School" of the 1930s. Other members at the time were Frank H. Knight, Lloyd W. Mints, and Aaron Director; Jacob Viner shared many of their views but did not consider himself a member. Simons more than the others translated their general attitudes into specific policy proposals, which he advanced forcefully in his own writing and defended in a series of strong reviews of the writings of the opposition.

---

9. Robert M. Haig, "The Concept of Income," in *The Federal Income Tax,* ed. R. M. Haig (New York, 1921).

Simons's great attraction for his colleagues, students, and sympathetic readers was a matter of personal and literary style as well as of substance. His writing was polished, ironical, free of technical jargon, statistics, or mathematics, rising above "mere" economic analysis to grand pronouncements on eternal subjects. It was not very difficult but difficult enough to leave the reader with a sense of accomplishment at having recognized its merits. He gave his readers and students a feeling of being initiated into a select club that had great insights that politicians, businessmen, and most economists were intellectually, morally, and ethically incapable of appreciating.

After World War II, and after his death in 1946, national discussion and, to some extent, policy turned in Simons's direction. There was no possibility of reverting to the negative conservativism of the prewar years. But with a greatly enlarged federal budget and debt, and with the experience of inflation, the naive expansionism of Keynes's American disciples was no longer an acceptable policy. In this gap, Simons's ideas filled a need. A "modern conservativism" emerged that accepted government responsibility for general economic stability, was strongly anti-inflationary, sought a rule to govern stabilization policy, relied on tax changes rather than expenditure changes when positive fiscal measures were needed, opposed protectionism, sought to weaken the power of labor unions, and accepted the progressive personal income tax as the main source of federal revenue. Simons's work contributed to this development. By the 1950s, some of his principal concepts had become common currency in policy discussion—the combination of positive measures with laissez faire, the rules-versus-authority issue, and the Haig-Simons definition of the tax base. Many of his colleagues and students came into positions from which they could influence public opinion and policy.

By 1960, a new-generation Chicago School had come into prominence. Typified by Milton Friedman and George Stigler, this group had been profoundly influenced by Simons as students but were departing substantially from his policy positions. Monetary history convinced them that Simons was wrong in opting for a price-level rule rather than a quantity-of-money rule for monetary policy. They concluded that antitrust activity, on which he had once placed so much emphasis, was on the whole destructive of competition. Whereas Simons never contemplated a peacetime federal budget exceeding 10 percent of the national income, they were living with one exceeding 20 percent, and that changed their views of many things. They came to doubt Simons's reliance on rational discussion as a way to improve government policy in a democracy; this led them, in the case of Friedman, to a search for constitutional amendments that would limit the political process or, in the case of Stigler, to concentrating on explaining rather than influencing the process. But still, they all retained the Simons vision of the good free society with a division of responsibility between the government and the market, and through them his voice was still heard forty years after his death. *(1987)*

34

The End of Economics As We Know It

E ver since Francis Fukuyama wrote his essay, "The End of History," I have been fascinated by the idea of writing something called "The End of Economics." But to talk about the end of economics, period, seems presumptuous, implying more knowledge of the past of economics and of its potential future than I have. So I settle for the more modest title, "The End of Economics as We Know It."

By "we" in this title, I mean the economists of my generation and the succeeding one, who have functioned in the past sixty years, especially those involved with public policy. We have lived through the period of the greatest self-confidence on the part of economists and highest esteem on the part of the public in the history of economics.

Confidence in Economists

The high point in this confidence and esteem was symbolized for me by the *Time* magazine of December 31, 1965, which had a picture of J. M. Keynes on the cover. The point of the cover story was that economists had solved the great problems of our time and had learned how to achieve economic stability and rapid growth. Since then, I suggest, it has been downhill.

At about the same time, in 1966, a professor at the University of Michigan published a book entitled *The Age of the Economist*. No one would write such a book today: the more likely title would be *The Age of the Spin Doctor.*

Fifty years ago, we all thought we knew what America's economic problem was. In that year, the Pabst Brewing Company, wanting to celebrate its hundredth anniversary with an act of public value, held a contest for essays to solve the great postwar problem, which was to maintain high employment. (I remember that well because I won the contest.) According to our view of the economic condition, we had an efficient and potentially very rich economy flawed by some mechanical deficiency that kept us from realizing our potential. If that deficiency were corrected, people would pursue their own interests rationally and effectively, and everything would be all right. Everyone would want to live by bourgeois values— studying and working hard, making provision for the future, and taking responsibility for their families.

We also thought we knew what the flaw in the system was and how to correct it: aggregate demand was inadequate or fluctuated too much. We also thought that the correction could be found in some combination of fiscal and monetary measures—the fiscal measures associated with the name of Keynes and the monetary measures, which came into prominence later, associated with the name of Milton Friedman.

The distinction between fiscal and monetary policy is not important for my story, although it has absorbed much of the attention of economists. My point is that many believed some macroeconomic button could be pushed to make the machine run smoothly without fussing with its internal structure or operation. This kind of thinking about what the problem was and where the solution lay was the basis for the Employment Act of 1946. That act established the Council of Economic Advisers to the president and the Joint Economic Committee in the Congress and was a testament to public faith in economics.

Skepticism toward Economic Policy Solutions

Belief in this identification of the problem and confidence in that solution persisted for a long time, but both began to fade after 1965. Skepticism set in first with respect to fiscal policy, during the Vietnam War. One problem was that economists had not forecast the economy and the effect of fiscal measures on it well enough to keep demand very close to a predetermined path. But there was a more fundamental difficulty, illustrated by President Johnson's reluctance to raise taxes to pay for the war and revealing what we should have known all along. Taxes and expenditures are not value-free counters to be put on the scales of the economy, or taken off, by economists to achieve their notion of balance. They are policies in which taxpayers and recipients of benefits have strong interests that they are unwilling to subordinate to an economist's mathematical model. And this unwillingness is correct, not ignorant.

While confidence in monetarism came along later and lasted longer, anyone who reads the newspapers can see that there is no longer any faith in monetary economics. Instead, faith has been displaced to the inscrutable oracle at the Federal Reserve. While this faith may be rewarded, it is not economics.

At the same time that we were losing faith in the ability of economics to solve the problem of inadequacy or instability of demand, it began to seem less overwhelming than we had thought since the Great Depression. Was this change due to the success of economics? We really do not know, but some research now suggests that the economy was just as stable before the Great Depression— say, from 1869 to 1929—as it has been since World War II. Only the Great Depression was unique. Otherwise, we have about the same degree of instability as we had before economists became so smart.

We have also become better adjusted to living with instability than we were. The problem in recessions, even in the Great Depression, was not that average incomes were absolutely low. The problem had two aspects. First, average incomes had fallen, so that even though not low, they were lower than people were used to and expected. Second, the average was very unevenly distributed, so that the burdens were concentrated on the unemployed. But today people are better able to cope with a drop in their incomes because they have more assets, mainly in the form of owned homes and durable goods, so that they can get along better with some decline of income. Moreover, the burden of unemployment has been somewhat socialized, partly the result of unemployment compensation but even more the result of two-worker families.

Economic Growth

In the past twenty years or so, the attention of economists and makers of economic policy has turned, or returned, to another problem: economic growth, or raising total output. This was the original Adam Smith problem, which he dealt with in *The Wealth of Nations*.

Why Adam Smith thought that increasing the wealth of nations was important is a little obscure. He apparently did not care much about increasing *per capita* incomes. The comment of a leading Smith scholar, Jacob Viner, is surprising in view of the picture we commonly have of Adam Smith as a great apostle of individualism. Viner says:

> He [Smith] also found value in increase of aggregate wealth because it makes possible an increase in handsome buildings and great avenues in the towns, the "magnificence" so extolled by the writers of classical antiquity and of the Renaissance, but he treated these as public rather than individual riches. Smith also included as an advantage of growth of aggregate wealth the progress of aesthetic and intellectual culture and of "civilization" in general, which he associated with communal enrichment.

But in 1928 along came Keynes, the great iconoclast, to question the traditional value placed on growth. He calculated that in 100 years, at foreseeable rates of growth, per capita income in the developed countries would be from four to eight times as high as it then was. He thought that when such a level of income was reached, further increase of income would not seem of much importance. We are now two-thirds of the way through Keynes's 100 years and three-fourths of the way to his forecast income level four times as high as in 1928. By his reasoning, we are close to the point at which more growth will be unimportant.

A Canadian economist, with the wonderful name of A. F. W. Plumptre, whom I knew during the war, disputed Keynes's conclusion. He said that wants are insatiable, so that even if the forecast increase of income occurred, people would want more. That argument, however, leads to a paradox. We will become so rich that either becoming richer will seem unimportant or we will see that becoming richer will bring us no closer to the satisfaction of our wants, which are infinite, so what is the point?

Moreover, at least two decades of worrying about economic growth have yielded very little knowledge about how to accelerate it. Probably most economists in the past fifteen years have thought that reducing budget deficits would speed up growth, but estimates of the size of the effect vary widely, with the most plausible estimates being quite small.

So, at least in my opinion, the instability problem and the growth problem—the staples of economics as we know it—are not the critical problems, nor are we confident of our ability to contribute much to their solution. The questions now are, What are the critical problems of a very rich and reasonably stable society, and what can economics contribute to dealing with them? In my opinion, economics as we know it is not well adapted to those problems and, indeed, has deliberately abstracted itself from them.

Traditional Economics

Economics has traditionally defined itself as the study of the behavior of individuals attempting to use their given resources and technology to maximize satisfaction of their given wants. In its descriptive aspect, economics tries to tell how individuals actually do behave in this effort. In its prescriptive aspect, economics tries to say how individuals and various institutions, especially government, should behave so that individuals will succeed in the effort to maximize the satisfaction of their given wants.

The assumption that the wants are given is critical. They are assumed to be given in several senses. One is that the wants are stable. If the wants are not stable, we cannot predict future behavior from observation of the past, which is what we try to do all the time. We also assume that the wants are given in the sense that they are the ultimate value, and no one is entitled to look behind them to judge their worth. The conclusion that a society in which people maximize the satisfaction of their given wants is a good society implies that these wants are the ultimate standard.

Subliminally or subconsciously, economists have assumed that the wants, or values, of individuals were those of an eighteenth-century Scottish philosopher or of a Cambridge professor in Victorian England: that is, people value the future highly, like to work and study, accept responsibility for their families, and are trustworthy, law-abiding, and peaceful.

From time to time, economists and others have pointed to the unreality and inadequacy of these views about wants. Without going into the implications of that, I want to concentrate on one aspect of the wants question that I see as a dominant problem of our time: the "values" problem, more properly called the "conflict of values" problem.

Conflicting Values

One can imagine a community of people, say, on an island in the South Pacific, none of whom share the straight puritanical values. They toil not, neither do they spin; they do not study and do not save. They are sexually promiscuous and neglect their children. Their per capita GDP is low and stagnant. They live short and possibly happy lives. Who is to say that there is a values problem on that island?

But imagine a society in which there is a sharp division of values. Suppose the society is divided into the X People and the Y People. The X People have predominantly, but not exclusively, the bourgeois or puritanical values. The Y People, perhaps in rebellion against the X People, do not. In particular, they value today's gratification much more than tomorrow's.

Within each group is an unequal distribution of native talents and income. Some of the Y People have higher incomes than some of the X People. But the average income of the Y People is less than that of the X People, even if the average talents in the two groups are equal. A Y Person has less income than an X Person with the same native talent because the Y Person invests less time and effort in cultivating the talent to make it productive and remunerative in the market.

This is a condition for serious conflict. Each side has disdain for the other but also a certain envy. Each side tries, in one way or another, to convert the other, and each side fears being corrupted or having its children corrupted by the other. The X People have a particular problem: they see the Y People living in what they regard as misery. They are compassionate enough to want to help relieve the misery, but they do not want to reward and encourage a way of life that they find repulsive.

The X People have another problem as well. In the most famous sentence in the history of economics, Adam Smith said: "It is not from the benevolence of the butcher, the brewer, or the baker, that we expect our dinner, but from their regard for their own interest." But we do depend on the butcher, baker, and brewer to see it as in their interest to get up in the morning and go to work rather than sleeping until noon. The X People and the Y People are parts of the same economy, and each gains from the industriousness and thriftiness of the other.

The Y People too have their problems. They have some ambivalence and feelings of self-reproach. They do not like all the outcomes of their behavior and believe that the X People have a responsibility to help change the outcomes. But they do not want to be lectured about their values or punished for their behavior.

Perhaps I have blundered into a field that properly belongs to sociologists and psychiatrists. But I have been emboldened to enter this field by reading an excellent article by Henry Aaron in the spring 1994 *Journal of Economic Perspectives,* although I cannot attribute to him any of my specific comments. I may be wrong in thinking that the problem I have tried to describe in a schematic way is very serious in America or even exists here. But suppose that I am correct that America is a rich country subject to only moderate instability and that the conflict of values has become the dominant problem. What would that mean for economics?

One possibility is that economics would be irrelevant to the major human and social problem of our time. We could resign ourselves to what Keynes said:

> But, chiefly, do not let us overestimate the importance of the economic problem, or sacrifice to its supposed necessities other matters of greater and more permanent significance. It should be a matter for specialists—like dentistry. If economists could manage to get themselves thought of as humble, competent people, on a level with dentists, that would be splendid.

It might be splendid, but it would also be the end of economics as we know it.

The other possibility is that economics could contribute to understanding and possibly solving the values problem. I believe that there is hope for this. Economists may have something to say about how economic conditions interact with and affect values and are in turn affected by them.

We might take as an example the interaction of economics and values in determining the number of children born to teenaged mothers. Suppose a certain community has a strong taboo against teenaged motherhood, so that the number of cases is small. Then with a change in economic conditions, like a change in welfare policy, the rewards increase (or economic costs are reduced) for being a teenaged mother. Despite the taboo, the number of cases increases. But as teenaged motherhood becomes a more common occurrence, it becomes more accepted. The taboo weakens, and the number of cases increases further. That is, the values have shifted. If the economic conditions then revert to what they were, by a reversal of the welfare policy, the number of cases will remain higher than in the initial condition, at least for a long time.

Economics and Values

I am not suggesting that economists should undertake to judge which values are good and which are not. Economists have no special qualifications for doing that. But economists should participate in a value-free study of values, because values affect many of the phenomena that economists have always considered their province—the rate of saving, for example—and values are in turn affected by what we have always considered "economic" variables.

But if economics is to contribute to the study of values, it will have to change in several ways:

- It will have to recognize the critical importance of the subject—of the character, distribution, and determinants of values.
- It will have to become more history minded; instead of searching only for timeless reversible functions, it will also have to study the one-directional path by which functional relations change.
- It will have to become used to collaborating with social scientists who are not economists.

If these should become the features of a future economics, that would mark the end of economics as we know it but also the beginning of a new economics. *(June 1994)*

About the Author

Herbert Stein earned his B.A. from Williams College and his Ph.D. from the University of Chicago. He was a member of the President's Council of Economic Advisers from 1969 to 1974 and was chairman from 1972. He is the A. Willis Robertson Professor of Economics Emeritus of the University of Virginia and a senior fellow of the American Enterprise Institute (AEI). He writes regularly for *The American Enterprise,* the magazine of AEI. He is also a member of the board of contributors of the *Wall Street Journal,* for which he writes frequently.

Among his publications are *An Illustrated Guide to the American Economy* (1992, with Murray Foss), *The Fiscal Revolution in America* (1969, rev. ed. 1990), *Washington Bedtime Stories* (1986), and *Governing the $5 Trillion Economy* (1989).

Acknowledgments

Most of the chapters in this volume were first published elsewhere in slightly different form. Listed below are the books, journals, or newspapers that originally published the material, followed by the title under which the chapter was published if changed.

Wall Street Journal:

"Adventures with Exchange Rates" ("Foreign Travels, Foreign-Exchange Travails"), August 27, 1990.

"The Age of Ignorance," June 11, 1993.

"A Crypto-Liberal Takes the Cure," October 6, 1988.

"The $50 Billion Option," June 12, 1992.

"Fugue for Talking Heads" ("Pundits, Set Your Metronome at Presto"), January 10, 1994.

"Memories of a Model Economist," November 23, 1992.

"On Doubling per Capita National Income" ("Growth Isn't Everything"), April 1, 1993.

"On Nixon's Economics," April 27, 1994.

"Remembering Adam Smith," April 6, 1994.

"What If You Call It a Tax?" ("The Tax vs. Expenditure Flap"), October 11, 1990.

"Will, War, and Bureaucrats," March 21, 1991.

The American Enterprise magazine:

"The Disintegration of Fiscal Policy" ("Budget Imperatives"), March/April 1993.

"Economics—The Dismal Science or Dentistry?" ("Economics: Still the Dismal Science"), January/February 1993.

"Economics in Washington—Fifty-five Years Ago" ("When Economics Came to Washington"), May/June 1993.

"The End of Economics as We Know It," September/October 1994.

"Industrial Policy, the New Old Idea" ("Recycling Industrial Policy"), July/August 1992.

"Jacob Viner, Master of the 'No School' School of Economics ("Master of the 'No School' School of Economics"), May/June 1992.

"Richard Nixon, Economics, and Me," July/August 1994.

"What Economic Policy Advisers Do," March/April 1991.

"Whose Growth?" November/December 1992.

Other publications:

"The Balance of Payments," *Fortune Encyclopedia of Economics.* Warner Books, New York, 1993.

"The Generational Transfer," *Newsday,* January 14, 1990.

"Henry Calvert Simons," *The New Palgrave: Dictionary of Economics.* Edited by John Eatwell, Murray Milgate, and Peter Newman. London: Macmillan Press Limited, 1989.

"Letters of a Father and Son about a Grandson and Son" ("Dear Son: I Fear for Your Boy's Future"; "Dear Pop: Me, Too"), *Newsday,* January 14, 1990.

"My Life as a Dee-Cline," *American Spectator,* April 1989.

"The Mythology of Tax Reduction" ("Myth & Math: How Cutting Taxes Trims the Truth"), *Washington Post,* August 30, 1992.

"The Triumph of the Adaptive Society," *American Economist,* Spring 1990.

"Twelve Years of the *AEI Economist*" ("Twelve Years of Policy"), *AEI Economist,* August 1989.

"The White House Mess" ("My Free Lunch: Mourning the White House Mess"), *Washington Post,* February 21, 1993.

A NOTE ON THE BOOK

This book was edited by the staff of the AEI Press.
The text was set in Century Old Style.
Coghill Composition, of Richmond, Virginia, set the type,
and Data Reproductions Corporation, of Rochester Hills, Michigan,
printed and bound the book, using permanent acid-free paper.

The AEI PRESS is the publisher for the American Enterprise Institute for Public Policy Research, 1150 17th Street, N.W., Washington, D.C. 20036; *Christopher C. DeMuth,* publisher; *Dana Lane,* director; *Ann Petty,* editor; *Leigh Tripoli,* editor; *Cheryl Weissman,* editor; *Lisa Roman,* editorial assistant (rights and permissions).